WIDE-AWAKE EDITION.

THE

LIFE AND PUBLIC SERVICES

OF

HON. ABRAHAM LINCOLN,

OF ILLINOIS,

AND

HON. HANNIBAL HAMLIN,

OF MAINE.

BOSTON:
THAYER & ELDRIDGE,
114 AND 116 WASHINGTON STREET.
1860.

GEO. C. RAND & AVERY, PRINTERS, 3 CORNHILL, BOSTON.

TABLE OF CONTENTS.

CHAPTER VI.

CHAPTER VII.

CHAPTER I.

CHAPTER II.

CHAPTER III.

CHAPTER IV.

APPENDIX.

INTRODUCTORY.

THE REPUBLICAN PARTY, by its National Nominating Convention, at Chicago, on Friday, May 18, placed before the American people these two, ABRAHAM LINCOLN, of Illinois, and HANNIBAL HAMLIN, of Maine, the latter one of the United States Senators from that State, as its candidates for PRESIDENT and VICE-PRESIDENT of this Republic. The nominations have additional interest at this particular period. Besides the fact that they are thus made the standard-bearers of the most vigorous political organization in the nation, there is also to be taken into account the manifold dissensions of their adversaries, which would seem to point the way to a certain Republican victory at the election in November next.

ABRAHAM LINCOLN, of Illinois, is a genuine scion of the "West-land," and may therefore fairly be regarded as a representative man. Born on the "dark and bloody ground" of Kentucky, he was "raised" in Illinois, being brought to that then Territory at a period when the foot of the white man had barely begun to tread its magnificent prairies.

With very limited opportunities of receiving an education, but much of that genial humor and quick sense of observation and appreciation, which is especially characteristic of our Western Pioneers, Abraham Lincoln stands to-day not only a representative of the early Western stock, the hunter, farmer, and pioneer, but an admirable example of what energy and ability can do for a man honestly using them in honorable pursuits.

Not only in character but in person, is Abraham Lincoln a type of the West. Tall and loose-jointed, with large bones, the person of the future Hoosier President will attract attention everywhere.

In personal appearance, Mr. Lincoln, or, as he is more familiarly termed among those who know him best, "Honest Abe," is long, lean, and wiry. In motion, he has a good deal of the elasticity and awkwardness which indicate the rough training of his early life, and his conversation savors strongly of Western idioms and pronunciation. His height is six feet three inches. His complexion is about that of an octoroon; his face, without being by any means beautiful, is genial looking, and good-humor seems to lurk in every corner of its innumerable angles. He has dark hair, tinged with gray; a good forehead; small eyes; a long, penetrating nose, with nostrils such as Napoleon always liked to find in his best generals, because they indicated a long head and clear thoughts; and a mouth which, aside from being of magnificent proportions, is probably his most expressive feature.

As a speaker, he is ready, precise, and fluent. His manner before a popular assembly is as he pleases to make it, being either superlatively ludicrous, or very impressive. He employs but little gesticulation, but, when he desires to make a point, produces a shrug of his shoulders, an elevation of his eyebrows, a depression of his mouth, and a general distortion of countenance, so comically awkward that it never fails to "bring down the house." His enunciation is slow and emphatic, and his voice, though sharp and powerful, at times has a frequent tendency to dwindle into a shrill and unpleasant sound; but, as before stated, the peculiar characteristic of his manner is the remarkable mobility of his features, the frequent contortions of which excite a merriment his words could not produce.

The Boston *Transcript* published the following in its issue of October 13, 1858. It describes Mr. Lincoln's appearance in the debate with Mr. Douglas, at Galesburg, Illinois, October 7, of the same year. The letter was written by the president of a college in that State, — a gentleman well known in New England, and particularly esteemed in Boston. After stating the reception of the rival champions of the two parties, this correspondent continued: —

"The men are entirely dissimilar. Mr. Douglas is a thick-set, finely-built, courageous man, and has an air of self-confidence that does not a little to inspire his supporters with hope. Mr. Lincoln is a tall, lank man, awkward, apparently diffident, and, when not speaking, has neither firmness in his countenance, nor fire in his eye. . . . .

"Mr. Lincoln has a rich, silvery voice, enunciates with great distinctness, and has a fine command of language. He commenced by a review of the points Mr. Douglas had made. In this he showed great tact, and his retorts, though gentlemanly, were sharp, and reached to the core of the subject in dispute. While he gave but little time to the work of review, we did not feel that anything was omitted which deserved attention.

"He then proceeded to defend the Republican party. Here he charged Mr. Douglas with doing nothing for freedom; with disregarding the rights and interests of the colored man; and, for about forty minutes, he spoke with a power that we have seldom heard equalled. There was a grandeur in his thoughts, a comprehensiveness in his arguments, and a binding force in his conclusions, which were perfectly irresistible. The vast throng were silent as death; every eye was fixed upon the speaker, and all gave him serious attention. He was the tall man eloquent; his countenance glowed with animation, and his eye glistened with an intelligence that made it lustrous. He was no longer awkward and ungainly, but graceful, bold, commanding."

"Honest old Abe," as Mr. Lincoln is commonly called by the great masses of the people of the "Prairie State," is decidedly a man to win upon the popular heart by the sturdy manliness of his character, and the simple integrity and straight-forward logic of his political opinions. The genuine though not reverential instincts of the Western people have fixed upon the Republican candidate an expressive, if not euphonious title, which is in decided contrast with the reputation an "old public functionary" will carry with him into a dishonored retirement. In one respect the name is a misnomer, as "Honest Abe" is by no means "old;" he being fifty-one years of age, and in the bloom of full and vigorous manhood.

Mr. Lincoln is by profession a lawyer, in which pursuit he has won a position and reputation at the Illinois bar second to none. His mind is eminently legal; as an advocate, he is clear, cogent, and logical; understands how to control a jury, and always presents himself well fortified in the legal points of any case he may undertake.

As a politician, he has always acted with the moderate Whigs of the Henry Clay school, and since the former parties of the country committed themselves fully to the interests of the Slave Propaganda, he has been found working with the party of free labor. Though decidedly opposed to slavery, as the speeches inserted in these pages show, Mr. Lincoln would not be classed as a radical Republican. His opposition to the "peculiar institution" seems rather to be based upon the politico-economical view of the subject than upon the moral grounds, though he by no means shirks that most important element of the question. The charge of desiring "negro equality," which would have been trumpeted against Mr. Seward, cannot be charged on Mr. Lincoln. He has distinctly stated his opposition to the exercise of suffrage, &c., by the Anglo-Africans of this continent. In this respect, he represents the average sentiment of the people among whom he lives.

Mr. Lincoln is one of the most effective of "stump speakers." He understands well how to move the hearts of a people more powerfully affected and controlled by the fiery eye, the working features, the speaking tongue, and the many magnetic elements which go to make up the orator, than possibly any other people on the face of the earth. "Honest old Abe" has the qualities of earnestness, enthusiasm, evident sincerity, large knowledge of men, quick perception of the humorous, and a ready application of his faculties to the surrounding circumstances. All these make him a powerful and popular speaker of the Western school.

Of the people, — sprung from their loins, proud of his origin, having carved out for himself his own fortune, — the whilom flat-boatman, farmer, clerk, storekeeper, captain of volunteers, serving gallantly in the Black Hawk War of 1832; the rising lawyer, active politician, and prominent leader of his party for many years, — the name, history, and character of Abraham Lincoln has in it many of the qualities that will stir the enthusiasm, and bring out the hardy masses of freemen, throughout the whole of the Northern and border States.

The Chicago *Press and Tribune* gives the following interesting particulars relative to the *personnel* of Mr. Lincoln. This journal being the leading Republican paper of the Northwest, and of Illinois in particular, its statements are worthy of notice, as coming from those speaking as with authority. The description of his person, and account of his habits, are especially interesting.

"Mr. Lincoln stands six feet four inches high in his stockings. His frame is not muscular, but gaunt and wiry; his arms are long, but not unreasonably so for a person of his height; his lower limbs are not disproportioned to his body. In walking, his gait, though firm, is never brisk. He steps slowly and deliberately, almost always with his head inclined forward, and his hands clasped behind his back. In matters of dress, he is by no means precise. Always clean, he is never fashionable; he is careless, but not slovenly. In manner, he is remarkably cordial, and, at the same time, simple. His politeness is always sincere, but never elaborate and oppressive. A warm shake of the hand, and a warmer smile of recognition, are his methods of greeting his friends. At rest, his features, though those of a man of mark, are not such as belong to a handsome man; but when his fine dark-gray eyes are lighted up by any emotion, and his features begin their play, he would be chosen from among a crowd as one who had in him not only the kindly sentiments which women love, but the heavier metal of which full-grown men and presidents are made. His hair is black, and, though thin, is wiry. His head sits well on his shoulders, but, beyond that, it defies description. It nearer resembles that of Clay than Webster; but it is unlike either. It is very large, and, phrenologically, well proportioned, betokening power in all its developments. A slightly Roman nose, a wide-cut mouth, and a dark complexion, with the appearance of having been weather-beaten, complete the description.

"In his personal habits, Mr. Lincoln is as simple as a child. He loves a good dinner, and eats with the appetite which goes with a great brain; but his food is plain and nutritious. He never drinks intoxicating liquors of any sort, not even a glass of wine. He is not addicted to tobacco in any of its shapes. He never was accused of a licentious act in all his life. He never uses profane language. He never gambles; we doubt if he ever indulges in any games of chance. He is particularly cautious about incurring pecuniary obligations for any purpose whatever; and, in debt, he is never content until the score is discharged. We presume he ows no man a dollar. He never speculates. The rage for the sudden acquisition of wealth never took hold of him. His gains from his profession have been moderate, but sufficient for his purposes. While others have dreamed of gold, he has been in pursuit of knowledge. In all his dealings, he has the reputation of being generous but exact, and, above all, religiously honest. He would be a bold man who would say that Abraham Lincoln ever wronged any one out of a cent, or ever spent a dollar that he had not honestly earned.

His struggles in early life have made him careful of money, but his generosity with his own is proverbial. He is a regular attendant upon religious worship, and, though not a communicant, is a pew-holder and liberal supporter of the Presbyterian Church in Springfield, to which Mrs. Lincoln belongs. He is a scrupulous teller of the truth, — too exact in his notions to suit the atmosphere of Washington as it now is. His enemies may say that he tells Black Republican lies; but no man ever charged that, in a professional capacity, or as a citizen dealing with his neighbors, he would depart from the scriptural command. At home, he lives like a gentleman of modest means and simple tastes. A good-sized house of wood, simply but tastefully furnished, surrounded by trees and flowers, is his own, and there he lives, at peace with himself, the idol of his family, and, for his honesty, ability, and patriotism, the admiration of his countrymen.

"If Mr. Lincoln is elected President, he will carry but little that is ornamental to the White House. The country must accept his sincerity, his ability, and his honesty in the mould in which they are cast. He will not be able to make as polite a bow as Frank Pierce, but he will not commence anew the agitation of the slavery question by recommending to Congress any Kansas-Nebraska bills. He may not preside at the Presidential dinners with the ease and grace which distinguish the "venerable public functionary," Mr. Buchanan; but he will not create the necessity for a Covode Committee, and the disgraceful revelations of Cornelius Wendell. He will take to the Presidential chair just the qualities which the country now demands to save it from impending destruction, — ability that no man can question, firmness that nothing can overbear, honesty that never has been impeached, and patriotism that never despairs."

LIFE AND PUBLIC SERVICES

OF

HON. ABRAHAM LINCOLN.

CHAPTER I.

Ancestors — Birth — Early Surroundings — Removal to Indiana — Education — Occupation — Settled in Illinois — Black Hawk War, etc.

THE ancestors of ABRAHAM LINCOLN were of the good old stock by whom the State of Pennsylvania was founded. Members of the Society of Friends, they lived in Berks County, Pennsylvania, and emigrated from thence to Rockingham County, Virginia. In 1781–2, the paternal grandfather of Mr. Lincoln removed to Kentucky, where a year or two later he was killed by the Indians. Descendants from the same stock still live in the eastern part of Pennsylvania.

Mr. Lincoln was born February 12, 1809, in Harden County, Kentucky. He is consequently now in the fifty-first year of his life. The early impressions of his childhood were formed amid the wilderness scenes of Kentucky, and among the rude, yet large-hearted men who were the pioneers of those days.

In 1816, when the subject of this memoir was about seven years of age, his parents removed with him to Spencer County, in the Territory of Indiana. Those of the present generation have but little idea of the character and surroundings of the Western people at that early period. The vast continental area, now covered with populous States, teeming with civilization and its results, blooming with cultivation, and blossoming beneath the busy brain and toiling hand of American industry, was then but a wide expanse of unknown prairie, whose far-off western horizon was supposed to dip its blue circle beyond the impassable American desert; long the bugbear of travellers, and now the exploded chimera of ignorant geographers. At this early period, the refining, educating influences of modern society were unknown. The preachers, what few there were, were mostly like the congregation, — uncultured backwoodsmen, whose rude eloquence was yet well fitted to uplift the mind of their uneducated hearers. Schools were even less frequent than the opportunities for religious instruction.

It was among such influences as these that our young pioneer grew up to carve out for himself a distinguished manhood. Mr. Lincoln barely received the rudimentary elements of a common English education. Probably six months will cover the whole period spent by him within the rude log walls of the schoolhouse of the paternal settlement. Endowed with quick faculties, ambition, and energy, the youth of Mr. Lincoln was not lost in idleness, or wasted in vain pursuits.

He remained in Indiana until 1830, working on the home farm, or engaged in other arduous occupations. During the period of youth and early manhood, he labored industriously, losing no opportunity of cultivating his mind, whether working on the farm, or drifting on the flat-boat down the Mississippi River.

In 1830, at the age of twenty-one, Mr. Lincoln removed to Macon County, Illinois. Here he remained for about a year, engaged in agricultural pursuits. At this period, he hired himself out to the neighboring farmers, and it is told of him that he mauled and split a large quantity of rails. During the sitting of the Republican Convention, much amusement was excited by the introduction of a banner supported by two worm-eaten rails, and inscribed as part of a lot of 3,000 made by Abraham Lincoln, in 1830, for a farmer in Macon County.

Mr. Lincoln removed to New Salem, then in Sagamore, now Chenard County, where he remained about one year. He was principally employed as a clerk in a store. Mr. Lincoln, in the first of his celebrated debates with Judge Douglas, held at

Ottawa, Illinois, August 21, 1858, alluded to this period of his life, in reply to this, Judge Douglas epitomized a history of Mr. Lincoln.

"In the remarks I have made on this platform, and the position of Mr. Lincoln upon it, I mean nothing personally disrespectful or unkind to that gentleman. I have known him for nearly twenty-five years. There were many points of sympathy between us when we first got acquainted. We were both comparatively boys, and both struggling with poverty in a strange land. I was a school-teacher in the town of Winchester, and he a flourishing grocery-keeper in the town of Salem. He was more successful in his occupation than I was in mine, and hence more fortunate in this world's goods. Lincoln is one of those peculiar men who perform with admirable skill everything which they undertake. I made as good a school-teacher as I could, and when a cabinet maker, I made a good bedstead and tables, although my old boss said I succeeded better with bureaus and secretaries than with anything else; but I believe that Lincoln was always more successful in business than I, for his business enabled him to get into the legislature. I met him there, however, and had a sympathy with him, because of the up-hill struggle we both had in life. He was then just as good at telling an anecdote as now. He could beat any of the boys wrestling, or running a footrace, in pitching quoits or tossing a copper; could ruin more liquor than all the boys of the town together, and the dignity and impartiality with which he presided at a horserace or fist-fight, excited the admiration and won the praise of everybody that was present and participated. I sympathized with him, because he was struggling with difficulties, and so was I. Mr. Lincoln served with me in the legislature in 1836, when we both retired, and he subsided, or became submerged, and he was lost sight of as a public man for some years. In 1846, when Wilmot introduced his celebrated proviso, and the Abolition tornado swept over the country, Lincoln again turned up as a member of Congress from the Sangamon District. I was then in the Senate of the United States, and was glad to welcome my old friend and companion. Whilst in Congress, he distinguished himself by his opposition to the Mexican war, taking the side of the common enemy against his own country; and when he returned home he found that the indignation of the people followed him everywhere, and he was again submerged or obliged to retire into private life, forgotten by his former friends. He came up again in 1854, just in time to make his Abolition or Black Republican platform, in company with Giddings, Lovejoy, Chase, and Fred Douglass, for the Republican party to stand upon."

Mr. Lincoln answered as follows: —

The judge is wofully at fault about his early friend Lincoln being a "grocery-keeper." I don't know as it would be a great sin, if I had been; but he is mistaken. Lincoln never kept a grocery anywhere in the world. It is true that Lincoln did work the latter part of one winter in a little still-house, up at the head of a hollow. And so I think my friend, the Judge, is equally at fault when he charges me, at the time when I was in Congress, of having opposed our soldiers who were fighting in the Mexican war. The judge did not make his charge very distinctly, but I can tell you what he can prove, by referring to the record. You remember I was an old Whig, and whenever the Democratic party tried to get me to vote that the war had been righteously begun by the President, I would not do it. But whenever they asked for any money or land-warrants, or anything to pay the soldiers there, during all that time, I gave the same vote that Judge Douglas did. You can think as you please as to whether that was consistent. Such is the truth; and the Judge has the right to make all he can out of it. But when he, by a general charge, conveys the idea that I withheld supplies from the soldiers who were fighting in the Mexican war, or did anything else to hinder the soldiers, he is, to say the least, grossly and altogether mistaken, as a consultation of the records will prove to him.

The Black Hawk Indian war broke out at this time. The

violence with which it raged for a period of ten months, created great excitement among the settlers. A company of volunteers was raised in New Salem, of which Abraham Lincoln was elected captain. He must have made his mark at this early date among his associates to have been raised to this post of confidence. The war terminated by the capture of Black Hawk, the Indian chief, and the total defeat of his warriors in August, 1832.

Mr. Lincoln, many years after, during his congressional career thus humorously alluded to his campaigning services.

"By the way, Mr. Speaker, did you know I was a military hero? Yes, sir, in the days of the Black Hawk war I fought, bled, and came away. Speaking of Gen. Cass's career, reminds me of my own. I was not at Sullivan's defeat, but I was about as near to it as Cass was to Hull's surrender; and like him I saw the place soon after. It is quite certain that I did not break my sword, for I had none to break; but I bent my musket pretty badly on one occasion. If Cass broke his sword, the idea is, he broke it in desperation. I bent the musket by accident. If General Cass went in advance of me in picking whortleberries, I guess I surpassed him in charges upon the wild onions. If he saw any live fighting Indians, it was more than I did, but I had a good many bloody struggles with the mosquitoes; and although I never fainted from loss of blood, I certainly can say, I was often very hungry."

This campaign cost a number of valuable lives, and the government over two million dollars. Like most of the wars and difficulties with Indian tribes, the conduct of the whites will not bear close inspection. The difficulties were mainly caused by dispossession of the lands from their aboriginal occupants. A portion of Black Hawk's tribe, the Sacs, under Keokuk, a chief friendly to the whites, sold all their lands east of the Mississippi. Black Hawk refused to move, and this was the primary cause of the war. There is but little doubt but that the Indian chief was at this time the leading spirit in a projected general attack by the Indians from Texas to the northern Mississippi, upon the frontier settlements of the United States.

It was generally believed that such a plan was formed. The capture of the leader, Black Hawk, put an end to all hopes of the kind, entertained by the native tribes. Black Hawk was taken to Washington, and after being kept prisoner at Fort Munroe for some months, was set at liberty by order of the President, General Jackson.

When Mr. Lincoln returned to Sangamon County, he learned the art of surveying, and prosecuted that profession until the financial crash of 1837 destroyed the value of real estate and ruined the business, — the result of which was that Lincoln's surveying apparatus was sold on an execution by the sheriff. Nothing daunted by this turn of ill-luck, he directed his attention to the law, and borrowing a few books from a neighbor, which he took from the office in the evening and returned in the morning, he learned the rudiments of the profession in which he has since become so distinguished, *by the light of a fire-place!*

The Cleveland *Leader* publishes the following touching events in the life of Abraham Lincoln, which is so interesting as illustrative of a noble character, that it is inserted herewith.

"As a western man, I wish space to give vent to my enthusiasm over the nomination of Hon. Abraham Lincoln, for President of the United States. Mr. Lincoln, or 'Old Abe,' as his friends familiarly call him, is a self-made man. A Kentuckian by birth, he emigrated to Illinois in his boyhood, where he earned his living at the anvil, devoting his leisure hours to study. Having chosen the law as his future calling, he devoted himself assiduously to its mastery, contending at every step with adverse fortune.. During this period of study, he found a home under the hospitable roof of one Armstrong, a farmer who lived in a loghouse some eight miles from the village of Petersburg, Menard County. Here, clad in homespun, with elbows out, and knees covered with patches, young Lincoln would master his lessons by the fire-light of the cabin, and then walk to town for the purpose of recitation. This man Armstrong was himself poor, but he saw the genius struggling in the young student, and opened to him his rude home, and bade him welcome to his coarse fare. How Lincoln graduated with promise, — how he has more than fulfilled that promise, — how honorably he acquitted himself alike on the battle-field, in defending our border settlements against the ravages of savage foes, and in the halls of our national legislature, are matters of history, and need no repetition here. But one little incident of a more private nature, standing as it does as a sort of sequel to some things already alluded to, I deem worthy of record.

"Some few years since the oldest son of Mr. Lincoln's old friend Armstrong, the chief support of his widowed mother, — the good old man having some time previously passed from earth, — was arrested on the charge of murder. A young man had been killed during a riotous *melée*, in the night time, at a camp-meeting, and one of his associates stated that the death-wound was inflicted by young Armstrong. A preliminary examination was gone into, at which the accuser testified so positively, that there seemed no doubt of the guilt of the prisoner, and therefore he was held for trial. As is too often the case, the bloody act caused an undue degree of excitement in the public mind. Every improper incident in the life of the prisoner,— each act which bore the least semblance of rowdyism,— each school-boy quarrel, — was suddenly remembered and magnified, until they pictured him as a fiend of the most horrible hue. As these rumors spread abroad, they were received as gospel truth, and a feverish desire for vengeance seized upon the infatuated populace, whilst only prison bars prevented a horrible death at the hands of a mob. The events were heralded in the county papers, painted in highest colors, accompanied by rejoicing over the certainty of punishment being meted out to the guilty party. The prisoner, overwhelmed by the circumstances under which he found himself placed, fell into a melancholy condition, bordering upon despair; and the widowed mother, looking through her tears, saw no cause for hope from earthly aid.

"At this juncture, the widow received a letter from Mr. Lincoln, volunteering his services in an effort to save the youth from the impending stroke. Gladly was his aid accepted, although it seemed impossible for even his sagacity to prevail in such a desperate case ; but the heart of the attorney was in his work, and he set about it with a will that knew no such word as fail. Feeling that the poisoned condition of the public mind was such as to preclude the possibility of impanelling an impartial jury in the court having jurisdiction, he procured a change of venue and a postponement of the trial. He then went studiously to work unravelling the history of the case, and satisfied himself that his client was the victim of malice, and that the statements of the accuser were a tissue of falsehoods.

"When the trial was called on, the prisoner, pale and emaciated, with hopelessness written on every feature, and accompanied by his half-hoping, half-despairing mother, — whose only hope was in a mother's belief of her son's innocence, in the justice of the God she worshipped, and in the noble counsel, who, without the hope of fee or reward upon earth, had undertaken the cause, — took his seat in the prisoner's box, and with a 'stony firmness' listened to the reading of the indictment. Lincoln sat quietly by, whilst the large auditory looked on him as though wondering what he could say in defence of one whose guilt they regarded as certain. The examination of the witnesses for the State was begun, and a well-arranged mass of evidence, circumstantial and positive, was introduced, which seemed to impale the prisoner beyond the possibility of extraction. The counsel for the defence propounded but few questions, and those of a character which excited no uneasiness on the part of the prosecutor, — merely, in most cases, requiring the main witnesses to be definite as to the time and place. When the evidence of the prosecution was ended, Lincoln introduced a few witnesses to remove some erroneous impressions in regard to the previous character of his client, who, though somewhat rowdyish, had never been known to commit a vicious act; and to show that a greater degree of ill-feeling existed between the accuser and the accused, than the accuser and the deceased.

"The prosecutor felt that the case was a clear one, and his opening speech was brief and formal. Lincoln arose, while a deathly silence pervaded the vast audience, and in a clear and moderate tone began his argument. Slowly and carefully he reviewed the testimony, pointing out the hitherto unobserved discrepancies in the statements of the principal witness. That which had seemed plain and plausible, he made to appear crooked as a serpent's path. The witness had stated that the affair took place at a certain hour in the evening, and that, by the aid of the brightly shining moon he saw the prisoner inflict the death-blow with a slung-shot. Mr. Lincoln showed that at the hour referred to, the moon had not yet appeared above the horizon, and consequently the whole tale was a fabrication.

"An almost instantaneous change seemed to have been wrought in the minds of his auditors, and the verdict of 'not guilty,' was at the end of every tongue. But the advocate was not content with this intellectual achievement. His whole being had for months been bound up in this work of gratitude and mercy, and, as the lava of the overcharged crater bursts from its imprisonment, so great thoughts and burning words leaped forth from the soul of the eloquent Lincoln. He drew a picture of the perjurer so horrid and ghastly that the accuser could sit under it no longer, but reeled and staggered from the court-room, whilst the audience fancied they could see the brand upon his brow. Then in words of thrilling pathos Lincoln appealed to the jurors as fathers of sons who might become fatherless, and as husbands of wives who might be widowed, to yield to no previous impressions, no ill-founded prejudice, but to do his client justice; and as he alluded to the debt of gratitude which he owed the boy's sire, tears were seen to fall from many eyes unused to weep.

"It was near night when he concluded by saying that if justice was done — as he believed it would be — before the sun should set, it would shine upon his client a free man. The jury retired, and the court adjourned for the day. Half an hour had not elapsed, when, as the officers of the court and the volunteer attorney sat at the tea-table of their hotel, a messenger announced that the jury had returned to their seats. All repaired immediately to the court-house, and whilst the prisoner was being brought from the jail, the court-room was filled to overflowing with citizens of the town. When the prisoner and his mother entered, silence reigned as completely as though the house were empty. The foreman of the jury, in answer to the usual inquiry from the court, delivered the verdict of 'Not Guilty!' The widow dropped into the arms of her son, who lifted her up and told her to look upon him as before, free and innocent. Then, with the words, 'Where is Mr. Lincoln?' he rushed across the room and grasped the hand of his deliverer, whilst his heart was too full for utterance. Lincoln turned his eyes toward the West, where the sun still lingered in view, and then, turning to the youth, said, 'It is not yet sundown, and you are free.' I confess that my cheeks were not wholly unwet by tears, and I turned from the affecting scene. As I cast a glance behind, I saw Abraham Lincoln obeying the divine injunction, by comforting the widowed and the fatherless."

CHAPTER II.

Entrance into Public Life — Election to State Legislature — Presidential Elector — Election to Congress — Action therein, etc.

MR. LINCOLN early identified himself with the Whig party, and was long a disciple and admirer of "Harry of the West." He belongs by character and association to that school of moderate, conservative men, who sought the peaceful extinction of the slave system by the gradually ameliorating influences of advancing sentiment and civilization. When the party with which he had so long acted was fully handed over to the will of the Slave Power, Mr. Lincoln, like Mr. Seward and others, tried to save it from complete destruction. Failing this, he was found among the first to work for the formation of a new organization, which should direct the uprising waves of public feeling on the subject of slavery aggressions.

After Mr. Lincoln's return, in 1832, from the Black Hawk campaign, he became a candidate for the State legislature, but was defeated.

In 1834, he was returned to the legislature by his party, and served for the next six years in the lower house, running the gauntlet of three elections and succeeding in each. In 1836, Mr. Douglas was returned to the legislature and sat on the Democratic side of the House. Here commenced that personal as well as political rivalry which still continues between these two eminent men.

At this period the fever of speculation was at its height throughout the West. A magnificent scheme of internal improvement was projected for Illinois. The credit of the State was beginning to stagger under its erroneous banking system, and the debts incurred to carry forward the projected canals and railroad. Mr. Lincoln was in favor of internal improvements, but his course was marked by judicious approval of plans well matured, likely to benefit the State and increase its prosperity.

Mr. Lincoln took up his residence at Springfield, the capitol of the State, and engaged in the practice of the law. He had studied during his first legislative term, and was admitted to the bar. He soon became a prominent and successful advocate.

The diligent attention necessary to secure success in his chosen profession did not prevent him from taking an active part in both local and national politics. He soon became one of the recognized leaders of the Whig party in the Northwest, and was placed on the Harrison and Clay electoral tickets in the Presidential campaigns of 1840 and 1844. In the latter canvass he took the stump for Henry Clay, and made a tour of Illinois, advocating his claim, to the Presidency.

He was elected in 1846 to the popular branch of the national Congress, from the central district of Illinois. The State legislature was Democratic, and at the same time Mr. Douglas was elected to the United States Senate. Mr. Lincoln took his seat in the Thirtieth Congress, in Dec., 1847. James K. Polk was President when Mr. Hamlin, at this session, first took his seat as Senator from Maine. He then acted with the Democratic party. The Mexican war was being waged. Much opposition existed to the administration on account thereof. The election as Speaker, by the House of Representatives, of Robert C. Winthrop, of Massachusetts, showed the President and Cabinet to be in a minority in that branch of Congress.

The sessions of the Thirtieth Congress were crowded with important events. The unjust war with Mexico, commenced mainly with a view to the extension of Slavery, was terminated on the 30th of May, 1848. By the treaty of peace, Mexico ceded to the United States the territory comprised in New Mexico and Upper California. The lower Rio Grande, from its mouth to El Paso, was made the boundary of Texas.

On the 22d of Dec. 1847, Mr. Lincoln introduced a resolution, calling upon the President to inform Congress whether the spot on which the first blood was shed, was on American soil or not. He voted steadily in opposition to the administration.

The question of organizing a Territorial Government in Oregon, came up for discussion during the first session of this Congress. Mr. Calhoun desired to insert in the Oregon bill, his doctrine, of no power in Congress to abolish slavery in the Territories. This brought up the whole subject. Mr. Douglas proposed in the Senate to extend the line of 36° 30", as laid down in the Wilmot proviso. This was one of that demagogue's first concessions to the South.

A bill for organizing Oregon, applying the conditions of the celebrated Northwest Ordinance of 1787, to the new Territory, was introduced into the House. The Slavery Prohibition provision was stricken out. Mr. Lincoln spoke and voted against the amendment. It was lost by a vote of 114 to 88. The bill passed the House on the 2d of August, 1848, by a vote of 127 to 70. In the Senate, Mr. Douglas moved to amend by extending the line of 36° 30", to the Pacific. This was agreed to, on the 12th of August. The amended bill was sent to the House, which disagreed by a vote of 121 to 82. Mr. Lincoln voted steadily throughout this contest in favor of congressional prohibition of slavery. He performed yeoman service during this session, making himself felt in the House, as a man of ability. His humorous, quick, keen oratorical powers made him a decided character, and when he rose to speak, the House, feeling sure that he would make his points clearly and say something worth hearing, always listened with attention. It was his custom to note down the points to which he wished to speak, and then trust to the glowing heat of his own mind for the sparks to fly whither they were meant. At first, his tone was slow and drawling, his manner heavy, but as he proceeded, he grew warm with argument. His features lighted up, his tone became clearer and more penetrating, and the orator, heated with his subject, would commence rapidly walking up and down the floor, one hand behind his coat-tail, the other gesticulating, while fast as the House subsided under some repartee or witty anecdote, another would come tumbling forth, always hitting point-blank where it was aimed.

The second session of the Thirtieth Congress was marked by an exciting debate, caused by the introduction of a resolution of thanks to General Taylor, and the army in Mexico, for the conduct of the war. Mr. Ashmun, of Massachusetts, (President of the Chicago Convention,) moved to amend an amendment which virtually indorsed the administration in commencing the war, by adding the words, "In a war unnecessarily and unconstitutionally begun by the President of the United States."

This amendment was finally carried, by a vote of 85 to 82, Mr. Lincoln voting in the affirmative. Throughout his congressional career, he steadily voted with the Whigs against the administration and its measures, as carried out in the Mexican war, and attempted to be enforced in the organization of Oregon.

Mr. Lincoln took an active part in the Whig Convention, which, in 1848, nominated General Taylor for the Presidency. He canvassed his own State for the nominee. He also visited New England during the campaign, and attended the Whig State Convention, at Worcester. He afterwards went to New Bedford, where he made a political address, of which the *Mercury* of September 15, 1848, contains the following mention: —

"Mr. Page, Chairman of the Executive Committee, introduced the Hon. Abraham Lincoln, member of Congress from Illinois, who had kindly yielded to the earnest solicitations of the Committee to come from Worcester to address our citizens. Mr. Lincoln enchained the attention of a delighted audience for nearly two hours. His speech covered the whole ground of the national election, and was marked by great originality, clear, conclusive, convincing reasoning, and enlivened by frequent flashes of genuine, racy, Western wit. We have rarely seen a more attentive or interested audience. In fact, he took the hours right between wind and water, and made a most admirable and effective speech, which cannot fail to make a lasting impression on his hearers, and to gain friends for that honest old man and tried patriot, as well as soldier, Zachary Taylor.

"After Mr. Lincoln finished his address, the audience gave him three hearty cheers, and repeated, with rousing cheers, for Taylor and Fillmore."

In the following year, he was the candidate of his party in the legislature for United States Senator, but the Whigs were in the minority.

CHAPTER III.

1854 — The Nebraska Bill Agitation in Illinois — Position of Mr. Lincoln — Speech at Peoria — Anti-Nebraska Convention — Campaign of 1856.

From 1849 to 1854, Mr. Lincoln was engaged assiduously in the practice of his profession, and, being deeply immersed in business, was beginning to lose his interest in politics, when the scheming ambition of an unscrupulous aspirant to the Presidency brought about the repeal of the Missouri Compromise. That act of baseness and perfidy aroused Mr. Lincoln, and he prepared for new efforts. He threw himself at once into the contest that followed, and fought the battle of freedom on the ground of his former conflicts in Illinois with more than his accustomed energy and zeal. Those who recollect the tremendous battle fought in Illinois that year will award to Abraham Lincoln fully three fourths of the ability and unwearying labor which resulted in the victory which gave Illinois her first Republican legislature, and placed Lyman Trumbull in the Senate of the United States. The first and greatest debate of that year came off between Lincoln and Douglas, at Springfield, during the progress of the State Fair, in October. The Chicago *Press and Tribune* describes the scene in the following graphic manner: —

The affair came off on the fourth day of October, 1854. The State Fair had been in progress two days, and the capital was full of all manner of men. The Nebraska bill had been passed on the previous twenty-second of May. Mr. Douglas had returned to Illinois to meet an outraged constituency. He had made a fragmentary speech in Chicago, the people filling up each hiatus in a peculiar and good-humored way. He called the people a mob; they called him a rowdy. The "mob" had the best of it, both then and at the election which succeeded. The notoriety of all these events had stirred up the politics of the State from bottom to top.

Hundreds of active politicians had met at Springfield, expecting a tournament of an unusual character, — Douglas, Breese, Kœrner, Lincoln, Trumbull, Matteson, Yates, Codding, John Calhoun, (of the order of the Candle-Box,) John M. Palmer, the whole house of the McConnells, Singleton, (known to fame in the Mormon war,) Thomas L. Harris, and a host of others. Several speeches were made before, and several after, the passage between Lincoln and Douglas, but that was justly held to be the event of the season.

We do not know whether a challenge to debate passed between the friends of the speakers or not, but there was a perfectly amicable understanding between Lincoln and Douglas that the former should speak two or three hours, and the latter reply in just as little or as much time as he chose. Mr. Lincoln took the stand at two o'clock, — a large crowd in attendance, and Mr. Douglas seated on a small platform in front of the desk. The first half hour of Mr. Lincoln's speech was taken up with compliments to his distinguished friend, Judge Douglas, and dry allusions to the political events of the past few years. His distinguished friend, Judge Douglas, had taken his seat, as solemn as the Cock-lane ghost, evidently with the design of not moving a muscle till it came his turn to speak. The laughter provoked by Lincoln's exordium, however, soon began to make him uneasy, and when Mr. Lincoln arrived at his (Douglas's) speech, pronouncing the Missouri Compromise "a sacred thing which no ruthless hand would ever be reckless enough to disturb," he opened his lips far enough to remark, "A first-rate speech!" This was the beginning of an amusing colloquy.

"Yes," continued Lincoln, "so affectionate was my friend's regard for this compromise line, that when Texas was admitted into the Union, and it was found that a strip extended north of 36°30′, he actually introduced a bill extending the line, and prohibiting slavery in the northern edge of the new State."

"And you voted against the bill," said Douglas.

"Precisely so," answered Lincoln; "I was in favor of running the line *a great deal further South.*"

"About this time," the speaker continued, "my distinguished friend introduced me to a particular friend of his, one David Wilmot, of Pennsylvania." [Laughter.]

"I thought," said Douglas, "you would find him congenial company."

"So I did," replied Lincoln. "I had the pleasure of voting for his proviso, in one way and another, about forty times. It was a

Democratic measure then, I believe. At any rate, General Cass scolded honest John Davis, of Massachusetts, soundly for talking away the last hours of the session, so that he (Cass) couldn't crowd it through. Apropos of General Cass; if I am not greatly mistaken, he has a prior claim to my distinguished friend to the authorship of popular sovereignty. The old gentleman has an infirmity for writing letters. Shortly after the scolding he gave John Davis, he wrote his Nicholson letter — "

Douglas, (solemnly.) "God Almighty placed man on the earth, and told him to choose between good and evil. That was the origin of the Nebraska Bill!"

Lincoln. "Well, the priority of invention being settled, let us award all credit to Judge Douglas for being the first to discover it."

It would be impossible, in these limits, to give an idea of the strength of Mr. Lincoln's argument. We deemed it by far the ablest effort of the campaign, — from whatever source. The occasion was a great one, and the speaker was every way equal to it. The effect produced on the listeners was magnetic. No one who was present will ever forget the power and vehemence of the following passage : —

"My distinguished friend says it is an insult to the emigrants to Kansas and Nebraska to suppose that they are not able to govern themselves. We must not slur over an argument of this kind, because it happens to tickle the ear. It must be met and answered. I admit that the emigrant to Kansas and Nebraska is competent to govern *himself*, but" (the speaker rising to his full height) "*I deny his right to govern any other person* WITHOUT THAT PERSON'S CONSENT." The applause which followed this triumphal refutation of a cunning falsehood was but an earnest of the victory at the polls which followed just one month from that day.

When Mr. Lincoln had concluded, Mr. Douglas strode hastily to the stand. As usual, he employed ten minutes in telling how grossly he had been abused, recollecting himself, he added, "though in a perfectly courteous manner," — abused in a perfectly courteous manner! He then devoted half an hour to showing that it was indispensably necessary to California emigrants, Santa Fe traders and others, to have organic acts provided for the territories of Kansas and Nebraska, — that being precisely the point which nobody disputes. Having established these premises to his satisfaction, Mr. Douglas launched forth into an argument wholly apart from the positions taken by Mr. Lincoln. He had about half finished at six o'clock, when an adjournment to tea was effected. The speaker insisted strenuously upon his right to resume in the evening, but we believe the second part of that speech has not been delivered to this day. After the Springfield passage, the two speakers went to Peoria, and tried it again, with identically the same results. A friend who listened to the Peoria debate, informed us that after Lincoln had finished, Douglas "hadn't much to say," — which we presume to have been Mr. Douglas's view of the case also, for the reason that he ran away from his antagonist and kept out of his way during the remainder of his campaign.

At Peoria, in the same summer, Mr. Lincoln made a speech, from which we extract.

THE SPREAD OF SLAVERY.

This is the *repeal* of the Missouri Compromise. The foregoing history may not be precisely accurate in every particular; but I am sure it is sufficiently so for all the uses I shall attempt to make of it, and in it we have before us the chief materials enabling us to correctly judge whether the repeal of the Missouri Compromise is right or wrong.

I think, and shall try to show, that it it wrong, — wrong in its direct effect, letting slavery into Kansas and Nebraska, and wrong in its prospective principle, allowing it to spread to every other part of the wide world, where men can be found inclined to take it.

This *declared* indifference, but, as I must think, covert *real* zeal for the spread of slavery, I cannot but hate. I hate it because of the monstrous injustice of slavery itself. I hate it because it deprives our Republican example of its just influence in the world; enables the enemies of free institutions, with plausibility, to taunt us as hypocrites; causes the real friends of freedom to doubt our sincerity, and especially because it forces so many really good men amongst ourselves into an open war with the very fundamental principles of civil liberty, criticising the Declaration of Independence, and insisting that there is no right principle of action but *self-interest.*

Before proceeding, let me say, I think I have no prejudice against the Southern people. They are just what we would be in their situation. If slavery did not now exist among them, they would not introduce it. If it did now exist among us, we should not instantly give it up. This I believe of the masses North and South. Doubtless there are individuals, on both sides, who would not hold slaves under any circumstances; and others who would gladly introduce slavery anew if it were out of existence. We know that some Southern men do free their slaves, go North, and become tip-top Abolitionists; while some Northern ones go South, and become most cruel slave-masters.

WHAT SHALL BE DONE?

When Southern people tell us they are no more responsible for the origin of slavery than we, I acknowledge the fact. When it is said that the institution exists, and that it is very difficult to get rid of it, in any satisfactory way, I can understand and appreciate the saying. I surely will not blame them for not doing what I should not know how to do myself. If all earthly power were given me, I should not know what to do, as to the existing institution. My first impulse would be to free all the slaves, and send them to Liberia — to their own native land. But a moment's reflection would convince me, that whatever of high hope (as I think there is) there may be in this, in the long run, its sudden execution is impossible. If they were all landed there in a day, they would all perish in the next ten days; and there are not surplus shipping and surplus money enough in the world to carry them there in many times ten days. What then? Free them all, and keep them among us as underlings? Is it quite certain that this betters their condition? I think I would not hold one in slavery at any rate; yet the point is not clear enough to me to denounce people upon. What next? Free them, and make them politically and socially our equals? My own feelings will not admit of this; and if mine would, we well know that those of the great mass of white people will not. Whether this feeling accords with justice and sound judgment, is not the sole question, if, indeed, it is any part of it. A universal feeling, whether well or ill founded, cannot be safely disregarded. We cannot, then, make them equals. It does seem to me that systems of gradual emancipation might be adopted; but for their tardiness in this, I will not undertake to judge our brethren of the South.

When they remind us of their constitutional rights, I acknowledge them, not grudgingly, but fully and fairly; and I would give them any legislation for the reclaiming of their fugitives, which should not, in its stringency, be more likely to carry a free man into slavery, than our ordinary criminal laws are to hang an innocent one.

But all this, to my judgment, furnishes no more excuse for permitting slavery to go into our own free territory, than it would for reviving the African slave-trade by law. The law which forbids the bringing of slaves *from* Africa, and that which has so long forbid the taking of them *to* Nebraska, can hardly be distinguished on any moral principle; and the repeal of the former could find quite as plausible excuses as that of the latter.

In October of the same year, a mass convention of the anti-Nebraska men was held at Springfield. The following resolutions were there adopted. The platform adopted was more radical than the sentiments then and since avowed by Mr. Lincoln,—

1. *Resolved*, That we believe this truth to be self-evident, that when parties become subversive of the ends for which they are established, or incapable of restoring the Government to the true principles of the Constitution, it is the right and duty of the people to dissolve the political bands by which they may have been connected therewith, and to organize new parties upon such principles and with such views as the circumstances and exigencies of the nation may demand.

2. *Resolved*, That the times imperatively demand the reorganization of parties, and, repudiating all previous party attachments, names, and predilections, we unite ourselves together in defence of the liberty and Constitution of the country, and will hereafter co-operate as the Republican party, pledged to the accomplishment of the following purposes: To bring the administration of the Government back to the control of first principles; to restore Nebraska and Kansas to the position of free territories; that as the Constitution of the United States vests in the States, and not in Congress, the power to legislate for the extradition of fugitives from labor, to repeal and entirely abrogate the Fugitive Slave Law; to restrict slavery to those States in which it exists; to prohibit the admission of any more slave States into the Union; to abolish slavery in the District of Columbia; to exclude slavery from all the territories over which the General Government has exclusive jurisdiction; and

to resist the acquirements of any more territories unless the practice of slavery therein forever shall have been prohibited.

3. *Resolved*, that in furtherance of these principles we will use such constitutional and lawful means as shall seem best adapted to their accomplishment, and that we will support no man for office, under the General or State Government, who is not positively and fully committed to the support of these principles, and whose personal character and conduct is not a guaranty that he is reliable, and who shall not have abjured old party allegiance and ties.

In 1855, Mr. Lincoln was again a candidate before the legislature for the United States senatorship, but was unsuccessful, Judge Trumbull being elected to the position he has since so ably filled.

The Republican party being fully organized with the gallant Fremont as its candidate for the Presidency, Mr. Lincoln was placed at the head of the State Electoral Ticket. He canvassed the State during that exciting campaign.

CHAPTER IV.

Nomination as Senator at Springfield — Speech of Acceptance — Challenge to Douglas — Correspondence.

THE Republican State Convention of Illinois, that met at Springfield, June 17, 1858, placed in nomination Abraham Lincoln as its candidate for the United States senatorship, soon to be vacated by the expiration of Judge Douglas's term. The latter came fresh from his celebrated Lecompton struggle, to fight both the Republican candidate and the friends of the administration. The strife was indeed an arduous one, and won the admiration of the "Little Giant's" most determined foes.

In accepting this nomination, tendered him by the Convention, Mr. Lincoln gives expression to the principles which he conceived should govern the coming canvass. He also analyzes the position of Senator Douglas and of both wings of the Democratic party. The speech will be found terse, logical, and vigorous. It reviews the position of the two branches of the Democracy, and exposes in a scathing manner the false premises and weaker deductions of his opponent. He commenced by enunciating, in the broadest manner —

THE IRREPRESSIBLE CONFLICT.

Mr. President and Gentlemen of the Convention: If we could first know where we are, and whither we are tending, we could better judge what to do, and how to do it. We are now far into the fifth year, since a policy was initiated with the avowed object, and confident promise, of putting an end to slavery agitation. Under the operation of that policy, that agitation has not only not ceased, but has constantly augmented. In my opinion, it will not cease, until a crisis shall have been reached and passed. "A house divided against itself cannot stand." I believe this government cannot endure permanently half slave and half free. I do not expect the Union to be dissolved; I do not expect the house to fall; but I do expect it will cease to be divided. It will become all one thing or all the other. Either the opponents of slavery will arrest the further spread of it, and place it where the public mind shall rest in the belief that it is in the course of ultimate extinction; or its advocates will push it forward, till it shall become alike lawful in all the States; old as well as new, North as well as South.

THE DRED SCOTT DECISION — ITS HISTORY.

Have we no tendency to the latter condition?

Let any one who doubts, carefully contemplate that now almost complete legal combination, — piece of machinery, so to speak, — compounded of the Nebraska doctrine, and the Dred Scott decision. Let him consider not only what work the machinery is adapted to do, and how well adapted; but also, let him study the history of its construction, and trace, if he can, or rather fail, if he can, to trace the evidences of design, and concert of action, among its chief architects, from the beginning.

The new year of 1854 found slavery excluded from more than half the States by State constitutions, and from most of the national territory by congressional prohibition. Four days later, commenced the struggle which ended in repealing that congressional prohibition. This opened all the national territory to slavery, and was the first point gained.

But, so far, Congress only had acted; and an indorsement by the people, real or apparent, was indispensable, to save the point already gained, and give chance for more.

This necessity had not been overlooked; but had been provided for, as well as might be, in the notable argument of "squatter sovereignty," otherwise called "sacred right of self-government," which latter phrase, though expressive of the only rightful basis of any government, was so perverted in this attempted use of it as to amount to just this: That if any *one* man choose to enslave *another*, no *third* man shall be allowed to object. That argument was incorporated into the Nebraska bill itself, in the language which follows: "It being the true intent and meaning of this act not to legislate slavery into any territory or State, nor to exclude it therefrom; but to leave the people thereof perfectly free to form and regulate their domestic institutions in their own way, subject only to the Constitution of the United States." Then opened the roar of loose declamation in favor of "Squatter Sovereignty," and "sacred right of self-government." "But," said opposition members, "let us amend the bill so as to expressly declare that the people of the territory may exclude slavery." "Not we," said the friends of the measure; and down they voted the amendment.

While the Nebraska bill was passing through Congress, a *law case* involving the question of a negro's freedom, by reason of his owner having voluntarily taken him into a free State, and then into a territory covered by the congressional prohibition, and held him as a slave for a long time in each, was passing through the U. S. Circuit Court for the District of Missouri; and both Nebraska bill and lawsuit were brought to a decision in the same month of May, 1854. The negro's name was "Dred Scott," which name now designates the decision finally made in the case. Before the then next presidential election, the law case came to, and was argued in, the Supreme Court of the United States; but the decision of it was deferred until after the election. Still, before the election, Senator Trumbull, on the floor of the Senate, requested the leading advocate of the Nebraska bill to state *his opinion* whether the people of a territory can constitutionally exclude slavery from their limits; and the latter answers: "That is a question for the Supreme Court."

The election came. Mr. Buchanan was elected, and the indorsement, such as it was, secured. That was the second point gained. The indorsement, however, fell short of a clear popular majority by nearly four hundred thousand votes, and so, perhaps, was not overwhelmingly reliable and satisfactory. The outgoing President, in his last annual message, as impressively as possible echoed back upon the people the weight and authority of the indorsement. The Supreme Court met again; did not announce their decision, but ordered a reargument. The presidential inauguration came, and still no decision of the court; but the incoming President, in his inaugural address, fervently exhorted the people to abide by the forthcoming decision, whatever it might be. Then, in a few days, came the decision.

The reputed author of the Nebraska bill finds an early occasion to make a speech at this capital indorsing the Dred Scott decision, and vehemently denouncing all opposition to it. The new President, too, seizes the early occasion of the Silliman letter to indorse and strongly construe that decision, and to express his astonishment that any different view had ever been entertained!

At length a squabble springs up between the President and the author of the Nebraska bill, on the mere question of *fact*, whether the Lecompton Constitution was or was not, in any just sense, made by the people of Kansas; and in that quarrel the latter declares that all he wants is a fair vote for the people, and that he cares not whether slavery be voted *down* or voted *up*. I do not understand his declaration that he cares not whether slavery be voted down or voted up, to be intended by him other than as an apt definition of the policy he would impress upon the public mind, — the principle for which he declares he has suffered so much, and is ready to suffer to the end. And well may he cling to that principle. If he has any parental feeling, well may he cling to it. That principle is the only shred left of his original Nebraska doctrine. Under the Dred Scott decision, "squatter sovereignty" squatted out of existence, tumbled down, like temporary scaffolding, — like the mould at the foundry served through one blast, and fell back into loose sand, — helped to carry an election, and then was kicked to the winds. His late joint struggle with the Republicans, against the Lecompton Constitution, involves nothing of the original Nebraska doctrine. That struggle was made on a point — the right of a people to make their own constitution — upon which he and the Republicans have never differed.

ITS WORKINGS AND OBJECTS.

The several points of the Dred Scott decision, in connection with Senator Douglas's "care not" policy, constitute the piece of machinery, in its present state of advancement. This was the third point gained. The working points of that machinery are: —

First, That no negro slave, imported as such from Africa, and no descendant of such slave, can ever be a citizen of any State, in the sense of that term as used in the Constitution of the United States.

This point is made in order to deprive the negro, in every possible event, of the benefit of that provision of the United States Constitution, which declares that "The citizens of each State shall be entitled to all privileges and immunities of citizens in the several States."

Secondly, That "subject to the Constitution of the United States," neither Congress nor a territorial legislature can exclude slavery from any United States territory. This point is made in order that individual men may fill up the territories with slaves, without danger of losing them as property, and thus to enhance the chances of permanency to the institution through all the future.

Thirdly, That whether the holding a negro in actual slavery in a free State, makes him free, as against the holder, the United States courts will not decide, but will leave to be decided by the courts of any slave State the negro may be forced into by the master. This point is made, not to be pressed immediately; but, if acquiesced in for a while, and apparently indorsed by the people at an election, then to sustain the logical conclusion that what Dred Scott's master might lawfully do with Dred Scott, in the free State of Illinois, every other master may lawfully do with any other one or one thousand slaves, in Illinois, or in any other free State.

Auxiliary to all this, and working hand in hand with it, the Nebraska doctrine, or what is left of it, is to educate and mould public opinion, at least Northern public opinion, not to care whether slavery is voted down or voted up. This shows exactly where we now are; and partially, also, whither we are tending.

THE CONSPIRACY.

It will throw additional light on the latter, to go back, and run the mind over the string of historical facts already stated. Several things will now appear less dark and mysterious than they did when they were transpiring. The people were to be left "perfectly free," "subject only to the Constitution." What the Constitution had to do with it, outsiders could not then see. Plainly enough now, it was an exactly fitted niche, for the Dred Scott decision to afterward come in, and declare the perfect freedom of the people to be just no freedom at all. Why was the amendment, expressly declaring the right of the people, voted down? Plainly enough now: the adoption of it would have spoiled the niche for the Dred Scott decision. Why was the court decision held up? Why even a Senator's individual opinion withheld, till after the presidential election? Plainly enough now: the speaking out then would have damaged the perfectly free argument upon which the election was to be carried. Why the outgoing President's felicitation on the indorsement? Why the delay of a reargument? Why the incoming President's advance exhortation in favor of the decision? These things look like the cautious patting and petting of a spirited horse preparatory to mounting him, when it is dreaded that he may give the rider a fall. And why the hasty after-indorsement of the decision by the President and others?

We cannot absolutely know that all these exact adaptations are the result of preconcert. But when we see a lot of framed timbers, different portions of which we know have been gotten out at different times and places and by different workmen, — Stephen, Franklin, Roger, and James, for instance, — and when we see these timbers joined together, and see they exactly make the frame of a house or a mill, all the tenons and mortices exactly fitting, and all the lengths and proportions of the different pieces exactly adapted to their respective places, and not a piece too many or too few, — not omitting even scaffolding, — or, if a single piece be lacking, we see the place in the frame exactly fitted and prepared yet to bring such piece in, — in such a case, we find it impossible not to believe that Stephen, and Franklin, and Roger, and James, all understood one another from the beginning, and all worked upon a common plan or draft drawn up before the first blow was struck.

It should not be overlooked that, by the Nebraska bill, the people of a *State* as well as territory, were to be left "perfectly free," "subject only to the Constitution." Why mention a State? They were legislating for territories, and not for or about States. Certainly the people of a State are and ought to be subject to the Constitution of the United States; but why is mention of this lugged into this merely territorial law? Why are the people of a territory and the people of a State therein lumped together, and their relation to the Constitution therein treated as being precisely the same? While the opinion of the court, by Chief Justice Taney, in the Dred Scott case, and the separate opinions of all the concurring judges, expressly declare that the Constitution of the United States neither permits Congress nor a territorial legislature to exclude slavery from any United States territory, they all omit to declare whether or not the same Constitution permits a State, or the people of a State to exclude it. *Possibly*, this is a mere omission; but who can be quite sure, if McLean or Curtis had sought to get into the opinion a declaration of unlimited power in the people of a State to exclude slavery from their limits, just as Chase and Mace sought to get such declaration, in behalf of the people of a territory, into the Nebraska bill; — I ask, who can be quite sure that it would not have been voted down in the one case as it had been in the other? The nearest approach to the point of declaring the power of a State over slavery, is made by Judge Nelson. He approaches it more than once, using the precise idea, and almost the language, too, of the Nebraska act. On one occasion, his exact language is, "Except in cases where the power is restrained by the Constitution of the United States, the law of the State is supreme over the subject of slavery within its jurisdiction." In what cases the power of the States is so restrained by the United States Constitution, is left an open question, precisely as the same question, as to the restraint on the power of the territories, was left open in the Nebraska act. Put this and that together, and we have another nice little niche, which we may, ere long, see filled with another Supreme Court decision, declaring that the Constitution of the United States does not permit a *State* to exclude slavery from its limits. And this may especially be expected if the doctrine of "care not whether slavery be voted down or voted up," shall gain upon the public mind sufficiently to give promise that such a decision can be maintained when made.

Such a decision is all that slavery now lacks of being alike lawful in all the States. Welcome, or unwelcome, such decision is probably coming, and will soon be upon us, unless the power of the present political dynasty shall be met and overthrown. We shall lie down pleasantly dreaming that the people of Missouri are on the verge of making their State free, and we shall awake to the reality instead, that the Supreme Court has made Illinois a slave State. To meet and overthrow the power of that dynasty, is the work now before all those who would prevent that consummation. That is what we have to do. How can we best do it?

THE SLAVE OLIGARCHY AND JUDGE DOUGLAS.

There are those who denounce us openly to their own friends, and yet whisper us softly, that Senator Douglas is the aptest instrument there is with which to effect that object. They wish us to *infer* all, from the fact that he now has a little quarrel with the present head of the dynasty; and that he has regularly voted with us on a single point, upon which he and we have never differed. They remind us that he is a great man, and that the largest of us are very small ones. Let this be granted. But "a living dog is better than a dead lion." Judge Douglas, if not a dead lion, for this work, is at least a caged and toothless one. How can he oppose the advances of slavery? He don't care anything about it. His avowed mission is impressing the "public heart" to *care nothing about it.* A leading Douglas Democratic newspaper thinks Douglas's superior talent will be needed to resist the revival of the African slave-trade. Does Douglas believe an effort to revive that trade is approaching? He has not said so. Does he really think so? But if it is, how can he resist it? For years he has labored to prove it a sacred right of white men to take negro slaves into the new territories. Can he possibly show that it is less a sacred right to buy them where they can be bought cheapest? And unquestionably they can be bought cheaper in Africa than in Virginia. He has done all in his power to reduce the whole question of slavery to one of a mere right of property; and as such, how can he oppose the foreign slave-trade,—how can he refuse that trade, in that "property" shall be "perfectly free,"—unless he does it as a protection to the home production? And as the home producers will probably not ask the protection, he will be wholly without a ground of opposition.

Senator Douglas holds, we know, that a man may rightfully be wiser to-day than he was yesterday, that he may rightfully change when he finds himself wrong. But can we, for that reason, run ahead, and infer that he will make any particular change, of which he, himself, has given no intimation? Can we safely base our action upon any such vague inference? Now, as ever, I wish not to misrepresent Judge Douglas's position, question his motives, or do aught that can be personally offensive to him. Whenever, if ever, he and we can come together on principle so that our cause may have assistance from his great ability, I hope to have interposed no adventitious obstacle. But clearly, he is not now with us; he does not pretend to be; he does not promise ever to be.

Our cause, then, must be intrusted to, and conducted by, its own undoubted friends,—those whose hands are free, whose hearts are in the work, who *do care* for the result. Two years ago the Re-

The canvass that ensued was one of the most memorable political contests in the history of this country. Mr. Lincoln's conduct of the Republican cause, against confessedly one of the most powerful and able of politicians now living, won for him, at once, a national reputation. It was his masterly *exposé* of the Democratic treachery to the Union, which caused him to be taken up by the Chicago Convention and made the standard-bearer of the party during the ensuing important contest.

Mr. Lincoln spoke twice in the canvass previous to the commencement of the joint debates between himself and Senator Douglas.

The following correspondence shows the arrangements for the joint debates, which, in the summer of 1858, made the people of the county generally look so eagerly to Illinois. The challenge for the joint discussion, as will be seen, proceeded from the Republican candidate.

Mr. Lincoln to Mr. Douglas.

CHICAGO, ILL., July 24, 1858.

Hon. S. A. DOUGLAS — *My Dear Sir:* Will it be agreeable to you to make an arrangement for you and myself to divide time, and address the same audiences, the present canvass? Mr. Judd, who will hand you this, is authorized to receive your answer; and, if agreeable to you, to enter into the terms of such arrangement.

Your obedient servant,

A. LINCOLN.

Mr. Douglas to Mr. Lincoln.

CHICACO, July 24, 1858.

Hon. A. LINCOLN — *Dear Sir:* Your note of this date, in which you inquire if it would be agreeable to me to make an arrangement to divide the time, and address the same audiences, during the present canvass, was handed me by Mr. Judd. Recent events have interposed difficulties in the way of such an arrangement.

I went to Springfield last week for the purpose of conferring with the Democratic State Central Committee upon the mode of conducting the canvass, and with them, and under their advice, made a list of appointments covering the entire period until late in

October. The people of the several localities have been notified of the times and places of the meetings. Those appointments have all been made for Democratic meetings, and arrangements have been made by which the Democratic candidates for Congress, for the legislature, and other offices, will be present, and address the people. It is evident, therefore, that these various candidates, in connection with myself, will occupy the whole time of the day and evening, and leave no opportunity for other speeches.

Besides, there is another consideration which should be kept in mind. It has been suggested recently that an arrangement had been made to bring out a third candidate for the United States Senate, who, with yourself, should canvass the State in opposition to me, with no other purpose than to insure my defeat, by dividing the Democratic party for your benefit. If I should make this arrangement with you, it is more than probable that this other candidate, who has a common object with you, would desire to become a party to it, and claim the right to speak from the same stand; so that he and you, in concert, might be able to take the opening and closing speech in every case.

I cannot refrain from expressing my surprise, if it was your original intention to invite such an arrangement, that you should have waited until after I had made my appointments, inasmuch as we were both here in Chicago together for several days after my arrival, and again at Bloomington, Atlanta, Lincoln, and Springfield, where it was well known I went for the purpose of consulting with the State Central Committee, and agreeing upon the plan of the campaign.

While, under these circumstances, I do not feel at liberty to make any arrangements which would deprive the Democratic candidates for Congress, State officers, and the legislature, from participating in the discussion at the various meetings designated by the Democratic State Central Committee, I will, in order to accommodate you as far as it is in my power to do so, take the responsibility of making an arrangement with you for a discussion between us at one prominent point in each Congressional District in the State, except the second and sixth districts, where we have both spoken, and in each of which cases you had the concluding speech. If agreeable to you, I will indicate the following places as those most suitable in the several Congressional Districts at which we should speak, to wit: Freeport, Ottawa, Galesburg, Quincy,

Alton, Jonesboro', and Charleston. I will confer with you at the earliest convenient opportunity in regard to the mode of conducting the debate, the times of meeting at the several places, subject to the condition, that where appointments have already been made by the Democratic State Central Committee at any of those places, I must insist upon you meeting me at the times specified.

Very respectfully, your most obedient servant,

S. A. DOUGLAS.

Mr. Lincoln to Mr. Douglas.

SPRINGFIELD, July 29, 1858.

Hon. S. A. DOUGLAS—*Dear Sir:* Yours of the 24th, in relation to an arrangement to divide time, and address the same audiences, is received; and, in apology for not sooner replying, allow me to say, that when I sat by you at dinner yesterday, I was not aware that you had answered my note, nor, certainly, that my own note had been presented to you. An hour after, I saw a copy of your answer in the Chicago Times, and, reaching home, I found the original awaiting me. Protesting that your insinuations of attempted unfairness on my part are unjust, and, with the hope that you did not very considerately make them, I proceed to reply. To your statement that "it has been suggested, recently, that an arrangement had been made to bring out a third candidate for the United States Senate, who, with yourself, should canvass the State in opposition to me," etc., I can only say that such suggestion must have been made by yourself, for, certainly, none such has been made by or to me, or otherwise, to my knowledge. Surely, you did not *deliberately* conclude, as you insinuate, that I was expecting to draw you into an arrangement of terms, to be agreed on by yourself, by which a third candidate and myself, "in concert, might be able to take the opening and closing speech in every case."

As to your surprise that I did not sooner make the proposal to divide time with you, I can only say I made it as soon as I resolved to make it. I did not know but that such proposal would come from you; I waited, respectfully, to see. It may have been well known to you that you went to Springfield for the purpose of agreeing on the plan of campaign; but it was not so known to me.

When your appointments were announced in the papers, extending only to the 21st of August, I, for the first time, considered it certain that you would make no proposal to me, and then resolved that, if my friends concurred, I would make one to you. As soon thereafter as I could see and consult with friends satisfactorily, I did make the proposal. It did not occur to me that the proposed arrangement could derange your plans after the latest of your appointments already made. After that, there was, before the election, largely over two months of clear time.

For you to say that we have already spoken at Chicago and Springfield, and that on both occasions I had the concluding speech, is hardly a fair statement. The truth rather is this: At Chicago, July 9, you made a carefully prepared conclusion on my speech of June 16th, Twenty-four hours after, I made a hasty conclusion on yours on the 9th. You had six days to prepare, and concluded on me again, at Bloomington, on the 16th. Twenty-four hours after, I concluded again on you at Springfield. In the mean time, you had made another conclusion on me at Springfield, which I did not hear, and of the contents of which I knew nothing when I spoke; so that your speech made in daylight, and mine at night, of the 17th, at Springfield, were both made in perfect independence of each other. The dates of making all these speeches will show, I think, that, in the matter of time for preparation, the advantage has all been on your side; and that none of the external circumstances have stood to my advantage

I agree to an arrangement for us to speak at the seven places you have named, and at your own times, provided you name the times at once, so that I, as well as you, can have to myself the time not covered by the arrangement. As to the other details, I wish perfect reciprocity, and no more. I wish as much time as you, and that conclusions shall alternate. That is all.

Your obedient servant,

A. LINCOLN.

P. S. As matters now stand, I shall be at no more of your exclusive meetings; and, for about a week from to-day, a letter from you will reach me at Springfield. A. L.

Mr. Douglas to Mr. Lincoln.

BEMENT, PIATT CO., ILL., July 30, 1858.

Dear Sir: Your letter, dated yesterday, accepting my proposition for a joint discussion at one prominent point in each Congressional District, as stated in my previous letter, was received this morning.

The times and places designated are as follows: —

Ottawa, La Salle County	August	21,	1858.
Freeport, Stephenson County	"	27,	"
Jonesboro', Union County	September	15,	"
Charleston, Coles County	"	18,	"
Galesburg, Knox County	October	7,	"
Quincy, Adams County	"	13,	"
Alton, Madison County	"	15,	"

I agree to your suggestion that we shall alternately open and close the discussion. I will speak at Ottawa one hour, you can reply, occupying an hour and a half, and I will then follow for half an hour. At Freeport, you shall open the discussion, and speak one hour, I will follow for an hour and a half, and you can then reply for half an hour. We will alternate in like manner in each successive place.

Very respectfully, your obedient servant,

S. A. DOUGLAS.

Hon. A. LINCOLN, Springfield, Ill.

Mr. Lincoln to Mr. Douglas.

SPRINGFIELD, July 31, 1858.

Hon. S. A. DOUGLAS — *Dear Sir:* Yours of yesterday, naming places, times, and terms, for joint discussions between us, was received this morning. Although, by the terms, as you propose, you take *four* openings and closes to my *three*, I accede, and thus close the arrangement. I direct this to you at Hillsboro', and shall try to have both your letter and this appear in the Journal and Register of Monday morning.

Your obedient servant,

A. LINCOLN.

CHAPTER V.

The Senatorial Debates — Position of the Candidates — The Second Debate, at Freeport — Arguments of Mr. Lincoln and Mr. Douglas.

The contest that ensued upon the acceptance of Mr. Lincoln's challenge, was certainly one of the most remarkable in our political history. The position of the two men, the circumstances under which they appeared before the public, and the peculiar uncertainty which seemed to hang over political affairs, all combined to rivet the attention of the country upon this extraordinary struggle.

Both men were remarkable for great native ability, and for having, by their own energy, placed themselves in the foremost ranks of their respective parties. One of them, Judge Douglas, is far more than an ordinary man in his own range of intellect. He is one of the ablest, most unscrupulous, and daring of politicians. Not by any means possessed of the qualities of a statesman, he yet has great power as a popular leader and a partisan advocate. The other, Mr. Lincoln, with much less of the politician and partisan, less adroit and cunning, has yet, by the clearness of his logical intellect, the sagacious honesty of his character, and the persistence and energy with which he enforces ideas and carries out his purpose, won for himself a strong and abiding hold in the heart and faith of the people.

The Democratic Senator had returned from Washington, fresh from his Lecompton fight, — a fight induced by policy, and not principle, on his part. He stood before the people black with broken pledges, and disgraced by the violated compacts which, for his own mad ambition, he had broken. It was necessary to meet and expose his duplicity and treachery. Well and ably was it performed by Mr. Lincoln.

The second of these debates, held at Freeport, August 27, is generally esteemed the most masterly of these expositions of the principles of both the great parties, as represented by Messrs. Lincoln and Douglas. It is herewith inserted entire.

SECOND JOINT DEBATE, AT FREEPORT.

MR. LINCOLN'S SPEECH, AUGUST 27, 1858.

Ladies and Gentlemen: On Saturday last, Judge Douglas and myself first met in public discussion. He spoke one hour, I an hour and a half, and he replied for half an hour. The order is now reversed. I am to speak an hour, he an hour and a half, and then I am to reply for half an hour. I propose to devote myself during the first hour to the scope of what was brought within the range of his half hour's speech at Ottawa. Of course there was brought within the scope in that half hour's speech something of his own opening speech. In the course of that opening argument, Judge Douglas proposed to me seven distinct interrogatories. In my speech of an hour and a half, I attended to some other parts of his speech, and incidentally, as I thought, answered one of the interrogatories then. I then distinctly intimated to him that I would answer the rest of his interrogatories on condition only that he should agree to answer as many for me. He made no intimation at the time of the proposition, nor did he in his reply allude at all to that suggestion of mine. I do him no injustice in saying that he occupied at least half of his reply in dealing with me as though I had *refused* to answer his interrogatories. I now propose that I will answer any of the interrogatories upon condition that he will answer questions from me not exceeding the same number. I give him an opportunity to respond. The Judge remains silent. I now say that I will answer his interrogatories whether he answers mine

4

or not; and that. after I have done so, I shall propound mine to him.

I have supposed myself, since the organization of the Republican party at Bloomington, in May, 1856, bound as a party man by the platforms of the party, then and since. If in any interrogatories which I shall answer I go beyond the scope of what is within these platforms, it will be perceived that no one is responsible but myself.

Having said thus much, I will take up the Judge's interrogatories as I find them printed in the Chicago *Times*, and answer them *seriatim*. In order that there may be no mistake about it, I have copied the interrogatories in writing, and also my answers to them. The first one of these interrogatories is in these words: —

Question 1. I desire to know whether Lincoln to-day stands, as he did in 1854, in favor of the unconditional repeal of the Fugitive Slave Law?

Answer. I do not now, nor ever did, stand in favor of the unconditional repeal of the Fugitive Slave Law.

Q. 2. I desire him to answer whether he stands pledged to-day, as he did in 1854, against the admission of any more slave States into the Union, even if the people want them?

A. I do not now, nor ever did, stand pledged against the admission of any more slave States into the Union.

Q. 3. I want to know whether he stands pledged against the admission of a new State into the Union with such a constitution as the people of that State may see fit to make?

A. I do not stand pledged against the admission of a new State into the Union with such a Constitution as the people of that State may see fit to make.

Q. 4. I want to know whether he stands to-day pledged to the abolition of slavery in the District of Columbia?

A. I do not stand to-day pledged to the abolition of slavery in the District of Columbia.

Q. 5. I desire him to answer whether he stands pledged to the prohibition of the slave-trade between the different States?

A. I do not stand pledged to the prohibition of the slave-trade between the different States.

Q. 6. I desire to know whether he stands pledged to prohibit slavery in all the territories of the United States, north as well as south of the Missouri Compromise line?

A. I am impliedly, if not expressly, pledged to a belief in the *right* and *duty* of Congress to prohibit slavery in all the United States territories.

Q. 7. I desire him to answer whether he is opposed to the acquisition of any new territory unless slavery is first prohibited therein?

A. I am not generally opposed to honest acquisition of territory; and, in any given case, I would or would not oppose such acquisition, accordingly as I might think such acquisition would or would not aggravate the slavery question among ourselves.

Now, my friends, it will be perceived upon an examination of these questions and answers, that so far I have only answered that I was not *pledged* to this, that, or the other. The Judge has not framed his interrogatories to ask me anything more than this, and I have answered in strict accordance with the interrogatories, and have answered truly that I am not *pledged* at all upon any of the points to which I have answered. But I am not disposed to hang upon the exact form of his interrogatory. I am rather disposed to take up at least some of these questions, and state what I really think upon them.

As to the first one, in regard to the Fugitive Slave Law, I have never hesitated to say, and I do not now hesitate to say, that I think, under the Constitution of the United States, the people of the Southern States are entitled to a congressional Fugitive Slave Law. Having said that, I have had nothing to say in regard to the existing Fugitive Slave Law, further than that I think it should have been framed so as to be free from some of the objections that pertain to it, without lessening its efficiency. And inasmuch as we are not now in an agitation in regard to an alteration or modification of that law, I would not be the man to introduce it as a new subject of agitation upon the general question of slavery.

In regard to the other question, of whether I am pledged to the admission of any more slave States into the Union, I state to you very frankly, that I would be exceedingly sorry ever to be put in a position of having to pass upon that question. I should be exceedingly glad to know that there would never be another slave State admitted into the Union; but I must add, that if slavery shall be kept out of the Territories during the territorial existence of any one given Territory, and then the people shall, having a fair chance and a clear field, when they come to adopt the Constitution, do such an extraordinary thing as to adopt a slave Constitution, uninfluenced by the actual presence of the institution among them, I see no alternative, if we own the country, but to admit them into the Union.

The third interrogatory is answered by the answer to the second, it being, as I conceive, the same as the second.

The fourth one is in regard to the abolition of slavery in the District of Columbia. In relation to that, I have my mind very distinctly made up. I should be exceedingly glad to see slavery abolished in the District of Columbia. I believe that Congress possesses the constitutional power to abolish it. Yet, as a member of Congress, I should not, with my present views, be in favor of *endeavoring* to abolish slavery in the District of Columbia, unless it would be upon these conditions: *First*, that the abolition should be gradual. *Second*, that it should be on a vote of a majority of qualified voters in the District; and *third*, that compensation should be made to unwilling owners. With these three conditions, I confess I would be exceedingly glad to see Congress abolish slavery in the District of Columbia, and, in the language of Henry Clay, "sweep from our capital that foul blot upon our nation."

In regard to the fifth interrogatory, I must say here, that, as to the question of the abolition of the slave-trade between the different States, I can truly answer, as I have, that I am *pledged* to nothing about it. It is a subject to which I have not given that mature consideration that would make me feel authorized to state a position so as to hold myself entirely bound by it. In other words, that question has never been prominently enough before me to induce me to investigate whether we really have the constitutional power to do it. I could investigate it if I had sufficient time, to bring myself to a conclusion upon that subject; but I have not done so, and I say so frankly to you here, and to Judge Douglas. I must say, however, that if I should be of opinion that Congress does possess the constitutional power to abolish the slave-trade among the different States, I should still not be in favor of the exercise of that power unless upon some conservative principle, as I conceive it akin to what I have said in relation to the abolition of slavery in the District of Columbia.

My answer as to whether I desire that slavery should be prohibited in all the territories of the United States, is full and explicit within itself, and cannot be made clearer by any comments of mine.

So I suppose in regard to the question whether I am opposed to the acquisition of any more territory, unless slavery is first prohibited therein, my answer is such that I could add nothing by way of illustration, or making myself better understood, than the answer which I have placed in writing.

Now in all this, the Judge has me, and he has me on the record. I suppose he had flattered himself that I was really entertaining one set of opinions for one place, and another set for another place, —that I was afraid to say at one place what I uttered at another. What I am saying here I suppose I say to a vast audience as strongly tending to Abolitionism as any audience in the State of Illinois, and I believe I am saying that, which, if it would be offensive to any persons and render them enemies to myself, would be offensive to persons in this audience.

I now proceed to propound to the Judge the interrogatories, so far as I have framed them. I will bring forward a new instalment when I get them ready. I will bring them forward now, only reaching to number four.

The first one is:—

Question 1. If the people of Kansas shall, by means entirely unobjectionable in all other respects, adopt a State Constitution, and ask admission into the Union under it, *before* they have the requisite number of inhabitants according to the English bill,—some ninety-three thousand,—will you vote to admit them?

Q. 2. Can the people of a United States Territory, in any lawful way, against the wish of any citizen of the United States, exclude slavery from its limits prior to the formation of a State Constitution?

Q. 3. If the Supreme Court of the United States shall decide that States cannot exclude slavery from their limits, are you in favor of acquiescing in, adopting, and following such decision as a rule of political action?

Q. 4. Are you in favor of acquiring additional territory, in disregard of how such acquisition may affect the nation on the slavery question?

As introductory to these interrogatories which Judge Douglas propounded to me at Ottawa, he read a set of resolutions which he said Judge Trumbull and myself had participated in adopting, in the first Republican State Convention, held at Springfield, in October, 1854. He insisted that I and Judge Trumbull, and perhaps the entire Republican party, were responsible for the doctrines contained in the set of resolutions which he read, and I understand that it was from that set of resolutions that he deduced the interrogatories which he propounded to me, using these resolutions as a sort of authority for propounding those questions to me. Now I say here, to-day, that I do not answer his interrogatories because of their springing at all from that set of resolutions which he read. I answered them because Judge Douglas saw fit to ask them. I do not now, nor never did, recognize any responsibility upon myself in that set of resolutions. When I replied to him on that occasion, I assured him that I never had anything to do with them. I repeat here, to-day, that I never, in any possible form, had anything to do with that set of resolutions. It turns out, I believe, that those resolutions were never passed in any Convention held in Springfield. It turns out that they were never passed at any Convention or any public meeting that I had any part in. I believe it turns out, in addition to all this, that there was not, in the fall of 1854, any Convention holding a session in Springfield, calling itself a Republican State Convention; yet it is true there was a Convention, or assemblage of men calling themselves a Convention, at Springfield, that did pass *some* resolutions; but so little did I really know of the proceedings of that Convention, or what set of resolutions they had passed, though having a general knowledge that there had been such an assemblage of men there, that when Judge Douglas read the resolutions, I really did not know but they had been the resolutions passed then and there. I did not question that they were the resolutions adopted; for I could not bring myself to suppose that Judge Douglas could say what he did upon this subject without *knowing* that it was true. I contented myself, on that occasion, with denying, as I truly could, all connection with them, not denying or affirming whether they were passed at Springfield. Now it turns out that he had got hold of some resolutions passed at some Convention or public meeting in Kane county. I wish to say here, that I don't conceive that in any fair and just mind this discovery relieves me at all. I had just as much to do with the Convention in Kane county as that at Springfield. I am just as much responsible for the resolutions at Kane county as those at Springfield, the amount of the responsibility being exactly nothing in either case; no more than there would be in regard to a set of resolutions passed in the moon.

I allude to this extraordinary matter in this canvass for some further purpose than anything yet advanced. Judge Douglas did not make his statement upon that occasion as matters that he believed to be true, but he stated them roundly as *being true*, in such form as to pledge his veracity for their truth. When the whole matter turns out as it does, and when we consider who Judge Douglas is,—that he is a distinguished Senator of the United States,—that he has served nearly twelve years as such,—that his character is not at all limited as an ordinary Senator of the United States, but that his name has become of world-wide renown—it is *most extraordinary* that he should so far forget all the suggestions of justice to an adversary, or of prudence to himself, as to venture upon the assertion of that which the slightest investigation would have shown him to be wholly false. I can only account for his having done so upon the supposition that that evil genius which has attended him through his life, giving to him an apparent astonishing prosperity, such as to lead very many good men to doubt there being any advantage in virtue over vice,—I say I can only account for it on the supposition that that evil genius has at last made up its mind to forsake him.

And I may add that another extraordinary feature of the Judge's conduct in this canvass — made more extraordinary by this incident -- is, that he is in the habit, in almost all the speeches he makes, of charging falsehood upon his adversaries, myself and others. I now ask whether he is able to find in anything that Judge Trumbull, for instance, has said, or in anything that I have said, a justification at all compared with what we have, in this instance, for that sort of vulgarity.

I have been in the habit of charging as a matter of belief on my part, that, in the introduction of the Nebraksa bill into Congress, there was a conspiracy to make slavery perpetual and national I have arranged, from time to time, the evidence which establishes and proves the truth of this charge. I recurred to this charge at Ottawa. I shall not now have time to dwell upon it at very great length; but, inasmuch as Judge Douglas in his reply of half an hour, made some points upon me in relation to it, I propose noticing a few of them.

The Judge insists that, in the first speech I made, in which I very distinctly made that charge, he thought for a good while I was in fun! — that I was playful, — that I was not sincere about it, — and that he only grew angry and somewhat excited when he found that I insisted upon it as a matter of earnestness. He says he characterized it as a falsehood as far as I implicated his *moral character* in that transaction. Well, I did not know, till he presented that view, that I had implicated his moral character. He is very much in the habit, when he argues me up into a position I never thought of occupying, of very cosily saying he has no doubt Lincoln is "conscientious" in saying so. He should remember that I did not know but what *he* was ALTOGETHER "CONSCIENTIOUS" in that matter. I can conceive it possible for men to conspire to do a good thing, and I really find nothing in Judge Douglas's course or arguments that is contrary to or inconsistent with his belief of a conspiracy to nationalize and spread slavery as being a good and blessed thing, and so I hope he will understand that I do not at all question but that in all this matter he is entirely "conscientious."

But to draw your attention to one of the points I made in this case, beginning at the beginning. When the Nebraska bill was introduced, or a short time afterward, by an amendment, I believe, it was provided that it must be considered "the true intent and meaning of this act not to legislate slavery into any State or territory, or to exclude it therefrom, but to leave the people thereof perfectly free to form and regulate their own domestic institutions in their own way, subject only to the Constitution of the United States." I have called his attention to the fact that when he and some others began arguing that they were giving an increased degree of liberty to the people in the territories over and above what they formerly had on the question of slavery, a question was raised whether the law was enacted to give such unconditional liberty to the people; and to test the sincerity of this mode of argument, Mr. Chase, of Ohio, introduced an amendment, in which he made the law — if the amendment were adopted — expressly declare that the people of the territory should have the power to exclude slavery if they saw fit. I have asked attention also to the fact that Judge Douglas and those who acted with him, voted that amendment down, notwithstanding it expressed exactly the thing they said was the true intent and meaning of the law. I have called attention to the fact that in subsequent times, a decision of the Supreme Court has been made, in which it has been declared that a territorial legislature has no constitutional right to exclude slavery. And I have argued and said that for men who did intend that the people of the territory should have the right to exclude slavery absolutely and unconditionally, the voting down of Chase's amendment is wholly inexplicable. It is a puzzle, — a riddle. But I have said that with men who did look forward to such a decision, or who had it in contemplation, that such a decision of the Supreme Court would or might be made, the voting down of that amendment would be perfectly rational and intelligible. It would keep Congress from coming in collision with the decision when it was made. Anybody can conceive that if there was an intention or expectation that such a decision was to follow, it would not be a very desirable party attitude to get into for the Supreme Court, — all or nearly all its members belonging to the same party, — to decide one way, when the party in Congress had decided the other way. Hence it would be very rational for men expecting such a decision, to keep the niche in that law clear for it. After pointing this out, I tell Judge Douglas that it looks to me as though here was the reason why Chase's amendment was voted down. I tell him that as he did it, and knows why he did it, if it was done for a reason different from this, *he knows what that reason was, and can tell us what it was.* I tell him, also, it will be vastly more satisfactory to the country for him to give some other plausible, intelligible reason *why* it was voted down than to stand upon his dignity and call people liars. Well, on Saturday, he did make his answer, and what do you think it was? He says if I had only taken upon myself to tell the whole truth about that amendment of Chase's, no explanation would have been necessary on his part, — or words to that effect. Now, I say here, that I am quite unconscious of having suppressed anything material to the case, and I am very frank to admit if there is any sound reason other than that which appeared to me material, it is quite fair for him to present it. What reason does he propose? That when Chase came forward with his amendment, expressly authorizing the people to exclude slavery from the limits of every territory, Gen. Cass proposed to Chase, if he (Chase) would add to his amendment that the people should have the power to *introduce* or exclude, they would let it go. This is substantially all of his reply. And because Chase would not do that, they voted his amendment down. Well, it turns out, I believe, upon examination, that General Cass took some part in the little running debate upon that amendment, and then ran away *and did not vote on it at all.* Is not that the fact? So confident, as I think, was General

Cass that there was a snake somewhere about, he chose to run away from the whole thing. This is an inference I draw from the fact that, though he took part in the debate, his name does not appear in the ayes and noes. But does Judge Douglas's reply amount to a satisfactory answer? [Cries of "yes," "yes," and "no," "no."] There is some little difference of opinion here. But I ask attention to a few more views bearing on the question of whether it amounts to a satisfactory answer. The men who were determined that that amendment should not get into the bill, and spoil the place where the Dred Scott decision was to come in, sought an excuse to get rid of it somewhere. One of these ways, — one of these excuses, — was to ask Chase to add to his proposed amendment a provision that the people might *introduce* slavery if they wanted to. They very well knew Chase would do no such thing, — that Mr. Chase was one of the men differing from them on the broad principle of his insisting that freedom was *better* than slavery, — a man who would not consent to enact a law, penned with his own hand, by which he was made to recognize slavery on the one hand and liberty on the other as *precisely equal;* and when they insisted on his doing this, they very well knew they insisted on that which he would not for a moment think of doing, and that they were only bluffing him. I believe (I have not, since he made his answer, had a chance to examine the journals or *Congressional Globe*, and therefore speak from memory) — I believe the state of the bill at that time, according to parliamentary rules, was such that no member could propose an additional amendment to Chase's amendment. I rather think this is the truth, — the Judge shakes his head. Very well. I would like to know, then, *if they wanted Chase's amendment fixed over, why somebody else could not offer to do it?* If they wanted it amended, why did they not offer the amendment? Why did they stand there taunting and quibbling at Chase? Why did they not *put it in themselves?* But to put it on the other ground; suppose that there was such an amendment offered, and Chase's was an amendment to an amendment; until one is disposed of by parliamentary law, you cannot pile another on. Then all these gentlemen had to do was to vote Chase's on, and then in the amended form in which the whole stood, add their own amendment to it if they wanted to put it in that shape. This was all they were obliged to do, and the ayes and noes show that there were thirty-six who voted it down, against ten who voted in favor of it. The thirty-six held entire sway and control. They could in some form or other have put that bill in the exact shape they wanted. If there was a rule preventing their amending it at the time, they could pass that, and then Chase's amendment being merged, put it in the shape they wanted. They did not choose to do so, but they went into a quibble with Chase to get him to add what they knew he would not add, and because he would not, they stand upon that flimsy pretext for voting down what they argued was the meaning and intent of their own bill. They left room thereby for this Dred Scott decision, which goes very far to make slavery national throughout the United States.

I pass one or two points I have because my time will very soon expire, but I must be allowed to say that Judge Douglas recurs again, as he did upon one or two other occasions, to the enormity of Lincoln, — an insignificant individual like Lincoln, — upon his *ipse dixit* charging a conspiracy upon a large number of members of Congress, the Supreme Court, and two Presidents, to nationalize slavery. I want to say that, in the first place, I have made no charge of this sort upon my *ipse dixit.* I have only arrayed the evidence tending to prove it, and presented it to the understanding of others, saying what I think it proves, but giving you the means of judging whether it proves it or. not. This is precisely what I have done. I have not placed it upon my *ipse dixit* at all. On this occasion, I wish to recall his attention to a piece of evidence which I brought forward at Ottawa on Saturday, showing that he had made substantially the *same charge* against substantially the *same persons*, excluding his dear self from the category. I ask him to give some attention to the evidence which I brought forward, that he himself had discovered a "fatal blow being struck" against the right of the people to exclude slavery from their limits, which fatal blow he assumed as in evidence in an article in the Washington *Union*, published "by authority." I ask by whose authority? He discovers a similar or identical provision in the Lecompton Constitution. Made by whom? The framers of that Constitution. Advocated by whom? By all the members of the party in the nation, who advocated the introduction of Kansas into the Union under the Lecompton Constitution.

I have asked his attention to the evidence that he arrayed to prove that such a fatal blow was being struck, and to the facts which he brought forward in support of that charge, — being identical with the one which he thinks so villainous in me. He pointed it not at a newspaper editor merely, but at the President and his Cabinet, and the members of Congress advocating the Lecompton Constitution and those framing that instrument. I must again be permitted to remind him, that although my *ipse dixit* may not be as great as his, yet it somewhat reduces the force of his calling my attention to the *enormity* of my making a like charge against him.

Go on, Judge Douglas.

MR. DOUGLAS'S SPEECH.

Ladies and Gentlemen: The silence with which you have listened to Mr. Lincoln, during his hour, is creditable to this vast audience, composed of men of various political parties. Nothing is more honorable to any large mass of people assembled for the purpose of a fair discussion, than that kind and respectful attention that is yielded not only to your political friends, but to those who are opposed to you in politics.

I am glad that at last I have brought Mr. Lincoln to the conclusion that he had better define his position on certain political questions to which I called his attention at Ottawa. He there showed no disposition, no inclination, to answer them. I did not present idle questions for him to answer merely for my gratification. I laid the foundation for those interrogatories by showing that they constituted the platform of the party whose nominee he is for the Senate. I did not presume that I had the right to catechise him as I saw proper, unless I showed that his party, or a majority of it, stood upon the platform and were in favor of the propositions upon which my questions were based. I desired simply to know, inasmuch as he had been nominated as the first, last, and only choice of his party, whether he concurred in the platform which that party had adopted for its government. In a few moments I will proceed to review the answers which he has given to these interrogatories; but in order to relieve his anxiety I will first respond to these which he has presented to me. Mark you, he has not presented interrogatories which have ever received the sanction of the party with which I am acting, and hence he has no other foundation for them than his own curiosity.

First, he desires to know if the people of Kansas shall form a

Constitution by means entirely proper and unobjectionable, and ask admission into the Union as a State, before they have the requisite population for a member of Congress, whether I will vote for that admission. Well, now, I regret exceedingly that he did not answer that interrogatory himself before he put it to me, in order that we might understand, and not be left to infer, on which side he is. Mr. Trumbull, during the last session of Congress, voted from the beginning to the end against the admission of Oregon, although a free State, because she had not the requisite population for a member of Congress. Mr. Trumbull would not consent, under any circumstances, to let a State, free or slave, come into the Union until it had the requisite population. As Mr. Trumbull is in the field, fighting for Mr. Lincoln, I would like to have Mr. Lincoln answer his own question, and tell me whether he is fighting Trumbull on that issue or not. But I will answer his question. In reference to Kansas, it is my opinion, that as she has population enough to constitute a slave State, she has people enough for a free State. I will not make Kansas an exceptional case to the other States of the Union. I hold it to be a sound rule of universal application to require a territory to contain the requisite population for a member of Congress, before it is admitted as a State into the Union. I made that proposition in the Senate in 1856, and I renewed it during the last session, in a bill providing that no territory of the United States should form a constitution and apply for admission, until it had the requisite population. On another occasion I proposed that neither Kansas, nor any other territory, should be admitted until it had the requisite population. Congress did not adopt any of my propositions containing this general rule, but did make an exception of Kansas. I will stand by that exception. Either Kansas must come in as a free State, with whatever population she may have, or the rule must be applied to all the other territories alike. I therefore answer at once, that it having been decided that Kansas has people enough for a slave State, I hold that she has enough for a free State. I hope Mr. Lincoln is satisfied with my answer; and now I would like to get his answer to his own interrogatory,—whether or not he will vote to admit Kansas before she has the requisite population. I want to know whether he will vote to admit Oregon before that territory has the requisite population. Mr. Trumbull will not, and the same reason that commits Mr. Trumbull against the admission of Oregon, commits him against

Kansas, even if she should apply for admission as a free State. If there is any sincerity, any truth, in the argument of Mr. Trumbull in the Senate, against the admission of Oregon, because she had not 93,420 people, although her population was larger than that of Kansas, he stands pledged against the admission of both Oregon and Kansas until they have 93,420 inhabitants. I would like Mr. Lincoln to answer this question. I would like him to take his own medicine. If he differs with Mr. Trumbull, let him answer his argument against the admissiou of Oregon, instead of poking questions at me.

The next question propounded to me by Mr. Lincoln is, can the people of a territory, in any lawful way, against the wishes of any citizen of the United States, exclude slavery from their limits prior to the formation of a State constitution? I answer emphatically, as Mr. Lincoln has heard me answer a hundred times from every stump in Illinois, that in my opinion the people of a territory can, by lawful means, exclude slavery from their limits prior to the formation of a State constitution. Mr. Lincoln knew that I had answered that question over and over again. He heard me argue the Nebraska bill on that principle all over the State in 1854, in 1855, and in 1856, and he has no excuse for pretending to be in doubt as to my position on that question. It matters not what way the Supreme Court may hereafter decide as to the abstract question, whether slavery may or may not, go into a territory under the Constitution, the people have the lawful means to introduce it or exclude it as they please, for the reason that slavery cannot exist a day or an hour anywhere, unless it is supported by local police regulations. Those police regulations can only be established by the local legislature, and if the people are opposed to slavery, they will elect representatives to that body, who will, by unfriendly legislation, effectually prevent the introduction of it into their midst. If, on the contrary, they are for it, their legislation will favor its extension. Hence, no matter what the decision of the Supreme Court may be on that abstract question, still, the right of the people to make a slave territory, or a free territory, is perfect and complete under the Nebraska bill. I hope Mr. Lincoln deems my answer satisfactory on that point.

In this connection, I will notice the charge which he has introduced in relation to Mr. Chase's amendment. I thought that I had chased that amendment out of Mr. Lincoln's brain at Ottawa; but, it seems, that still haunts his imagination, and he is not yet satisfied. I had supposed that he would be ashamed to press that question further. He is a lawyer, and has been a member of Congress, and has occupied his time, and amused you, by telling you about parliamentary proceedings. He ought to have known better than to try to palm off his miserable impositions upon this intelligent audiance. The Nebraska bill provided that the legislative power, and authority of the said territory, should extend to all rightful subjects of legislation, consistent with the organic act, and the Constitution of the United States. It did not make any exception as to slavery, but gave all the power, that it was possible for Congress to give, without violating the Constitution, to the territorial legislature, with no exception or limitation on the subject of slavery at all. The language of that bill, which I have quoted, gave the full power and the full authority over the subject of slavery, affirmatively and negatively, to introduce it or exclude it, so far as the Constitution of the United States would permit. What more could Mr. Chase give by his amendment? Nothing. He offered his amendment for the identical purpose for which Mr. Lincoln is using it, to enable demagogues in the country to try and deceive the people.

His amendment was to this effect. It provided that the legislature should have the power to exclude slavery: and General Cass suggested, "why not give the power to introduce as well as exclude?" The answer was, they have the power already in the bill to do both. Chase was afraid his amendment would be adopted if he put the alternative proposition, and so make it fair both ways, but would not yield. He offered it for the purpose of having it rejected. He offered it, as he has himself avowed over and over again, simply to make capital out of it for the stump. He expected that it would be capital for small politicians in the country, and that they would make an effort to deceive the people with it; and he was not mistaked; for Lincoln is carrying out the plan admirably. Lincoln knows that the Nebraska bill, without Chase's amendment, gave all the power which the Constitution would permit. Could Congress confer any more? Could Congress go beyond the Constitution of the country? We gave all a full grant, with no exception in regard to slavery one way or the other. We left that question as we left all others, to be decided by the people for themselves, just as they pleased. I will not occupy my time on this question. I have argued it before, all over Illinois. I have argued it in this beautiful city of Freeport; I have argued in the North, the South, the East, and the West, avowing the same sentiments and the same principles. I have not been afraid to avow my sentiments up here, for fear I would be trotted down into Egypt.

The third question which Mr. Lincoln presented, is, if the Supreme Court of the United States shall decide that a State of this Union cannot exclude slavery from its own limits, will I submit to it? I am amazed that Lincoln should ask such a question. ("A schoolboy knows better,") Yes, a schoolboy does know better. Mr. Lincoln's object is to cast an imputation upon the Supreme Court. He knows that there never was but one man in America, claiming any degree of intelligence or decency, who ever for a moment pretended such a thing. It is true that the Washington *Union*, in an article published on the 17th of last December, did put forth that doctrine, and I denounced the article on the floor of the Senate, in a speech which Mr. Lincoln now pretends was against the President. The *Union* had claimed that slavery had a right to go into the free States, and that any provision in the Constitution or laws of the free States to the contrary were null and void. I denounced it in the Senate, as I said before, and I was the first man who did. Lincoln's friends, Trumbull, and Seward, and Hale and Wilson, and the whole Black Republican side of the Senate, were silent. They left it to me to denounce it. And what was the reply made to me on that occasion? Mr. Toombs, of Georgia, got up and undertook to lecture me on the ground that I ought not to have deemed the article worthy of notice, and ought not to have replied to it; that there was not one man, woman or child south of the Potomac, in any slave State, who did not repudiate any such pretension. Mr. Lincoln knows that that reply was made on the spot, and yet now he asks this question. He might as well ask me, suppose Mr. Lincoln should steal a horse, would I sanction it; and it would be as genteel in me to ask him, in the event he stole a horse, what ought to be done with him. He casts an imputation upon the Supreme Court of the United States, by supposing that they would violate the Constitution of the United States. I tell him that such a thing is not possible. It would be an act of moral treason that no man on the bench could ever descend to. Mr. Lincoln, himself, would never in his partisan feelings, so far forget what was right, as to be guilty of such an act.

The fourth question of Mr. Lincoln is, are you in favor of

acquiring additional territory, in disregard as to how such acquisition may affect the Union on the slavery questions? This question is very ingeniously and cunningly put.

The Black Republican creed lays it down expressly, that under no circumstances shall we acquire any more territory unless slavery is first prohibited in the country. I ask Mr. Lincoln whether he is in favor of that proposition. Are you (addressing Mr. Lincoln) opposed to the acquisition of any more territory, under any circumstances, unless slavery is prohibited in it? That he does not like to answer. When I ask him whether he stands up to that article in the platform of his party, he turns, Yankee-fashion, and without answering it, asks me whether I am in favor of acquiring territory without regard to how it may affect the Union on the slavery question. I answer, that whenever it becomes necessary, in our growth and progress, to acquire more territory, that I am in favor of it, without reference to the question of slavery; and when we have acquired it, I will leave the people free to do as they please, either to make it slave or free territory, as they prefer. It is idle to tell me or you that we have territory enough. Our fathers supposed that we had enough when our territory extended to the Mississippi River, but a few years' growth and expansion satisfied them that we needed more, and the Louisiana Territory, from the west branch of the Mississippi to the British Possessions, was acquired. Then we acquired Oregon, then California and New Mexico. We have enough now for the present, but this is a young and a growing nation. It swarms as often as a hive of bees, and as new swarms are turned out each year, there must be hives in which they can gather and make their honey. In less than fifteen years, if the same progress that has distinguished this country for the last fifteen years, continues, every foot of vacant land between this and the Pacific ocean, owned by the United States, will be occupied. Will you not continue to increase at the end of fifteen years as well as now? I tell you, increase, and multiply, and expand, is the law of this nation's existence. You cannot limit this great Republic by mere boundary lines, saying, "thus far shalt thou go, and no further." Any one of you gentlemen might as well say to a son twelve years old, that he is big enough, and must not grow any larger, and in order to prevent his growth put a hoop around him to keep him to his present size. What would be the result? either the hoop must burst and be rent asunder, or the child must die.

5

So it would be with this great nation. With our natural increase, growing with a rapidity unknown in any other part of the globe, with the tide of emigration that is fleeing from despotism in the old world, to seek refuge in our own, there is a constant torrent pouring into this country that requires more land, more territory upon which to settle; and just as fast as our interests and our destiny require additional territory in the North, in the South, or on the Islands of the ocean, I am for it, and when we acquire it, will leave the people, according to the Nebraska bill, free to do as they please on the subject of slavery and every other question.

I trust now that Mr. Lincoln will deem himself answered on his four points. He racked his brain so much in devising these four questions that he exhausted himself, and had not strength enough to invent the others. As soon as he is able to hold a council with his advisers, Lovejoy, Farnsworth, and Fred Douglass, he will frame and propound others. [" Good, good."] You Black Republicans, who say good, I have no doubt think that they are all good men. I have reason to recollect that some people in this country think that Fred Douglass is a very good man. The last time I came here to make a speech, while talking from the stand to you, people of Freeport, as I am doing to-day, I saw a carriage, and a magnificent one it was, drive up and take a position on the outside of the crowd; a beautiful young lady was sitting on the box-seat, whilst Fred Douglass and her mother reclined inside, and the owner of the carriage acted as driver. I saw this in your own town. [" What of it ? "] All I have to say of it is this, that if you, Black Republicans, think that the negro ought to be on a social equality with your wives and daughters, and ride in a carriage with your wife, whilst you drive the team, you have perfect right to do so. I am told that one of Fred Douglass's kinsmen, another rich black negro, is now travelling in this part of the State making speeches for his friend Lincoln as the champion of black men. [" What have you to say against it? "] All I have to say on that subject is, that those of you who believe that the negro is your equal and ought to be on an equality with you socially, politically, and legally, have a right to entertain those opinions, and of course will vote for Mr. Lincoln.

I have a word to say on Mr. Lincoln's answer to the interrogatories contained in my speech at Ottawa, and which he has pretended to reply to here to-day. Mr. Lincoln makes a great parade of the fact that I quoted a platform as having been adopted by the

Black Republican party at Springfield in 1854, which, it turns out, was adopted at another place. Mr. Lincoln loses sight of the thing itself in his ecstasies over the mistake I made in stating the place where it was done. He thinks that that platform was not adopted on the right "spot."

When I put the direct questions to Mr. Lincoln to ascertain whether he now stands pledged to that creed, — to the unconditional repeal of the Fugitive Slave Law, a refusal to admit any more slave States into the Union, even if the people want them, a determination to apply the Wilmot Proviso, not only to all the territory we now have, but all that we may hereafter acquire, he refused to answer, and his followers say, in excuse, that the resolutions upon which I based my interrogatories were not adopted at the "*right spot.*" Lincoln and his political friends are great on "*spots.*" In Congress, as a representative of this State, he declared the Mexican war to be unjust and infamous, and would not support it, or acknowledge his own country to be right in the contest, because he said that American blood was not shed on American soil, in the "*right spot.*" And now he cannot answer the questions I put to him at Ottawa, because the resolutions I read were not adopted at the "*right spot.*" It may be possible that I was led into an error as to the *spot* on which the resolutions I then read were proclaimed, but I was not and am not in error as to the fact of their forming the basis of the creed of the Republican party when that party was first organized. I will state to you the evidence I had, and upon which I relied for my statement that the resolutions in question were adopted at Springfield on the 5th of October, 1854. Although I was aware that such resolutions had been passed in this district, and nearly all the northern Congressional Districts and County Conventions, I had not noticed whether or not they had been adopted by any State Convention. In 1856, a debate arose in Congress between Major Thomas L. Harris, of the Springfield District, and Mr. Norton, of the Joliet District, on political matters connected with our State, in the course of which, Major Harris quoted those resolutions as having been passed by the first Republican State Convention that ever assembled in Illinois. I knew that Major Harris was remarkable for his accuracy, that he was a very conscientious and sincere man, and I also noticed that Norton did not question the accuracy of this statement. I therefore took it for granted that it was so, and the other day, when I concluded to use the resolutions at Ottawa, I wrote to Charles H. Lanphier, editor of the *State Register*, at Springfield, calling his attention to them, telling him that I had been informed that Major Harris was lying sick at Springfield, and desiring him to call upon him and ascertain all the facts concerning the resolutions, the time and place where they were adopted. In reply, Mr. Lanphier sent me two copies of his paper, which I have here. The first is a copy of the *State Register*, published at Springfield, Mr. Lincoln's own town, on the 16th of October, 1854, only eleven days after the adjournment of the Convention, from which I desire to read the following:—

"During the late discussions in this city, Lincoln made a speech, to which Judge Douglas replied. In Lincoln's speech he took the broad ground that, according to the Declaration of Independence, the whites and blacks are equal. From this he drew the conclusion, which he several times repeated, that the white man had no right to pass laws for the government of the black man without the nigger's consent. This speech of Lincoln's was heard and applauded by all the Abolitionists assembled in Springfield. So soon as Mr. Lincoln was done speaking, Mr. Codding arose and requested all the delegates to the Black Republican Convention to withdraw into the Senate chamber. They did so, and after long deliberation, they laid down the following Abolition platform as the platform on which they stood. We call the particular attention of all our readers to it."

Then follows the identical platform, word for word, which I read at Ottawa. Now, that was published in Mr. Lincoln's own town, eleven days after the Convention was held, and it has remained on record up to this day never contradicted.

When I quoted the resolutions at Ottawa, and questioned Mr. Lincoln in relation to them, he said that his name was on the committee that reported them, but he did not serve, nor did he think he served, because he was, or thought he was, in Tazewell county at the time the Convention was in session. He did not deny that the resolutions were passed by the Springfield Convention. He did not know better, and evidently thought that they were, but afterwards his friends declared that they had discovered that they varied in some respects from the resolutions passed by that Convention. I have shown you that I had good evidence for believing that the resolutions had been passed at Springfield. Mr. Lincoln ought to have known better; but not a word is said about his ignorance on the subject, whilst I, notwithstanding the circumstances, am accused of forgery.

Now, I will show you that if I have made a mistake as to the place where these resolutions were adopted, — and when I get down to Springfield, I will investigate the matter, and see whether or not I have,— that the principles they enunciate were adopted as the Black Republican platform [" white, white"] in the various counties and Congressional Districts throughout the north end of the State in 1854. This platform was adopted in nearly every county that gave a Black Republican majority for the legislature in that year, and here is a man [pointing to Mr. Denio, who sat on the stand near Deacon Bross] who knows as well as any living man that it was the creed of the Black Republican party at that time. I would be willing to call Denio as a witness, or any other honest man belonging to that party. I will now read the resolutions adopted at the Rockford Convention on the 30th of August, 1854, which nominated Washburne for Congress. You elected him on the following platform: —

"*Resolved*, That the continued and increasing aggressions of slavery in our country are destructive of the best rights of a free people, and that such aggressions cannot be successfully resisted without the united political action of all good men.

"*Resolved*, That the citizens of the United States hold in their hands peaceful, constitutional, and efficient remedy against the encroachments of the slave power, the ballot-box, and, if that remedy is boldly and wisely applied, the principles of liberty and eternal justice will be established.

"*Resolved*, That we accept this issue forced upon us by the slave power, and, in defence of freedom, will co-operate and be known as Republicans, pledged to the accomplishment of the following purposes: —

"To bring the Administration of the Government back to the control of first principles; to restore Kansas and Nebraska to the position of free Territories; to repeal and entirely abrogate the Fugitive Slave Law; to restrict slavery to those States in which it exists; to prohibit the admission of any more slave States into the Union; to exclude slavery from all the territories over which the General Government has exclusive jurisdiction, and to resist the acquisition of any more Territories unless the introduction of slavery therein forever shall have been prohibited.

"*Resolved*, That in furtherance of these principles we will use such constitutional and lawful means as shall seem best adapted to their accomplishment, and that we will support no man for office under the General or State Government who is not positively committed to the support of these principles, and whose personal character and conduct is not a guaranty that he is reliable, and shall abjure all party allegiance and ties.

"*Resolved*, That we cordially invite persons of all former political parties whatever, in favor of the object expressed in the above resolutions, to unite with us in carrying them into effect."

Well, you think that is a very good platform, do you not? If you do, if you approve it now, and think it is all right, you will not join with those men who say that I libel you by calling these your principles, will you? Now, Mr. Lincoln complains: Mr. Lincoln charges that I did you and him injustice by saying that this was the platform of your party. I am told that Washburne made a speech in Galena last night, in which he abused me awfully for bringing to light this platform, on which he was elected to Congress. He thought that you had forgotten it, as he and Mr. Lincoln desires to. He did not deny but that you had adopted it, and that he had subscribed to and was pledged by it, but he did not think it was fair to call it up and remind the people that it was their platform.

But I am glad to find that you are more honest in your abolitionism than your leaders, by avowing that it is your platform, and right in your opinion.

In the adoption of that platform, you not only declared that you would resist the admission of any more slave States, and work for the repeal of the Fugitive Slave Law, but you pledged yourselves not to vote for any man for State or Federal offices who was not committed to these principles. You were thus committed. Similar resolutions to those were adopted in your County Convention here; and now, with your admissions that they are your platform and embody your sentiments, now as they did then, what do you think of Mr. Lincoln, your candidate for the U. S. Senate, who is attempting to dodge the responsibility of this platform, because it was not adopted in the right spot. I thought that it was adopted in Springfield, but it turns out it was not, that it was adopted at Rockford, and in the various counties which comprise this Congressional District. When I get into the next district, I will show that the same platform was adopted there, and so on through the State, until I nail the responsibility of it upon the back of the Black Republican party throughout the State.

A voice — " Couldn't you modify and call it brown ? "

Mr. Douglas — Not a bit. I thought that you were becoming a little brown when your members in Congress voted for the Crittenden-Montgomery bill, but since you have backed out from that position and gone back to Abolitionism, you are black and not brown.

Gentlemen, I have shown you what your platform was in 1854. You still adhere to it. The same platform was adopted by nearly all the counties where the Black Republican party had a majority in 1854. I wish now to call your attention to the action of your representatives in the legislature when they assembled together at Springfield. In the first place, you must remember that this was the organization of a new party. It is so declared in the resolutions themselves, which say that you are going to dissolve all old party ties and call the new party Republican. The old Whig party was to have its throat cut from ear to ear, and the Democratic party was to be annihilated and blotted out of existence, whilst in lieu of these parties the Black Republican party was to be organized on this Abolition platform. You know who the chief leaders were in breaking up and destroying these two great parties. Lincoln on the one hand and Trumbull on the other, being disappointed politicians, and having retired or been driven to obscurity by an outraged constituency because of their political sins, formed a scheme to abolitionize the two parties and lead the old line Whigs and old line Democrats captive, bound hand and foot, into the Abolition camp. Giddings, Chase, Fred Douglass, and Lovejoy, were here to christen them whenever they were brought in. Lincoln went to work to dissolve the old line Whig party. Clay was dead, and although the sod was not yet green on his grave, this man undertook to bring into disrepute those great Compromise measures of 1850, with which Clay and Webster were identified. Up to 1854 the old Whig party and the Democratic party had stood on a common platform so far as this slavery question was concerned. You Whigs and we Democrats differed about the bank, the tariff, distribution, the specie circular and the sub-treasury, but we agreed on this slavery question, and the true mode of preserving the peace and harmony of the Union. The Compromise measures of 1850 were introduced by Clay, were defended by Webster, and supported by

Cass, and were approved by Fillmore, and sanctioned by the National men of both parties. They constituted a common plank upon which both Whigs and Democrats stood. In 1852 the Whig party, in its last National Convention at Baltimore, indorsed and approved these measures of Clay, and so did the National Convention of the Democratic party held that same year. Thus the old line Whigs and the old line Democrats stood pledged to the great principle of self-government, which guaranties to the people of each territory the right to decide the slavery question for themselves. In 1854, after the death of Clay and Webster, Mr. Lincoln, on the part of the Whigs, undertook to abolitionize the Whig party, by dissolving it, transferring the members into the Abolition camp, and making them train under Giddings, Fred Douglass, Lovejoy, Chase, Farnsworth, and other Abolition leaders. Trumbull undertook to dissolve the Democratic party by taking old Democrats into the Abolition camp. Mr. Lincoln was aided in his efforts by many leading Whigs throughout the State. Your member of Congress, Mr. Washburne, being one of the most active. Trumbull was aided by many renegades from the Democratic party, among whom were John Wentworth, Tom Turner, and others, with whom you are familiar.

[Mr. Turner, who was one of the moderators, here interposed and said that he had drawn the resolutions which Senator Douglas had read.]

Mr. Douglas — Yes, and Turner says that he drew these resolutions. ["Hurra for Turner," "Hurra for Douglas."] That is right, give Turner cheers for drawing the resolutions if you approve them. If he drew those resolutions he will not deny that they are the creed of the Black Republican party.

Mr. Turner — "They are our creed exactly."

Mr. Douglas — And yet Lincoln denies that he stands on them. Mr. Turner says that the creed of the Black Republican party is the admission of no more slave States, and yet Mr. Lincoln declares that he would not like to be placed in a position where he would have to vote for them. All I have to say to friend Lincoln is, that I do not think there is much danger of his being placed in such a position. As Mr. Lincoln would be very sorry to be placed in such an embarrassing position, as to be obliged to vote on the admission of any more slave States, I propose, out of mere kindness, to relieve him from any such necessity.

When the bargain between Lincoln and Trumbull was completed

for abolitionizing the Whig and Democratic parties, they "spread" over the State, Lincoln still pretending to be an old line Whig, in order to "rope" in the Whigs, and Trumbull pretending to be as good a Democrat as he ever was, in order to coax the Democrats over into the Abolition ranks. They played the part that "decoy ducks" play down on the Potomac River. In that part of the country they make artificial ducks, and put them on the water in places where the wild ducks are to be found, for the purpose of decoying them. Well, Lincoln and Trumbull played the part of these "decoy ducks," and deceived enough old line Whigs and old line Democrats to elect a Black Republican legislature. When that legislature met, the first thing it did was to elect, as Speaker of the House, the very man who is now boasting that he wrote the Abolition platform on which Lincoln will not stand. I want to know of Mr. Turner, whether or not, when he was elected, he was a good embodiment of Republican principles?

Mr. Turner — "I hope I was then, and am now."

Mr Douglas — He swears that he hopes he was then, and is now. He wrote that Black Republican platform, and is satisfied with it now. I admire and acknowledge Turner's honesty. Every man of you know that what he says about these resolutions being the platform of the Black Republican party is true, and you also know that each one of these men who are shuffling, and trying to deny it, are only trying to cheat the people out of their votes for the purpose of deceiving them still more after the election. I propose to trace this thing a little further, in order that you can see what additional evidence there is to fasten this revolutionary platform upon the Black Republican party. When the legislature assembled, there was an United States Senator to elect in the place of Gen. Shields, and before they proceeded to ballot, Lovejoy insisted on laying down certain principles by which to govern the party. It has been published to the world, and satisfactorily proven, that there was, at the time the alliance was made between Trumbull and Lincoln to abolitionize the two parties, an agreement that Lincoln should take Shield's place in the United States Senate, and Trumbull should have mine so soon as they could conveniently get rid of me. When Lincoln was beaten for Shield's place, in a manner I will refer to in a few minutes, he felt very sore and restive; his friends grumbled, and some of them came out and charged that the most infamous treachery had been practised against him; that the bargain was that Lincoln was to have had Shield's place, and Trumbull was to have waited for mine, but that Trumbull, having the control of a few abolitionized Democrats, he prevented them from voting for Lincoln, thus keeping him within a few votes of an election, until he succeeded in forcing the party to drop him and elect Trumbull. Well, Trumbull having cheated Lincoln, his friends made a fuss, and in order to keep them and Lincoln quiet, the party were obliged to come forward, in advance, at the last State election, and make a pledge that they would go for Lincoln, and nobody else. Lincoln could not be silenced in any other way.

Now there are a great many Black Republicans of you who do not know this thing was done. ["White, white," and great clamor.] I wish to remind you that while Mr. Lincoln was speaking, there was not a Democrat vulgar and blackguard enough to interrupt him. But I know that the shoe is pinching you. I am clinching Lincoln now, and you are scared to death for the result. I have seen this thing before. I have seen men make appointments for joint discussions, and the moment their man has been heard, try to interrupt and prevent a fair hearing of the other side. I have seen your mobs before, and defy your wrath. [Tremendous applause.] My friends, do not cheer, for I need my whole time. The object of the opposition is to occupy my attention in order to prevent me from giving the whole evidence, and nailing this double dealing on the Black Republican party. As I have before said, Lovejoy demanded a declaration of principles on the part of the Black Republicans of the legislature before going into an election for United States Senator. He offered the following preamble and resolutions which I hold in my hand: —

"WHEREAS, Human slavery is a violation of the principles of natural and revealed rights; and whereas, the fathers of the Revolution, fully imbued with the spirit of these principles, declared freedom to be the inalienable birthright of all men; and whereas, the preamble to the Constitution of the United States avers that that instrument was ordained to establish justice, and secure the blessings of liberty to ourselves and our posterity; and whereas, in furtherance of the above principles, slavery was forever prohibited in the old Northwest Territory, and more recently in all that territory lying west and north of the State of Missouri, by the act of the Federal Government; and whereas, the repeal of the prohibition last referred to was contrary to the wishes of the people of Illinois, a violation of an implied compact, long deemed sacred by the citizens of the United States, and a wide departure from the uniform action of the General Government in relation to the extension of slavery; therefore,

"*Resolved, by the House of Representatives, the Senate concurring therein*, That our Senators in Congress be instructed, and our Representatives requested to introduce, if not otherwise introduced, and to vote for a bill to restore such prohibition to the aforesaid territories, and also to extend a similar prohibition to all territory which now belongs to the United States, or which may hereafter come under their jurisdiction.

"*Resolved*, That our Senators in Congress be instructed, and our Representatives requested, to vote against the admission of any State into the Union, the constitution of which does not prohibit slavery, whether the territory out of which such State may have been formed shall have been acquired by conquest, treaty, purchase, or from original territory of the United States.

"*Resolved*, That our Senators in Congress be instructed, and our Representatives requested, to introduce, and vote for a bill to repeal an act entitled 'an act respecting fugitives from justice, and persons escaping from the service of their masters;' and, failing in that, for such a modification of it as shall secure the right of *habeas corpus*, and trial by jury, before the regularly constituted authorities of the State, to all persons claimed as owing service or labor."

Those resolutions were introduced by Mr. Lovejoy immediately preceding the election of Senator. They declared, first, that the Wilmot Proviso must be applied to all territory north of 36 deg. 30 min. Secondly, that it must be applied to all territory south of 36 deg. 30 min. Thirdly, that it must be applied to all territory now owned by the United States; and finally, that it must be applied to all territory hereafter to be acquired by the United States. The next resolution declares that no more slave States shall be admitted into this Union, under any circumstances whatever, no matter whether they are formed out of territory now owned by us, or that we may hereafter acquire, by treaty, by Congress, or in any manner whatever. The next resolution demands the unconditional repeal of the Fugitive Slave Law, although its unconditional repeal would leave no provision for carrying out that clause of the Constitution of the United States, which guaranties the surrender of fugitives. If they could not get an unconditional repeal, they demanded that that law should be so modified as to make it as nearly useless as possible. Now, I want to show you who voted for these resolutions. When the vote was taken on the first resolution it was decided in the affirmative,— yeas 41, nays 32. You will find that this is a strict party vote, between the Democrats on the one hand, and the Black Republicans on the other. [Cries of "White, white," and clamor.] I know your name, and always call things by their right name. The point I wish to call your attention to, is this: that these resolutions were adopted on the 7th day of February, and that on the 8th they went into an election for a United States Senator, and that day every man who voted for these resolutions, with but two exceptions, voted for Lincoln for the United States Senate. ["Give us their names."] I will read the names over to you if you want them, but I believe your object is to occupy my time.

On the next resolution the vote stood, — yeas 33, nays 40, and on the third resolution, — yeas 35, nays 47. I wish to impress it upon you, that every man who voted for those resolutions, with but two exceptions, voted on the next day for Lincoln for United States Senator. Bear in mind that the members who thus voted for Lincoln, were elected to the legislature, pledged to vote for no man for office under the State or Federal Government, who was not committed to this Black Republican platform. They were all so pledged. Mr. Turner, who stands by me, and who then represented you, and who says that he wrote those resolutions, voted for Lincoln, when he was pledged not to do so unless Lincoln was in favor of those resolutions. I now ask Mr. Turner [turning to Mr. Turner], did you violate your pledge in voting for Mr. Lincoln, or did he commit himself to your platform before you cast your vote for him?

I could go through the whole list of names here, and show you that all the Black Republicans in the legislature, who voted for Mr. Lincoln, had voted on the day previous for these resolutions. For instance, here are the names of Sargent and Little, of Jo Daviess and Carroll, Thomas J. Turner of Stephenson, Lawrence of Boone, and McHenry, Swan of Lake, Pinckney of Ogle county, and Lyman of Winnebago. Thus you see every member from your Congressional District voted for Mr. Lincoln, and they were pledged not to vote for him unless he was committed to the doctrine of no more slave States, the prohibition of slavery in the territories, and the repeal of the Fugitive Slave Law. Mr. Lincoln tells you to-day that he is not pledged to any such doctrine. Either Mr. Lincoln was then committed to those propositions, or Mr. Turner violated his pledges to you when he voted for him. Either Lincoln was pledged to each one of those propositions, or else every Black Republican representative from this congressional district violated his pledge of honor to his constituents by voting for him. I ask you which horn of the dilemma will you take? Will you hold Lincoln up to the platform of his party, or will you accuse every representative you had in the legislature of violating his pledge of honor to his constituents? There is no escape for you. Either Mr. Lincoln was committed to those propositions, or your members violated their faith. Take either horn of the dilemma you choose. There is no dodging the question; I want Lincoln's answer. He says he was not pledged to repeal the Fugitive Slave Law, that he does not quite like to do it; he will not introduce a law to repeal it, but thinks there ought to be some law; he does not tell what it ought to be; upon the whole, he is altogether undecided, and don't know what to think or do. That is the substance of his answer upon the repeal of the Fugitive Slave Law. I put the question to him distinctly, whether he indorsed that part of the Black Republican platform which calls for the entire abrogation and repeal of the Fugitive Slave Law. He answers no! that he does not indorse that; but he does not tell what he is for, or what he will vote for. His answer is, in fact, no answer at all. Why cannot he speak out, and say what he is for and what he will do?

In regard to there being no more slave States, he is not pledged to that. He would not like, he says, to be put in a position where he would have to vote one way or another upon that question. I pray you, do not put him in a position that would embarrass him so much. Gentlemen, if he goes to the Senate, he may be put in that position, and then which way will he vote?

[A voice—"How will you vote?"]

Mr. Douglas—I will vote for the admission of just such a State as by the form of their constitution the people show they want; if they want slavery, they shall have it; if they prohibit slavery, it shall be prohibited. They can form their institutions to please themselves, subject only to the Constitution; and I for one stand ready to receive them into the Union. Why cannot your Black Republican candidates talk out as plain as that when they are questioned?

I do not want to cheat any man out of his vote. No man is deceived in regard to my principles if I have the power to express myself in terms explicit enough to convey my ideas.

Mr. Lincoln made a speech when he was nominated for the United States Senate which covers all these Abolition platforms. He there lays down a proposition so broad in its abolitionism as to cover the whole ground.

"In my opinion it [the slavery agitation] will not cease until a crisis shall have been reached and passed. 'A house divided against itself cannot stand.' I believe this Government cannot endure permanently half slave and half free. I do not expect the house to fall, but I do expect it will cease to be divided. It will become all one thing or all the other. Either the opponents of slavery will arrest the further spread of it, and place it where the public mind shall rest in the belief that it is in the course of ultimate extinction, or its advocates will push it forward till it shall become alike lawful in all the States,—old as well as new, North as well as South."

There you find that Mr. Lincoln lays down the doctrine that this Union cannot endure divided as our fathers made it, with free and slave States. He says they must all become one thing, or all the other; that they must all be free or all slave, or else the Union cannot continue to exist. It being his opinion that to admit any more slave States, to continue to divide the Union into free and slave States, will dissolve it, I want to know of Mr. Lincoln whether he will vote for the admission of another slave State.

He tells you the Union cannot exist unless the States are all free or all slave; he tells you that he is opposed to making them all slave, and hence he is for making them all free, in order that the Union may exist; and yet he will not say that he will not vote against another slave State, knowing that the Union must be dissolved if he votes for it. I ask you if that is fair dealing? The true intent and inevitable conclusion to be drawn from his first Springfield speech is, that he is opposed to the admission of any more slave States under any circumstances. If he is so opposed, why not say so? If he believes this Union cannot endure divided into free and slave States, that they must all become free in order to save the Union, he is bound, as an honest man, to vote against any more slave States. If he believes it he is bound to do it. Show me that it is my duty in order to save the Union to do a particular act, and I will do it if the Constitution does not prohibit it. I am not for the dissolution of the Union under any circumstances. I will pursue no course of conduct that will give just cause for the dissolution of the Union. The hope of the friends of freedom throughout the world rests upon the perpetuity of this Union. The down-trodden and oppressed people who are suffering under European despotism all look with hope and anxiety to the American Union as the only resting-place and permanent home of freedom and self government.

Mr. Lincoln says that he believes that this Union cannot continue to endure with slave States in it, and yet he will not tell you distinctly whether he will vote for or against the admission of any more slave States, but says he would not like to be put to the test. I do not think he will be put to the test. I do not think that the people of Illinois desire a man to represent them who would not like to be put to the test on the performance of a high constitutional duty. I will retire in shame from the Senate of the United States when I am not willing to be put to the test in the performance of my duty. I have been put to severe tests. I have stood by my principles in fair weather and in foul, in the sunshine and in the rain. I have defended the great principles of self-government here among you when Northern sentiment ran in a torrent against me, and I have defended that same great principle when Southern sentiment came down like an avalanche upon me. I was not afraid of any test they put to me. I knew I was right,—I knew my principles were sound,—I knew that the people would see in the end that I had done right, and I knew that the God of heaven would smile upon me if I was faithful in the performance of my duty.

Mr. Lincoln makes a charge of corruption against the Supreme Court of the United States, and two Presidents of the United States, and attempts to bolster it up by saying that I did the same against the Washington *Union*. Suppose I did make that charge of corruption against the Washington *Union*, when it was true, does that justify him in making a false charge against me and others? That is the question I would put. He says that at the time the Nebraska bill was introduced, and before it was passed, there was a conspiracy between the Judges of the Supreme Court, President Pierce, President Buchanan and myself by that bill, and the decision of the court to break down the barrier and establish slavery all over the Union. Does he not know that that charge is historically false as against President Buchanan? He knows that Mr. Buchanan was at that time in England, representing this country with distinguished ability at the Court of St. James, that he was there for a long time before, and did not return for a year or more after. He knows that to be true, and that fact proves his charge to be false as against Mr. Buchanan. Then again, I wish to call his attention to the fact that at the time the Nebraska bill was passed, the Dred Scott case was not before the Supreme Court at all; it was not upon the docket of the Supreme Court; it had not been brought there, and the judges in all probability knew nothing of it. Thus the history of the country proves the charge to be false as against them. As to President Pierce, his high character as a man of integrity and honor is enough to vindicate him from such a charge; and as to myself, I pronounce the charge an infamous lie, whenever and wherever made, and by whomsoever made. I am willing that Mr. Lincoln should go and rake up every public act of mine, every measure I have introduced, report I have made, speech delivered, and criticise them, but when he charges upon me a corrupt conspiracy for the purpose of preserving the institutions of the country, I brand it as it deserves. I say the history of the country proves it to be false, and that it could not have been possible at the time. But now he tries to protect himself in this charge, because I made a charge against the Washington *Union*. My speech in the Senate, against the Washington *Union*, was made because it advocated a revolutionary doctrine, by declaring that the free States had not the right to prohibit slavery within their own limits. Because I made that charge against the Washington *Union*, Mr. Lincoln says it was a charge against Mr. Buchanan. Suppose it was; is Mr. Lincoln the peculiar defender of Mr. Buchanan? Is he so interested in the Federal Administration, and so bound to it, that he must jump to the rescue and defend it from every attack that I may make against it? I understand the whole thing. The Washington *Union*, under that most corrupt of all men, Cornelius Wendell, is advocating Mr. Lincoln's claim to the Senate. Wendell was the printer of the last Black Republican house of representatives; he was a candidate before the present Democratic house, but was ignominiously kicked out, and then he took the money which he had made out of the public printing by means of the Black Republicans, bought the Washington *Union*, and is now publishing it in the name of the Democratic party, and advocating Mr. Lincoln's election to the Senate. Mr. Lincoln therefore considers an attack upon Wendell and his corrupt gang as a personal attack upon him. This only proves what I have charged, that there is an alliance between Lincoln and his supporters, and the Federal office-holders of this State, and presidential aspirants out of it, to break me down at home.

Mr. Lincoln feels bound to come in to the rescue of the Washington *Union*. In that speech which I delivered in answer to the Washington *Union*, I made it distinctly against the *Union*, and against the *Union* alone. I did not choose to go beyond that. If I have occasion to attack the President's conduct, I will do it in language that will not be misunderstood. When I differed with the President, I spoke out so that you all heard me. That question passed away; it resulted in the triumph of my principle by allowing the people to do as they please, and there is an end of the controversy. Whenever the great principle of self-government — the right of the people to make their own constitution, and come into the Union with slavery or without it, as they see proper, shall again arise, you will find me standing firm in defence of that principle, and fighting whoever fights it. If Mr. Buchanan stands, as I doubt not he will, by the recommendation contained in his message, that hereafter all State constitutions ought to be submitted to the people before the admission of the State into the Union, he will find me standing by him firmly, shoulder to shoulder, in carrying it out. I know Mr. Lincoln's object; he wants to divide the Democratic party, in order that he may defeat me and get to the Senate."

Mr. Douglas's time here expired, and he stopped on the moment.

MR. LINCOLN'S REJOINDER.

My Friends: It will readily occur to you that I cannot, in half an hour, notice all the things that so able a man as Judge Douglas can say in an hour and a half; and I hope, therefore, if there be anything that he has said upon which you would like to hear something from me, but which I omit to comment upon, you will bear in mind that it would be expecting an impossibility for me to go over his whole ground. I can but take up some of the points that he has dwelt upon, and employ my half hour specially on them.

The first thing I have to say to you is a word in regard to Judge

Douglas's declaration about the "vulgarity and blackguardism" in the audience, — that no such thing, as he says, was shown by any Democrat while I was speaking. Now, I only wish, by way of reply on this subject, to say that while *I* was speaking, *I* used no "vulgarity or blackguardism" toward any Democrat.

Now, my friends, I come to all this long portion of the Judge's speech, — perhaps half of it, — which he has devoted to the various resolutions and platforms that have been adopted in the different counties in the different congressional districts, and in the Illinois legislature, — which he supposes are at variance with the positions I have assumed before you to-day. It is true that many of these resolutions are at variance with the positions I have here assumed. All I have to ask is that we talk reasonably and rationally about it. I happen to know, the Judge's opinion to the contrary notwithstanding, that I have never tried to conceal my opinions, nor tried to deceive any one in reference to them. He may go and examine all the members who voted for me for United States Senator in 1855, after the election of 1854. They were pledged to certain things here at home, and were determined to have pledges from me, and if he will find any of these persons who will tell him anything inconsistent with what I say now, I will resign, or rather retire from the race, and give him no more trouble. The plain truth is this: At the introduction of the Nebraska policy, we believed there was a new era being introduced in the history of the Republic, which tended to the spread and perpetuation of slavery. But in our opposition to that measure we did not agree with one another in everything. The people in the north end of the State were for stronger measures of opposition than we of the central and southern portions of the State, but we were all opposed to the Nebraska doctrine. We had that one feeling and that one sentiment in common. You at the north end met in your conventions and passed your resolutions. We in the middle of the State and further south did not hold such conventions and pass the same resolutions, although we had in general a common view and a common sentiment. So that these meetings which the Judge has alluded to, and the resolutions he has read from, were local, and did not spread over the whole State. We at last met together in 1856, from all parts of the State, and we agreed upon a common platform. You, who held more extreme notions, either yielded those notions, or if not wholly yielding them, agreed to yield them practically, for the sake of embodying the opposition to the measures which the opposite party were pushing forward at that time. We met you then, and if there was anything yielded, it was for practical purposes. We agreed then upon a platform for the party throughout the entire State of Illinois, and now we are all bound as a party, *to that platform*. And I say here to you, if any one expects of me, in the case of my election, that I will do anything not signified by our Republican platform and my answers here to-day, I tell you very frankly that person will be deceived. I do not ask for the vote of any one who supposes that I have secret purposes or pledges that I dare not speak out. Cannot the Judge be satisfied? If he fears, in the unfortunate case of my election, that my going to Washington will enable me to advocate sentiments contrary to those which I expressed when you voted for and elected me, I assure him that his fears are wholly needless and groundless. Is the Judge really afraid of any such thing? I'll tell you what he is afraid of. *He is afraid we'll all pull together*. This is what alarms him more than anything else. For my part, I do hope that all of us, entertaining a common sentiment in opposition to what appears to us a design to nationalize and perpetuate slavery, will waive minor differences on questions which either belong to the dead past or the distant future, and all pull together in this struggle. What are your sentiments? If it be true, that on the ground which I occupy, — ground which I occupy as frankly and boldly as Judge Douglas does his, — my views, though partly coinciding with yours, are not as perfectly in accordance with your feelings as his are, I do say to you in all candor, go for him and not for me. I hope to deal in all things fairly with Judge Douglas, and with the people of the State, in this contest. And if I should never be elected to any office, I trust I may go down with no stain of falsehood upon my reputation, — notwithstanding the hard opinions Judge Douglas chooses to entertain of me.

The Judge has again addressed himself to the abolition tendencies of a speech of mine, made at Springfield in June last. I have so often tried to answer what he is always saying on that melancholy theme, that I almost turn with disgust from the discussion, — from the repetition of an answer to it. I trust that nearly all of this intelligent audience have read that speech. If you have, I may venture to leave it to you to inspect it closely, and see whether it contains any of those "bugaboos" which frighten Judge Douglas.

The Judge complains that I did not fully answer his questions. If I have the sense to comprehend and answer those questions, I have done so fairly. If it can be pointed out to me how I can more fully and fairly answer him, I aver I have not the sense to see how it is to be done. He says I do not declare I would in any event vote for the admission of a slave State into the Union. If I have been fairly reported, he will see that I did give an explicit answer to his interrogatories. I did not merely say that I would dislike to be put to the test; but I said clearly, if I were put to the test, and a territory from which slavery had been excluded should present herself with a State constitution sanctioning slavery, — a most extraordinary thing, and wholly unlikely to happen, — I did not see how I could avoid voting for her admission. But he refuses to understand that I said so, and he wants this audience to understand that I did not say so. Yet it will be so reported in the printed speech that he cannot help seeing it.

He says if I should vote for the admission of a slave State, I would be voting for a dissolution of the Union, because I hold that the Union cannot permanently exist half slave and half free. I repeat, that I do not believe this Government *can* endure, permanently, half slave and half free; yet I do not admit, nor does it at all follow, that the admission of a single slave State will permanently fix the character and establish this as a universal slave nation. The Judge is very happy indeed in working up these quibbles. Before leaving the subject of answering questions, I aver as my confident belief, when you come to see our speeches in print, that you will find every question which he has asked me, more fairly and boldly and fully answered than he has answered those which I put to him. Is not that so? The two speeches may be placed side by side; and I will venture to leave it to impartial judges whether his questions have not been more directly and circumstantially answered than mine.

Judge Douglas says he made a charge upon the editor of the Washington *Union alone*, of entertaining a purpose to rob the States of their power to exclude slavery from their limits. I undertake to say, and I make the direct issue, that he did *not* make his charge against the editor of the *Union* alone. I will undertake to prove by the record here, that he made that charge against more and higher dignitaries than the editor of the Washington *Union.* I am quite aware that he was shirking and dodging around the form in which he put it, but I can make it manifest that he levelled his "fatal blow" against more persons than this Washington editor. Will he dodge it now, by alleging that I am trying to defend Mr. Buchanan against the charge? Not at all. Am I not making the same charge myself? I am trying to show that you, Judge Douglas, are a witness on my side. I am not defending Buchanan, and I will tell Judge Douglas that in my opinion, when he made that charge, he had an eye farther north than he was to-day. He was then fighting against people who called *him* a Black Republican and an Abolitionist. It is mixed all through his speech, and it is tolerably manifest that his eye was a great deal farther north than it is to-day. The Judge says that though he made this charge, Toombs got up and declared there was not a man in the United States, except the editor of the *Union*, who was in favor of the doctrines put forth in that article. And thereupon, I understand that the Judge withdrew the charge. Although he had taken extracts from the newspaper, and then from the Lecompton Constitution, to show the existence of a conspiracy to bring about a "fatal blow," by which the States were to be deprived of the right of excluding slavery, it all went to pot as soon as Toombs got up and told him that it was not true. It reminds me of the story that John Phœnix, the Californian railroad surveyor, tells. He says they started out from the Plaza to the Mission of Dolores. They had two ways of determining distances. One was by a chain and pin taken over the ground. The other was by a "go-it-ometer, — an invention of his own, — a three-legged instrument, with which he computed a series of triangles between the points. At night he turned to the chain-man to ascertain what distance they had come, and found that by some mistake he had merely dragged the chain over the ground without keeping any record. By the "go-it-ometer" he found he had made ten miles. Being skeptical about this, he asked a drayman who was passing how far it was to the plaza. The drayman replied it was just half a mile, and the surveyor put it down in his book, — just as Judge Douglas says, after he had made his calculations and computations, he took Toombs's statement. I have no doubt that after Judge Douglas had made his charge, he was as easily satisfied about its truth as the surveyor was of the drayman's statement of the distance of the plaza. Yet it is a fact that the man who put forth all that matter, which Douglas deemed a "fatal blow" at State sovereignty, was elected by the Democrats as public printer.

Now, gentlemen, you may take Judge Douglas's speech of March 22d, 1858, beginning about the middle of page 21, and reading to the bottom of page 24, and you will find the evidence on which I say that he did not make his charge against the editor of the *Union* alone. I cannot stop to read it, but I will give it to the reporters. Judge Douglas said: —

"Mr. President, you here find several distinct propositions advanced boldly by the Washington *Union* editorially, and apparently *authoritatively*, and every man who questions any of them is denounced as an abolitionist, a freesoiler, a fanatic. The propositions are, first, that the primary object of all government, at its original institution, is the protection of persons and property; second, that the Constitution of the United States declares that the citizens of each State shall be entitled to all the privileges and immunities of citizens in the several States; and that, therefore, thirdly, all State laws, whether organic or otherwise, which prohibit the citizens of one State from settling in another with their slave property, and especially declaring it forfeited, are direct violations of the original intention of the Government and Constitution of the United States; and fourth, that the emancipation of the slaves of the Northern States was a gross outrage on the rights of property, inasmuch as it was involuntarily done on the part of the owner."

"Remember that this article was published in the *Union* on the 17th of November, and on the 18th appeared the first article giving the adhesion of the *Union* to the Lecompton Constitution. It was in these words: —

"'KANSAS AND HER CONSTITUTION. — The vexed question is settled. The problem is solved. The dead point of danger is passed. All serious trouble to Kansas affairs is over and gone' —

"And a column, nearly, of the same sort. Then, when you come to look into the Lecompton Constitution, you find the same doctrine incorporated in it which was put forth editorially in the *Union*. What is it?

"'ARTICLE 7, *Section* 1. The right of property is before and higher than any constitutional sanction; and the right of the owner of a slave to such slave and its increase is the same and as invariable as the right of the owner of any property whatever.'

"Then in the schedule is a provision that the Constitution may be amended after 1864 by a two thirds vote.

"'But no alteration shall be made to affect the right of property in the ownership of slaves.'

"It will be seen by these clauses in the Lecompton Constitution, that they are identical in spirit with this *authoritative* article in the Washington *Union* of the day previous to its indorsement of this Constitution.

"When I saw that article in the *Union* of the 17th of November, followed by the glorification of the Lecompton Constitution on the 18th of November, and this clause in the Constitution asserting the doctrine that a State has no right to prohibit slavery within its limits, I saw that there was a *fatal blow* being struck at the sovereignty of the States of this Union."

Here he says, "Mr. President, you here find several distinct propositions advanced boldly, and apparently *authoritatively.*" By whose authority, Judge Douglas? Again, he says in another place, "It will be seen by these clauses in the Lecompton Constitution, that they are identical in spirit with this *authoritative* article." *By whose authority?* Who do you mean to say authorized the publication of these articles? He knows that the Washington *Union* is considered the organ of the administration. *I* demand of Judge Douglas *by whose authority* he meant to say those articles were published, if not by the authority of the President of the United States and his Cabinet? I defy him to show whom he referred to, if not to these high functionaries in the Federal Government. More than this, he says the articles in that paper and the provisions of the Lecompton Constitution are "identical," and being identical, he argues that the authors are co-operating and conspiring together. He does not use the word "conspiring," but what other construction can you put upon it? He winds up with this: —

"When I saw that article in the *Union* of the 17th of November, followed by the glorification of the Lecompton Constitution on the 18th of November, and this clause in the Constitution asserting the doctrine that a State has no right to prohibit slavery within its limits, I saw that there was a *fatal blow* being struck at the sovereignty of the States of this Union."

I ask him if all this fuss was made over the editor of this newspaper? It would be a terribly "*fatal* blow" which a single man could strike, when no President, no Cabinet officer, no member of

Congress, was giving strength and efficiency to the moment. Out of respect to Judge Douglas's good sense, I must believe that he didn't manufacture his idea of the "fatal" character of that blow out of such a miserable scapegrace as he represents that editor to be. But the Judge's eye is farther South now. Then, it was very peculiarly and decidedly North. His hope rested on the idea of visiting the great "Black Republican" party, and making it the tail to his new kite. He knows he was then expecting from day to day to turn Republican, and place himself at the head of our organization. He has found that these despised "Black Republicans" estimate him by a standard which he has taught them none too well. Hence he is crawling back into his old camp, and you will find him eventually installed in full fellowship among those whom he was then battling, and with whom he now pretends to be at such fearful variance. [Loud applause, and cries of "go on, go on."] I cannot, gentlemen, my time has expired.

CHAPTER VI.

Re-election of Mr. Douglas—Fraudulent districting—Canvass in Ohio—Speeches by Mr. Lincoln—Speech at New York, &c.

THE circumstances attending the re-election of Mr. Douglas to the United States Senate by the Illinois legislature, elected at the close of the canvass previously described, are too fresh in the public mind to need much detail here. Mr. LINCOLN was largely triumphant on the popular vote. The Republican members of that legistature having on the total vote of the State, a majority over the Douglas Democrats of about five thousand. Yet, Douglas had a majority of the body, and was therefore re-elected. This result was accomplished through a fraudulent districting of the State by a previous legislature, whereby small democratic districts had the same and even larger representation than densely populated ones, which were largely Republican. The "gerrymandering" was successful in defeating the Free Labor candidate.

Mr. Lincoln spoke twice in Ohio during the gubernatorial canvass of the following year. Gov. Dennison was the representative of the Republicans, and Judge Ranney of the Democrats. The latter gentleman is one of the ablest men in the Anti-Lecompton ranks.

The fight between the Illinois Senator and the Administration, continuing with the same bitterness of spirit at first manifested, the Ohio canvass was looked to with much interest. Senator Douglas had just issued his celebrated Harper article, and it had been assailed by Attorney-General Black. Mr. Douglas took the stump in Ohio in support of Ranney. The Republicans placed Mr. Lincoln in the field against him, as the man best fitted to cope with the "Little Giant." Undoubtedly, from the experience of the previous year, he was thoroughly acquainted with the tortuous sinuosities of the Senator's sophistical and declamatory periods. Mr. Lincoln performed the duty assigned him, and in two speeches, delivered in September, 1859, at Columbus and Cincinnati, respectively, demolished effectually the framework of Douglas's argument.

Mr. Lincoln spoke several times during the last winter to large audiences in the Eastern States. He delivered an effective oration on "National Politics" at the Cooper Institute, New York, before the Young Men's Republican Club, of that city, which was largely attended. A New York correspondent of a far-western paper, thus describes the speaker, the speech, and its effects: —

"The tall form of the Westerner, towering as it ought to do, a full head and shoulders above the New Yorkers who surrounded him, and nearly doubling on the fat, jolly, and jocund Gen. Nye, — his small, compact head, dark complexion, and beardless face, too, furnishing a striking contrast to the great head, grim, grand countenance, and white beard of the venerable poet Bryant, while the dark piercing eye, close-cut hair, and ears set back almost out of sight, and the quick, vigilant manner, and plain Western dress, all combined to give him a decidedly striking and characteristic personality. His voice is sharp and shrill, pitched on a very high key, but at times, full, powerful, and sonorous; his manner is high-toned and courteous, his features capable of an infinite variety of expression; his enunciation slow and emphatic; his argument candid, closely reasoned, logical, and speaking with a generous humor. Altogether, he made the best impression, and stirred up the greatest enthusiasm of any public speaker I have heard for many a day."

CHAPTER VII.

National Republican Convention — Preparations at Chicago — The Wigwam — General Enthusiasm — Organization — Speech of the President — Nominations — Ballotings — Choice of Lincoln — Vice-President — Hamlin, etc.

The second National nominating Convention of the Republican party, met at Chicago, on the 16th of May. The assembling of the first, at Philadelphia, in June 1856, marked an era in national politics.

The outrages of the slave oligarchy in Kansas, and the manly character and life of the gallant Republican standard-bearer, John Charles Fremont, stirred up such a generous burst of enthusiasm as seldom before made the heart of a great nation beat to a noble cause. The young men were felt in that campaign. Men grave and reverend, bearing honored names in literature, sciences, and politics, came forward from their retirement to speak for the choice of the aroused North. The results of that glorious campaign are well known. Though defeated, it was but a Waterloo victory for the foe.

The Republican party showed, by the immense vote given for its candidates, how great a hold its principles had upon the public mind. This hold has not decreased, but rather become intensified, in the intervening four years. The reassembling of the party in convention, was looked forward to with the most eager interest.

The people of Chicago made every preparation to accommodate the hosts, who were westward wending their way, in the most liberal manner. Never before had the "Garden City" witnessed such animating scenes. It is reported that at least forty thousand strangers visited the city during the sitting of the Convention. The delegates numbered 465, and comprised representatives from all the Northern, and six of the slave States, viz. Maryland, Kentucky, Delaware, Virginia, Texas, and Missouri, and from the territories of Kansas and Nebraska, and the District of Columbia.

The candidates for President, most prominent, were Seward, of New York; Abraham Lincoln, of Illinois; Salmon P. Chase and Judge Wade, of Ohio; Edward Bates, of Missouri; and Mr. Cameron, of Pennsylvania. The friends of each were earnest and zealous in behalf of their choice, but Mr. Seward's and Mr. Lincoln's names created the greatest amount of enthusiasm.

The Republicans of Chicago had erected a huge temporary building for the use of the Convention. The "Wigwam," as it was called, covered a space of 600 feet by 180, and the height was between 50 and 60 feet. The building would hold about 10,000 persons, and was divided into platform, ground-floor, and gallery. The stage upon which the delegates and members of the press were seated, held about 1,800 persons; the ground-floor and galleries about 8,000. The floor rested on an inclined platform, so that those in the rear were able to see the stage as well as the spectators in the front. A large gallery was reserved for the ladies, and which was filled every day to overflowing.

At 12, M., on Wednesday the 16th of May, Gov. Morgan, of New York, Chairman of the National Committee, called the Convention to order, and nominated David Wilmot, of Pa., as President, *pro tem.*

A permanent organization was effected in the afternoon,—Hon. George Ashmun, of Massachusetts, being chosen President, and the following gentlemen Vice-Presidents and Secretaries:—

VICE-PRESIDENTS.

S. F. Hersey, Maine.
Wm. Hall, New Hampshire.
Wm. Heberd, Vermont.
John Beard, Indiana.
David Davis, Illinois.
Thos. W. Ferry, Michigan.

Ensign H. Kellogg, Mass.
R. G. Hazard, Rhode Island.
E. F. Cleveland, Connecticut.
Wm. O. Noyes, New York.
E. Z. Rogers, New Jersey.
Thaddeus Stevens, Penn.
John C. Clark, Delaware.
Wm. L. Marshall, Maryland.
Richard Crawford, Virginia.
George D. Burgess, Ohio.
Hans Crocker, Wisconsin.
Henry P. Schotte, Iowa.
Aaron Goodrich, Minnesota.
Henry T. Blow, Missouri.
W. D. Gallagher, Kentucky
W. T. Chandler, Texas.
A. A. Sargent, California.
Joel Burlingame, Oregon.
Wm. Ross, Kansas.
George Harrington, Dist. Col
A. S. Paddock, Nebraska.

SECRETARIES.

Chas. A. Wing, Maine.
Nathl. Hubbard, New Hamp.
R. R. Hazard, R. Island.
H. H. Starkweather, Conn.
C. O. Rogers, Massachusetts.
Theodore M. Pomeroy, N. Y.
Edward Bettie, N. Jersey.
J. Bollman Bell, Penn.
Benj. C. Hopkins, Delaware.
William E. Coale, Maryland.
A. W. Campbell, Virginia.
Horace Z. Beebe, Ohio.
D. D. Pellate, Indiana.
S. Davis, Illinois.
Wm. M. Stoughton, Mich.
L. T. Trisby, Wisconsin.
W. R. Allison, Iowa.
D. A. Secamb, Minnesota.
J. J. Kidd, Missouri.
John J. Hawes, Kentucky.
Dunbar Henderson, Texas.
D. J. Staples, California.
Eli Thayer, Oregon.
John A. Martin, Kansas.
H. R. Hitchcock, Nebraska.

Mr. Ashmun, in taking the Chair, spoke as follows : —

Gentlemen of the Convention, Republicans and Americans: My first duty is to express to you my deep sense of this distinguished mark of your confidence, and in the spirit in which it is offered I accept of it. I am sensible of the difficulties which surround the position, but I am cheered and sustained by the faith that the same generosity which brought me here will carry me through the discharge of my duties. I will not shrink from the position which is at the same time the post of danger as well as honor. (Applause.) Gentlemen, we have come here to-day at the call of the country, from widely separated homes, to fulfil a great and important duty.

No ordinary call has brought us together. Nothing but a momentous question would have called this vast multitude together, — nothing but the deep sense of danger into which the Government is fast running, could have rallied the people thus in this city to-day for the purpose of rescuing the Government from the deep degradation into which it has fallen. (Loud applause.) We have come here at the call of the country for the purpose of preparing for the most solemn duty that freemen can perform. We have here, in our ordinary capacity as delegates of the people, to prepare for the formation and carrying on of a new administration, and with the help of God we will do it. (Loud applause.) No mere controversy about miserable abstractions brought us here to-day. We do not come here on any idle question. The sacrifice which we have made in an extended journey, and the time we have devoted to it, would not have been made except on some solemn call. The stern look which I see on every face, and the earnest behavior which has been manifested in all the preliminary discussion, show that all have a true and deep sense of the solemn obligations which are resting upon us. Gentlemen, it does not belong to me to make any extended address, but rather to assist in the details of the business which belongs to the Convention; but allow me to say I think we have a right here to-day, in the name of the American people, to impeach the administration of our General Government of the highest crimes that can be committed against a constitutional government, against a free people, and against humanity. (Prolonged cheers.) The catalogue of its crimes it is not for me to recite; it is written on every page of the history of the present administration of the Government, and I care not how many paper protests the President may send into the House of Representatives. (Laughter and applause.) We here, as a grand inquest of the nation, will find out for him and his confederates, not only a punishment terrible and sure, but a remedy that shall be satisfactory. (Loud applause.) Before proceeding to business, the Convention will allow me to congratulate you and the people on the striking features which I think must have been noticed by everybody who has mixed in the preliminary discussions of the people who have gathered in this beautiful city; it is that brotherly kindness and generous emulation which have marked every conversation and every discussion, showing a desire for nothing save the country's good. Earnest, warm. generous preferences are expressed; ardent hopes and fond purposes are declared, but not during the three days I have spent among you all have I heard one unkind word uttered by one man against another. I hail it as an augury of success, and if during the proceedings of the Convention you will unite to perpetuate that feeling and allow it to pervade all your proceedings, I declare to you that it will be the surest and brightest omen of our success, whoever may be the standard-bearer in the great contest that is pending. (Applause.) In that spirit, gentlemen, let us now proceed to business — to the great work which the American people have given into our hands to do. (Loud cheers.)

On Thursday, the 17th, the Committee on Resolutions reported the following platform, which was adopted amid the wildest enthusiasm.

PLATFORM OF THE REPUBLICAN PARTY.

Resolved, That we, the delegated representatives of the Republican Electors of the United States, in Convention assembled, in the discharge of the duty we owe to our constituents and our country, unite in the following declarations: —

First, That the history of the nation during the last four years has fully established the propriety and necessity of the organization and perpetuation of the Republican party, and that the causes which called it into existence are permanent in their nature, and now more than ever before demand its peaceful and constitutional triumph.

Second: That the maintenance of the principles promulgated in the Declaration of Independence, and embodied in the Federal Constitution, is essential to the preservation of our Republican institutions; that the Federal Constitution, the rights of the States, and the union of the States, must and shall be preserved; and that we reassert "these truths to be self-evident, that all men are created equal; that they are endowed by their Creator with certain unalienable rights; that among these are life, liberty, and the pursuit of happiness. That to secure these rights, governments are instituted among men, deriving their just powers from the consent of the governed."

Third: That to the union of the States this nation owes its unprecedented increase in population; its surprising development of material resources; its rapid augmentation of wealth; its happiness at home, and its honor abroad: and we hold in abhorrence all schemes for disunion, come from whatever source they may; and we congratulate the country that no Republican member of Congress has uttered or countenanced a threat of disunion, so often made by Democratic members of Congress without rebuke and with applause from their political associates; and we denounce those threats of disunion, in case of a popular overthrow of their ascendency, as denying the vital principles of a free government, and as an avowal of contemplated treason, which it is the imperative duty of an indignant people strongly to rebuke and forever silence.

Fourth: That the maintenance inviolate of the rights of the States, and especially the right of each State to order and control its own domestic institutions, according to its own judgment exclusively, is essential to that balance of power on which the perfection and endurance of our political faith depends, and we denounce the lawless invasion by armed force of any State or Territory, no matter under what pretext, as among the gravest of crimes.

Fifth: That the present Democratic administration has far exceeded our worst apprehensions in its measureless subserviency to the exactions of a sectional interest, as is especially evident in its desperate exertions to force the infamous Lecompton Constitution upon the protesting people of Kansas, — in construing the personal relation between master and servant to involve an unqualified property in persons, — in its attempted enforcement everywhere, on land and sea, through the intervention of Congress and the Federal Courts of the extreme pretentions of a purely local interest, and in its general and unvarying abuse of the power intrusted to it by a confiding people.

Sixth: That the people justly view with alarm the reckless extravagance which pervades every department of the Federal Government; that a return to rigid economy and accountability is indispensable to arrest the system of plunder of the public treasury by favored partisans; while the recent startling developments of fraud and corruption at the Federal metropolis, show that an entire change of administration is imperatively demanded.

Seventh: That the new dogma that the Constitution of its own force carries slavery into any or all the Territories of the United States, is a dangerous political heresy, at variance with the explicit provisions of that instrument itself, with contemporaneous exposition, and with legislative and judicial precedent, is revolutionary in its tendency and subversive of the peace and harmony of the country.

Eighth: That the normal condition of all the territory of the United States is that of freedom; that as our republican fathers, when they had abolished slavery in all our national territory, ordained that no person should be deprived of life, liberty, or property, without the process of law, it becomes our duty, by legislation, whenever such legislation is necessary, to maintain this provision of the Constitution against all attempt to violate it; and we deny the authority of Congress, of a territorial legislature, or of any individuals, to give legal existence to slavery in any territory of the United States.

Ninth: That we brand the recent reopening of the African slave-trade, under the cover of our national flag, aided by perversions of judicial power, as a crime against humanity, a burning shame to our country and age, and we call upon Congress to take prompt and efficient measures for the total and final suppression of that execrable traffic.

Tenth: That in the recent vetoes by their Federal Governors of the acts of the legislatures of Kansas and Nebraska, prohibiting slavery in those Territories, we find a practical illustration of the boasted Democratic principle of non-intervention and popular sovereignty, embodied in the Kansas and Nebraska bill, and a denunciation of the deception and fraud involved therein.

Eleventh: That Kansas should of right be immediately admitted as a State under the Constitution recently formed and adopted by her people, and accepted by the House of Representatives.

Twelfth: That while providing revenue for the support of the General Government by duties upon imposts, sound policy requires such an adjustment of these imposts as to encourage the development of the industrial interest of the whole country, and we commend that policy of national exchanges which secures to the working-men liberal wages, to agriculture remunerating prices, to mechanics and manufacturers an adequate reward for their skill, labor and enterprise, and to the nation commercial prosperity and independence.

Thirteenth: That we protest against any sale or alienation to others of the public lands held by actual settlers, and against any view of the free Homestead policy which regards the settlers as paupers or supplicants for public bounty, and we demand the passage by Congress of the complete and satisfactory Homestead measure which has already passed the House.

Fourteenth: That the Republican party is opposed to any change in our Naturalization laws, or any State legislation by which the rights of citizenship hitherto accorded to immigrants from foreign lands shall be abridged or impaired; and in favor of giving a full and efficient protection to the rights of all classes of citizens, whether native or naturalized, both at home or abroad.

Fifteenth: That appropriations by Congress for river and harbor improvements of a national character, required for the accommodation and security of an existing commerce, are authorized by the Constitution, and justified by an obligation of the government to protect the lives and property of its citizens.

Sixteenth: That a railroad to the Pacific Ocean is imperatively demanded by the interests of the whole country; that the Federal Government ought to render immediate and efficient aid in its construction, and that as preliminary thereto, a daily overland mail should be promptly established.

Seventeenth: Finally, having thus set forth our distinctive principles and views, we invite the co-operation of all citizens, however differing on other questions, who substantially agree with us, in their affirmance and support.

Ballotings for candidate commenced on Friday, the third day of the session. William M. Evarts, of New York, placed in nomination the name of William H. Seward; Mr. Judd, of Illinois, that of Abraham Lincoln; Mr. Dudley, of New Jersey, that of William L. Dayton; Gov. Reeder, of Pennsylvania, the name of Simon Cameron; Mr. Carter, of Ohio, Salmon P. Chase; Frank P. Blair, Jr., of Missouri, Edward Bates; and Tom Corwin, of Ohio, Judge McLean. Much excitement and cheering followed, as delegates from various States seconded the different nominations. The following summary shows the results of the three ballots taken by the Convention: —

FIRST BALLOT.

For Mr. Seward	173½	For Mr. McLean	12
For Mr. Lincoln	102	For Mr. Collamer	10
For Mr. Cameron	50½	For Mr. Wade	3
For Mr. Chase	49	For Mr. Sumner	1
For Mr. Bates	48	For Mr. Reed	1
For Mr. Dayton	14	For Mr. Fremont	1

Whole number of votes, 465; necessary to a choice, 233.

SECOND BALLOT.

For Mr. Seward	184½	For Mr. Dayton	10
For Mr. Lincoln	181	For Mr. McLean	8
For Mr. Chase	42½	For Mr. Cameron	2
For Mr. Bates	35	For Mr. Clay	2

THIRD BALLOT.

For Mr. Lincoln	354	For Mr. Dayton	1
For Mr. Seward	110½	For Mr. McLean	½

Intelligence of the nomination was now conveyed to the men on the roof of the building, who immediately made the outside multitude aware of the result. The first roar of the cannon soon mingled itself with the cheers of the people, and the same moment a man appeared in the hall, bringing a large painting of Mr. Lincoln. The scene at this time surpassed description, — 11,000 people inside, and 20,000 or 30,000 outside, were yelling and shouting at once. Two cannon sent forth roar after roar in quick succession. Delegates tore up the sticks and boards bearing the names of the several States, and waved them aloft over their heads, and the vast multitude before the platform were waving hats and handkerchiefs. The whole scene was one of the wildest enthusiasm.

When silence was restored, William M. Evarts came forward to the Secretary's table, and spoke as follows: —

Mr. Chairman, Gentlemen of the National Convention, — The State of New York, by a full delegation, with complete unanimity of purpose at home, came to this Convention, and presented as its choice one of its citizens who had served the State from boyhood up, and labored for it and loved it. We came here a great State, with, as we thought, a great statesman — (applause) — and our love for the great Republic from which we are all delegates, — the great Republic of the American Union; and our love for the great Republican party of the Union, and our love of our statesman and candidate, made us think we did our duty to the country and the whole country in expressing our preference and love for him. (Applause.) But, gentlemen, it was from Gov. Seward that most of us learned to love Republican principles and the Republican party. (Cheers.) His fidelity to the country, the Constitution and the laws; his fidelity to the party and the principles that majorities govern; his interest in the advancement of our party to its victory, that our country may rise to its true glory, induce me to declare that I speak his sentiments, as I do the united opinion of our delegation, when I move, sir, as I do now, that the nomination of Abraham Lincoln, of Illinois, as the Republican candidate for the suffrages of the whole country for the office of Chief Magistrate of the American Union be made unanimous. (Applause, and three cheers for New York.)

In the afternoon the Convention balloted for Vice-President. Mr. Wilder, of Kansas, named John Hickman, of Pennsylvania; Mr. Lewis, of Pennsylvania, seconded the nomination; Mr. Carter, of Ohio, named Hannibal Hamlin, of Maine; Mr. Boutwell, of Massachusetts, named N. P. Banks, of Massachusetts; Mr. Smith, of Indiana, named Cassius M. Clay; Mr. Lowry, of Pennsylvania, named Gov. Reeder, of Pennsylvania.

The balloting resulted as follows: —

FIRST BALLOT.

For Mr. Hamlin	194	For Mr. Davis	8
For Mr. Clay	101½	For Mr. Houston	6
For Mr. Hickman	58	For Mr. Dayton	3
For Mr. Reeder	51	For Mr. Reed	1
For Mr. Banks	38½		

SECOND BALLOT.

For Mr. Hamlin	367	For Mr. Clay	86
For Mr. Hickman	13		

Speeches were made by delegates from the various States, in favor of the Ticket, Platform, and general success of the Republican party.

The Convention, after completing the business, by the appointment of a National Executive Committee, adjourned *sine die*, with nine cheers for the candidates.

The telegraph flashed the intelligence throughout the Union, and ratification meetings were held in nearly all of the cities and towns of the Northern States the same evening.

The Republican Convention has done its work. Their platform and candidates are before the people.

Throughout the Northern States, the nominations were enthusiastically received. In the Empire State, which had confidently looked for the nomination of her favorite son, William H. Seward, the effect of the news was at first that of surprise, and then of hearty approval. In Pennsylvania, by the votes of those delegates, Mr. Lincoln was virtually placed before the country, the intelligence was greeted with the utmost enthusiasm. So throughout the doubtful States. In the West, the excitement rose to fever-heat.

At Springfield, the home of Mr. Lincoln, the enthusiasm on receiving the news of his nomination, verged on wildness. Guns were fired, bonfires blazed, offices, stores, and dwelling-houses were illuminated, an impromptu torchlight procession formed, and the Republican candidate greeted with a serenade. Mr. Lincoln, in returning thanks, spoke of the demonstration thus made, not as personal to himself, but rather as a tribute to the principles which he was held worthy enough to represent.

The Committee, appointed by the Republican National Convention, comprising the president, Mr. Ashmun, and the chairman of the State delegations, to officially announce to Hon. Abraham Lincoln his nomination, arrived at Springfield, Saturday night, the 19th, and proceeded to Mr. Lincoln's residence, where Mr. Ashmun, in a brief speech, presented Mr. Lincoln a letter, announcing his nomination. Mr. Lincoln replied as follows: —

Mr. Chairman, and Gentlemen of the Committee, — I tender you, and through you, the Republican National Convention, and all people represented in it, my profoundest thanks for the high honor done me, which you formally announce. Deeply and even painfully sensible of the great responsibility which is inseparable from that honor, a responsibility which I could almost wish could have fallen upon some one of the far more eminent and experienced statesmen, whose distinguished names were before the Convention, I shall, by your leave, consider more fully the resolutions of the Convention, denominated the platform, and without unreasonable delay, respond to you, Mr. Chairman, in writing, not doubting that the platform will be found satisfactory, and the nomination accepted. Now I will not defer the pleasure of taking you and each of you by the hand."

The various members of the Committees were severally introduced and welcomed by the future President of this Union.

At Washington, Judge Douglas declared that there would not be a pound of gunpowder or a tar-barrel left in Illinios. If the remark had been of all the Western States, it would have been equally true. These popular outbursts are but a token of those to come. The "ides of November" will without doubt see the victorious Republican hosts dragging the men chosen to represent them in triumph to the White House.

H. Hamlin

LIFE AND PUBLIC SERVICES

OF

HON. HANNIBAL HAMLIN,

OF MAINE.

Yours Truly
H. Hamlin

INTRODUCTORY.

Mr. Hamlin is a true son of New England. All the characteristics of the Yankee, he possesses in the highest degree. Born among the immense forests of Maine, his appearance is that of the genuine Down-easter, — a type of character of which much has been said, but had little justice done it either by native or foreign writers. It is a character which combines shrewdness and cunning with intellectual strength; the craftiness of the Jew with the moral heroism of a Luther; and a physical development, so affluent of bone and muscle, so wiry and virile as to be able to carry on its work with credit and power, whether seen in driving logs down the turbulent Penobscot, or sitting in the senatorial chair arranging treaties with the nations of the earth, who come, like the Japanese princes of the East, to link themselves to the triumphal car of the young giants of the West. The physique of Senator Hamlin is very striking. He is about six feet in height, and well proportioned; the features are a little heavy when not animated by conversation, but his coal-black eye,

> " A glorious one,
> Bright as a diamond in the sun,"

relieves all dulness of face by its piercing eagle-like glance. His complexion is somewhat yellow and bilious, his hair dark, and his head has remarkable phrenological developments, among which the perceptive and reasoning faculties appear with the greatest prominence. He has a slight stoop of the shoulders, and is rather awkward, as a whole, in his carriage and gesticulations; but all this is soon forgot under the magic of his conversation or speech. He is careless, and almost slovenly in his dress, and the plentiful use of tobacco, which he chews incessantly when he is not smoking, stains his bosom with the juice of the weed. He is none of your kid-glove gentry, but is large handed and open palmed to every member of the free, unwashed democracy. A traveller through the town of his residence may see him any summer, about haying-time, in the fields in his shirt-sleeves, like the commonest laborer; and in his social intercourse with men he pays but little regard to the conventionalities of so-called polite society. He is "free, fresh, savage," as Walt. Whitman says, and thinks just as much of you, in shabby attire, as if you were faultlessly clad in shining broadcloth.

As a stump speaker he has few equals. It is on the stump that his peculiar powers are seen to the best advantage. He abounds in felicitous anecdotes, which, if sometimes coarse, are none the less good; and his quickness at repartee is remarkable, and sometimes overwhelming. One of his sharp things in this line, we remember, occurred in a speech which he delivered in Faneuil Hall, Boston, during a gubernatorial campaign. He had just concluded a terrific denunciation of the administration, and the Democratic party generally, and, just as the applause subsided, a solitary hiss was heard. He paused, and looking, with all the lurking comic-devil in his eyes, at the spot from which this serpent-like noise had proceeded, he said, with that nasal twang of which he is master: "Is that a hiss I hear?" The manner in which this was said, and which it is impossible to describe, convulsed the audience with laughter, and then, gathering himself up, he gave the unfortunate hisser a final and annihilating shot, thus: "It is said that the hiss of a goose once saved Rome, but it wont save modern Democracy." It is needless to say that this last sally was received with renewed merriment.

This is only a mere glance at his style when on the rostrum or the stump, as it is called, in the West. His speeches are full of the sharpest hits, and the most convincing logic. We have thus briefly described the Hon. Hannibal Hamlin, of Maine, ex-Governor, and present representative of Maine in the United States Senate.

This is the man on whom the people of Maine have lavished every honor within their gift as a State, and it is no more than just to say, that he has sustained himself in every position in which he has been placed with rare ability, and done great credit to himself, and his native State. It is needless to add that he is to be the next Vice-President of the United States, and as presiding officer of the first legislative body in the world, he will amply sustain the dignity of the position, and reflect great honor on the gallant body of northern freemen he so ably represents.

LIFE AND PUBLIC SERVICES

OF

HON. HANNIBAL HAMLIN.

CHAPTER I.

Date of Birth — Profession — Political Faith — Entrance to Public Life — Election to State Legislature, etc.

THE career of HANNIBAL HAMLIN, Representative in the U. S. Senate from the State of Maine, and the candidate of the Republican party for Vice-President, is so intimately associated from his long public services with the political history of the country, from 1840 down, that to tell the leading facts would involve the necessity of using more space than our little volume contains. We must therefore content ourselves with briefly and succinctly noting the leading points.

Senator Hamlin was born August 27, 1809, in Paris, Oxford County, Maine. He is consequently about six months younger than Mr. Lincoln, his associate on the Republican ticket. He resides in Hampden, Penobscot County.

Mr. Hamlin's father was a thriving and leading physician, and gave his sons an excellent education. The subject of this sketch passed honorably through his early educational career, and, with the necessary preliminary study, was admitted to the bar soon after reaching his majority.

He entered soon into active political life, identifying himself with the vigorous Democratic party of that period; not then as now, the abject instrument of the designs of the Southern oligarchy. He was but twenty-six years of age when first returned by his party to the State legislature. He served in that body for the next four years; during three of which, he was the Speaker of its House of Representatives.

In 1843, he was elected a Representative to the Twenty-eighth Congress. He served during both sessions, and was re-elected to the Twenty-ninth Congress.

While sitting in the national House of Representatives, the absorbing subject of public interest was the question of annexing Texas. Mr. Hamlin early identified himself by his votes, speeches, and other public action, with the Freesoil element of his party, on the resolutions of Mr. Brown, of Tenn., (providing for the annexation, with a provision that the States to be formed therefrom might come into the Union with or without slavery,) which was amended by Mr. Douglas, of Ill., to the effect that the provisions of the Missouri Compromise should be extended to the Texas territory; and in all States formed out of it north of 36° 30′, slavery should be prohibited; when the vote came up on its final passage, Mr. Hamlin, with the northern Freesoil members of both great parties voted against both the original resolution and amendment. With most of his party, he voted for receiving Texas, when that republic accepted the proposal of annexation; and again affirmatively his vote was recorded for the final admission of the "Lone Star" State.

In the Twenty-ninth Congress, Mr Hamlin's vote as strongly indicates his anti-slavery proclivities, though party ties still had their effect upon his action. His vote will be found recorded against Mr. Boyd's, of Ky., resolution declaring war against Mexico. His action throughout this Congress was of the same stamp.

CHAPTER II.

Return Home — State Legislature Election to the United States Senate — Admission of Oregon — Compromise of 1850 — Mr. Hamlin's votes — The Nebraska Bill — Abandonment of the Democratic Party — Election as Governor — Return to the Senate, &c.

On the adjournment of Congress in 1847, he returned to Maine and was elected a member of the House of Representatives of the State legislature. He served in this body during that term, and was elected by it to the United States Senate for a period of four years, May 26, 1848, to fill a vacancy caused by the decease of John Fairfield.

He took his seat in that body, and in consequence was a member and participant in the contest for the organization of Oregon, and the celebrated compromise struggle of 1850, caused by the proposition to admit California. Mr. Hamlin's vote stands recorded in favor of Northern principles.

He voted for the bill organizing the Territory of Oregon, containing the provisions of the ordinance of 1787, prohibiting slavery therein: and steadily opposed Mr. Douglas's amendment to extend the line of 36° 30′ to the Pacific.

During the continuance of the compromise struggle of 1850, Mr. Hamlin voted against Clay's omnibus bill, and most of its provisions. He voted for the admission of California with her constitution excluding slavery; against the organization of the territories of New Mexico and Utah, without slavery-excluding provisions; and for the abolition of the slave-trade in the District of Columbia. His vote is not recorded upon the final passage of the Fugitive Slave Bill.

On the 25th of July, 1851, Mr. Hamlin was re-elected to

the United States Senate for the term of six years. He still continued to act with the Democratic party, having advocated the election of President Pierce, and supported his administration up to the period that, under the lead of Senator Douglas, that party abrogated the Missouri Compromise by the passage of the Nebraska Bill in 1854.

Senator Hamlin's celebrated speech in the summer of '56, in which he abandoned his old party associates, they having abandoned their principles, will be remembered for the enthusiasm it excited throughout the North. It was the first gun of the Fremont campaign. In his own State Senator Hamlin instantly became the popular idol. Subsequent events mark how the people repay those who are true to them, and to the impulses of freedom.

Mr. Hamlin was the nominee of the Republican party of Maine, for the governorship, during the canvass of 1856. His name created the greatest enthusiasm; and Maine, the first of the States to lead off, in recording her opposition to Democratic treachery at Washington and Federal tyranny on the prairies of Kansas, rolled up a majority of 18,000 for the man of her choice.

He was inaugurated Governor of Maine, January 7, 1857, resigned his seat in the United States Senate on the same day; on the sixteenth of the same month he was reëlected to the United States Senate for another term of six years, and on February 20, resigned the governorship and took his seat in the national capitol. The annals of politics do not show another instance of such honors showered so thickly upon a statesman as in the case of Senator Hamlin.

CHAPTER III.

United States Senate — The Lecompton Contest — Mr. Hamlin's position — "Mudsills" — Answer to Senator Hammond, of S. C. — The Laborers of the North.

THROUGHOUT the exciting Lecompton contest, Mr. Hamlin bore himself gallantly in behalf of free labor. He spoke in answer to Senator Hammond's insolent speech of March, 1858, wherein the arrogant slaveocrat characterized the working-men of the free States as hirelings, and the "mudsills of society."

Mr. Hamlin commenced his reply on the ninth of March and continued it through the next day.

We make the following extracts: —

THE LECOMPTON CONSTITUTION AND ITS INFAMY.

Mr. HAMLIN said — Mr. President: I do not often trespass on the patience of the Senate. I do so now from no personal inclination of my own. Indeed, but for the obligation which is imposed upon me by the people whom I represent, I would forego, on the present occasion, any suggestions which I might deem it proper to make, and give a silent vote upon the views which have been presented, and shall be presented, by other senators, upon the question now pending. The importance of the question, however, is such as imposes an obligation upon me to speak in vindication of the rights of the people I represent. The magnitude of the question is a sufficient apology.

Since I have held a seat in this body, indeed in the history of the whole country, I think no question has been presented to us for our deliberation and consideration, equal in importance and magnitude to that which is now before us. I regret, sir, I deeply regret, the aspect in which it is presented. In all this body, were I to put the question, how many are there who approve the act which is about to be consummated here, in their judgment? how many of all that hold seats here, could give an affirmative answer? The tyranny of party, the despotism of party, come in to the rescue, and men here are about to do an act, which in their judgment and their hearts they disapprove. There is no despotism on earth like the despotism of party and party associations. We should, as freemen, do no act that does not command the approval of the judgment.

What is the act which a firm and settled majority in this Senate have determined shall be done? In all the history of time, in all the records of the past, no act of equal political turpitude, in my judgment, can be found, save one to which I may allude.

THE UNION.

Mr. President: I have no laudations to bestow on this Union. It needs none. Its eulogy is written in the history of the past. I choose that my acts shall speak for me, rather than the words I utter. I would, sir, that it should remain a monument forever to guide the nations of the world. I would, sir, that this government should be perpetuated for all coming time; and no act of mine, no instrumentality of mine, shall be exerted or given except for that perpetuation. I would that our nation should stand a moral monument to enlighten other nations; but I cannot resist the conclusion that if we are to bow to the unlimited power of party despotism, if we are to do acts, which, in our judgments and in our hearts we reprobate, the day, the hour, of our downfall is as certain as that of other nations which have preceded us. I do not mean that it will come now, or even within my day, or the day of the youngest of us. Great as may be the wrongs which you may perpetrate, the recuperative energies of our country may overcome them; but, in the course of time, this incessant arrogation of executive and governmental power must produce its effect; and the institutions which we have reared, when their foundation shall have been subverted by executive power, must crumble and decay. That act which is before us, that bill upon which we are to vote, is one of the measures which is calculated, if not designed, to produce that event. Who that believes that nations, like individuals, must answer to a higher power for the wrongs they perpetrate, who that believes that the sins committed by a nation are to be answered for as the sins of an individual, can doubt that, if the present course of things be persisted in, a fearful retribution must follow?

After alluding to the former and present positions of the South upon the tariff, and other questions, in illustration of the change of sentiment by those States, the Senator proceeds to show the designs of the founders of the government, and the action of the South at that period.

SOUTHERN CHANGE OF FRONT.

I pass from the consideration of these two questions to one of a broader character. I pass to the consideration of what was the original design of our government in its foundation, and what was the action of the South at that period of time. I know the South has changed her views. I do not know that I complain of it. I know the effect of habit, association, companionship, and interest, upon the lives, the conduct, and the opinions of men. I can be more charitable to those men of the South than I can be to their allies in the North; and God forbid that I should say one word to or of them, when we have such a class existing in the North as we have all around us. No, sir; I might say that I love them in comparison with the class of men at the North who are faithless to all the instincts of humanity, of association, of education, and all their surroundings. I know the force and the power of those influences. God knows what might be our opinions if we were born and educated at the South; I do not. Had I been born in Turkey, I do not know that I might not have been a Mussulman. But it is humiliating to us, it is mortifying, but it is an admission to be made, that you train our politicians at the North, and make them subservient to all your behests. It is a humiliating admission to make, but still it belongs to the frailty of humanity, and I hope, in the progress of time, we shall be compensated for the admission by finding, when government is restored to its original position, that that class of people do not live entirely at the North. While it is a matter of regret, and of deep regret, that we have such a class of men among us, while I mourn over it, I am consoled with the reflection that light is dawning in the distant South; that the patriotic, the noble men of that region are coming to the rescue, and telling us that they have hearts and sympathies that beat in unison with our own, and, that they, with us, ask only that this government be administered upon the principles on which our fathers founded it.

But, sir, what was the early action of the government to which I have referred, and upon which our government was based? It was the principle of freedom. I know too well, and I confess I feel somewhat embarrassed under the circumstances, that I can utter no new truth here; but what, I ask, is the history of this government in relation to the principles upon which it was founded? I say that it was founded, and it was designed to be based on the principles of free government. When our Constitution was formed, nobody doubted, everybody expected, that the institution of slavery, so deleterious in its effects, would fade away. Times have changed. The invention of the cotton-gin made the production of cotton profitable; and, with that power which belongs to the pocket-nerve, public sentiment has changed in the South, and too much in the North. The production of cotton became profitable, and with that profit came the change. A temporary and evanescent benefit has led to this change, not a permanent benefit. Madison told us, in the convention which framed the Constitution, that it was wrong to admit that man could hold property in man; that he would not incorporate that idea into the Constitution. We had the maxims and the teachings of Jefferson, and all the wisest and best men of the South against slavery. I have no time to stop now to quote authorities, they are

"Thick as autumnal leaves."

They all concurred in the doctrine that it was an institution that carried along with it blight and mildew; and your eloquent Pinkney, of Maryland, told you that it scorched the green earth upon which its footsteps fell.

Under that view of the case, the ordinance from the brain of Thomas Jefferson, was adopted. In the precise form in which it passed into a legal enactment, I know it came from Nathan Dane, of New England; but the idea was that of the South; the principle was originated by Thomas Jefferson; and the only distinction between the restriction of Jefferson in 1784, and Dane, in 1787, was this: Jefferson proposed that slavery should be prohibited from all your territories then belonging to the United States, and all that should be acquired. The proviso of Dane restricted it in the territories then belonging to the United States, and provided that fugitives from service should be surrendered. If the doctrine of Jefferson had been maintained as presented in 1784, there would have been quiet in the country, and none of the agitations which we have witnessed would have occurred.

This was the doctrine of the South, then; she presented it to us for our approval and adoption. How stands the South to-day? She has repudiated the doctrines of her fathers, and comes here asserting that our government is founded on the great principle of human servitude,— a system that degrades the white man who labors beside the slave.

. . . .

REPEAL OF THE MISSOURI COMPROMISE.

"Mr. President, I come now to another point which, in my judgment, implies vastly more than legislative faith. I come to the repeal of the Missouri Compromise. Whose measure was that? From what section of the country did it come? By whose votes was it imposed upon the country? Every man knows — it is historical — that the Missouri Compromise was a southern measure. Its passage was celebrated by public meetings all over the South. They held it as their peculiar measure. It was, in truth, the suggestion of Mr. McLane, from a southern State; and it was adopted finally upon the suggestion of Mr. Pinckney, a Senator from a southern State. His life shows the fact. The letter which he wrote upon the occasion states that, in the committee of conference between the two branches of Congress, he suggested it. Upon his suggestion it was adopted; and then public meetings were held through all the South, and they were jubilant over its success Now, sir, one of their own men declared that it should be an act irrepealable. I do not contend that it was such except in good faith. The Missouri Compromise line was, therefore, the act of the South; and in that act the North had always acquiesced. Who abrogated the restriction? It was adopted by almost all the votes of the South; and only here and there a man from the North to support it, and who were known no more forever, as will be those at the North who support this measure. It was a southern measure in essence and in substance. The North did not vote for it. Why? Because it was a partial departure from the original design of the government; because it did not come up to the doctrine of 1787. But after it had been adopted the North, for more than a third of a century, acquiesced in it. After the South had secured, under that compromise, all the advantage that could accrue to her and her peculiar institutions, she comes into this Hall, and she asks, she demands, and she obtains, a repeal of all that was beneficial to the North. We are told by the Senator from South Carolina that we can rely upon the South; that her plighted faith has never been broken! Sir, I will not quote what is so familiar upon my lips in relation to the South, but I will quote it as to what they call the Democratic party: "their faith is Punic, and branded to a proverb."

But, sir, it is not in a party aspect alone that I propose to view this question. A broader and a wider view is before me. It is not the South as a party, and in a party aspect, that has violated this time-honored compact, and I say has violated her faith; but she has extended her power to the court below. I think, on the whole, "the court below" is an appropriate term. She seized upon the Executive and bound him in her manacles. She holds the government in all its departments. You have got the legislative power in your control; you have got the executive in your control; you have got the judiciary in your power. How you got the two latter I do not precisely undertake to say, — by political complicity and collusion, any how. Search all the records of your country, examine all the messages that have ever been presented to us, and not one can be found where an Executive has undertaken to foreshadow the opinions of the judiciary, until you come to the inaugural address of the present President of the United States, — not one; and in that political collusion and complicity, I affirm that the object was to rob the people and the States of the rights that belong to them.

PROSTITUTION OF THE JUDICIARY.

Now, sir, with how much grace, or with how much truth, can the Senator from South Corolina affirm that the plighted faith of the South has never been broken? This opinion of the court — mark the word I use; I do not call it the decision of the court, for I regard it only as the opinion of the judges individually — is given upon a question which they tell us gravely is not before them. They erect a structure for which they have no foundation. They gravely and judicially tell us that they have no jurisdiction of the matter, and that they volunteer an opinion as to what they would decide if the question was before them. That is all there is of it; there is nothing more. I concur with Justice McLean, who said that he would treat it as no decision at all. There is not a lawyer in this body, there is not a lawyer in the country, who does not know that when the court determine that they have no jurisdiction in the matter, they have no right to determine the question which lies behind the issue of jurisdiction. I regret, sir, I deeply regret, that that court should have gone outside of its appropriate jurisdiction for the purpose of seeking an occasion on which to issue or make public their private opinions. I had before looked at that court with high respect; but I hold that they had no more right to decide upon that question than we have to decide for them. It was a political question purely; and it is one of those questions in regard to which Thomas Jefferson so early and so ably warned us against judicial interference. But why quote Thomas Jefferson? He is obsolete on the other side of the Chamber.

They had no more authority to decide a political question for us, than we had to decide a judicial question for them. Keep each branch of the government within the sphere of its own duties. We make laws, they interpret them; but it is not for them to tell us what are the limits within which we shall confine ourselves in our action; or, in other words, what is a political constitutional right of this body, any more than it is for us to tell them what is a judicial right that belongs to them. Of all despotisms upon earth, the despotism of a judiciary is the worst. It is a life estate. When that court shall make the decision foreshadowed in this opinion, they will be regarded on the pages of history as exceeding in infamy the famed Jeffreys, of England. His decisions did not undertake to grasp the liberties of a people, but were confined to individuals. Our court, broader in their grasp, undertake to usurp the rights of a nation. Jeffreys will be forgotten when the opinions of this court shall have grown into a judicial decision. Sir, that will never be. There is a peculiar fact that belongs to that court; I have been unable to find a decision contravening the party in power. While I am no prophet, I can read when "coming events cast their shadows before." We are to have the power; we are to restore the government to what our fathers made it; we are to place it upon its original basis; and the court will come back to the original basis.

. . . .

WHO CONTROLS THE DEMOCRATIC PARTY.

All parties, I have said, are directed more or less by certain influences within their organization. The Democratic party, so called, is in the control of South Carolina. I remember when Mr. Calhoun offered his resolutions here, only a few years ago, in relation to the powers of government over slavery in the territories. I refer to the resolutions which he offered about the days of the compromise. The Senator from New York [Mr. Seward] remembers how they were laughed and scouted from the Senate. They are in the Senate to-day; they are the basis of your Democratic party; they are now triumphant in every branch of the government; they are triumphant here; they are triumphant in the other branch of Congress, one of its very worthy and distinguished members being its presiding officer. They are here by your action, and you fasten your power upon the Executive at the other end of the avenue. Democracy in 1858 means the nullification doctrines of South Carolina in times gone by. It is so. I say you have the Senate, and you have the Congress. I have no earthly doubt as to what is to be the fate of this measure in this branch of the government. I have no doubt as to what will be its fate in the other House. I affirm, therefore, that you have got this branch of the government. That you have the Executive is clear. While he told his subordinate, the Governor of Kansas, that he must insist upon the submission of the Lecompton Constitution to the people for their vote of approval or rejection, he has yielded all, and tells you now that you must adopt the constitution, notwithstanding there is ten thousand majority against it. You have the Supreme Court, because they say, in their opinion, that,—"For more than a century before the adoption of the Constitution they had regarded negroes as beings of an inferior order, and possessed of no rights" — mark the words — "which a white man was bound to respect."

Is there a beast that toils in any State, — I speak of beasts, — where legislation has not thrown around it a protecting care that it shall not be abused by its owner? Is there a slave State where slavery exists intensified, where your legislation have not protected the rights of persons in the slave? It is an inhuman expression, it is historically untrue besides.

But, sir, what you call the Democracy have improved upon that doctrine. If you will pass this bill, (and who doubts that you will?) they come to the same conclusion; and they go further; for, while the court decide that colored men have no rights that you are bound to respect, they affirm that majorities of white men in the territories have no rights that the Democratic party are bound to respect. That is the conclusion. It is the logical conclusion from your acts. The court, I thought, went a great way. It is a revolting, — I repeat once more, — it is an inhuman expression. They said that was the sentiment of the revolutionary times. I mean to quote them correctly. I say it is historically incorrect. But, improving on that doctrine, that black men, for a century before the Constitution, had no rights that a white man was bound to respect, modern Democracy claims that a majority of free white men in your territories have no rights that it is bound to respect.

Mr Durkee. That is the doctrine of progress?

Mr. Hamlin. That is the doctrine of progress, as my friend says. Yes, sir, it is the doctrine of progress: but such a progress! I think it is that kind of progress that the boy made in going to his daily toils at school. There had been snow and rain, and the ground was very slippery, and he arrived at a very late hour. On being reprimanded by his instructor for not getting there earlier, he said that on taking a step forward, he always fell two steps behind. "Then pray, sir, how did you ever arrive?" "Why, after struggling a long while, I turned around and went backwards." [Laughter.]

The speaker proceeded to answer the insulting allusions of the South Carolinian, and thus rebuked his reference to Northern working-men. The courteous tone of the Senator added to the force of the earnest sarcasm, wherewith allusion was made to the source whence Mr. Hammond drew his conclusions relative to the industrial classes of the North.

THE LABORERS OF THE NORTH.

In my judgment, the Senator from South Carolina,— I assure him I say it in kindness,— has mistaken the character of our laborers and their position. I do not think he would designedly assign them a position to which they do not belong; and I have said, that in my opinion, he has come to the conclusion that our laborers occupy precisely the same position as those whom he sees in his own vicinity. I do not say that even that is so; but I say such is my conclusion. I am frank to admit that I know very little of the character of the laborers who toil beside the slave, but I have seen something of it. I have seen what has satisfied me that they have little intelligence; that they were poorly clothed; and that, while they felt themselves above them, they were actually, in the social scale, below the slaves. I remember, Sir, that upon the banks of the Potomac, I once heard a negro taunt a white man, that he was so poor, that he had not a master; and when I looked at the poor white man, I confess, I thought there was some truth in the taunt.

Now, my word for it, the Senator from South Carolina has mistaken the character of our population, and our laborers. I stand here the representative of Northern laborers. I wish they had a better and abler representative in my stead; but such as I am, they have sent me here; such as I am I will vindicate their rights.

The debate continued on the following day, Wednesday, March 10. Mr. Hamlin thus proceeded to rebuke the insults of the haughty South Carolinian.

When the Senator from South Carolina undertakes to draw imaginary distinctions between classes of laborers, he goes back to the old, the worn, the rotten, the discarded system of ages that have long since passed. I tell that Senator what is true, that we draw no imaginary distinctions between our different classes of laborers, — none whatever. "Manual laborers!" Well, Sir, who are the manual laborers of the North, that are degraded and placed beside the slave of the South by the Senator from South Carolina? Who are our manual laborers? Sir, all classes in our community are manual laborers; and, to a greater or less extent, they are hireling manual laborers. They constitute, I affirm, a majority of our community,— those who labor for compensation. I do not know, I confess I cannot understand, that distinction which allows a man to make a contract for the service of his brains, but denies him the right to make a contract for the service of his hands. There is no distinction between them. We draw none; we make none. Who are that class of citizens in our community, who are its hirelings? That is the term. I do not know whether he designs it as opprobrious; but that is the term with which he designates our laborers of the North. This is modern Democracy!

Who are our "hireling manual laborers" of the North? I can tell the Senator they are not the mudsills of our community. They are the men who clear away our forests. They are the men who make the green hill-sides blossom. They are the men who build our ships, and who navigate them. They are the men who build our towns, and who inhabit them. They are the men who constitute the great mass of our community. Sir, they are not only the pillars that support our government, but they are the capitals that adorn the very pillars. They are not to be classed with the slave. Our laboring men have homes; they have wives; they have little ones, dependent upon them for support and maintenance; and they are just so many incentives, and so much stimulus, to action. The laboring man, with us, knows for whom he toils; and when he toils, he knows he is to return to that home, where comfort and pleasure, and all the domestic associations, cluster around the social hearth-stone. Northern laborers are "hirelings," and are to be classed with the negro slave!

Besides that, the men who labor in our communities are the men whom we clothe with power. They are the men who exercise the prerogatives of the State. They are the men who, after having been clothed with power there, are sent abroad to represent us elsewhere. They do our legislation at home. They support the State. They are the State. They are men, — high-minded men. They read; they watch you in these halls every day; and, through all our community, the doings of this branch, and of the other, are as well understood, and perhaps even better, than we understand them ourselves. I affirm that, throughout our community, the proceedings of Congress are more extensively and accurately read than even by ourselves. These are the men who are to be classed by the side of the slave! I think it is true that in about every three generations, at most, the wheel entirely performs its revolutions. You rarely find a fortune continuing beyond three generations, in this country, in the same family.

That class of our community, constituting a very large majority, has been designated here as hireling laborers, — white slaves. Why, sir, does labor imply slavery? Because they toil, because they pursue a course which enables them to support their wives and their families, even if it be by daily manual labor, does that necessarily imply servitude? Far from it. I affirm that the great portion of our laborers at the North own their homes, and they labor to adorn them. They own their homes, and if you will visit them, you will find in many of them a portion, at least, of the literature of the times, which shows that they read; you will find there evidences to satisfy you, beyond all doubt, that they are intelligent, and that they are, in truth and in fact, precisely what I have described them to be, — the pillars of the State, the State itself, and the very ornaments and capitals that adorn the columns. With them the acquisition of knowledge is not a crime.

I have quoted all that the Senator from South Carolina has said on this point, for the purpose of giving the widest circulation I can to the declarations he has made. He has mistaken, I doubt not, the character of our laborers by judging them from what he has seen in his own vicinity, and what, in my judgment, is produced by that very state of servitude which is there existing. It is my duty to vindicate our laborers. My only regret is that I can do it no more efficiently.

Mr. Hamlin proceeds to review the history of the Democratic party down from its formation, and the relations the South stood in regard to its principles and action. He contrasted, in a forcible manner, the sentiments of the Jefferson Democracy, and those freedom-hating organizations which has usurped the honored name.

The remainder of the speech is mostly occupied by a statistical statement, forcibly put, of the difference of products, exports, and imports between the two great sections of the Union. These statements are conclusive on the effects of slave institutions to deteriorate the material wealth and social progress of any community adopting them.

The closing periods are filled with eloquent denunciation of the tyranny sought to be practised on Kansas. Alluding to the argument that the Lecompton swindle was made under the forms of law, Mr. Hamlin forcibly said: —

Forms of law! God knows there is nothing but form in it, — forms of law! Long years ago the mother country undertook to oppress these colonies by forms of law, but not as unjustly as we have ruled the people of Kansas; and she persecuted that great and noble patriot, John Hampden, under the forms of law, and for his love of liberty. There is one other act which has been perpetrated under the forms of law, to which I will allude, and then I shall have done.

Under the forms of law, despotism is created. Under the forms of law, all the wrongs of which the mind of man can conceive have been perpetrated. Under the forms of law, and in the name of liberty, liberty itself has been stricken down. In the name and under the forms of law, the Son of man was arraigned and stretched upon the cross. Under the forms of law, you are about to do an act here, unequalled in turpitude by anything that has been recorded in all the progress of time, save that event to which I have just alluded. In all history, save the crucifixion of Christ, there is no act that will stand upon the record of its pages in after time, of equal turpitude with this act. The purpose of it is to extend human slavery; and I may well inquire —

> "Is this the day for us to sow
> The soil of a virgin empire with slavery's seeds of woe;
> To feed with our fresh life-blood the old world's cast off crime,
> Dropped like some monstrous early birth from the tired lap of time."

CHAPTER IV.

Nomination as Vice-President—Mr. Hamlin's experience fits him for the position—Acceptance of Nomination—Public Serenade at Washington—Disturbance, &c.

Mr. Hamlin has still three years of his term in the Senate to serve. He is a member of the Committee on Commerce and on the District of Columbia. His long legislative experience renders him a most valuable colleague, and has admirably fitted him to preside over the body of which for nine years he has been a member. He is not a man of brilliant oratorical powers, but possesses decided executive and administrative faculties, which combined with ripe experience, will make him an important member of Mr. Lincoln's administration.

The reception on Friday, the 18th of May, of the news of Mr. Hamlin's nomination, at Washington, created much feeling among his friends. His rooms were thronged on Saturday, and in the evening a public serenade was given him. He occupies rooms at the Washington House, which on this occasion was illuminated from garret to cellar. The following report of the proceedings is taken from the special despatches to the New York Herald: —

At half-past nine o'clock, the procession arrived in front of the hotel, and was greeted with three lusty cheers. After the inspiring air, "Hail to the Chief," so familiar on similar occasions, had been performed by the band, loud calls were made for Mr. Hamlin.

Mr. B. B. French then came forward on the balcony, amid a number of ladies and gentlemen, and said: —

My friends, I have the pleasure of introducing Senator Hamlin, who has been nominated at the Chicago Convention to be one of the standard-bearers of the Republican party. (Loud cheers.) We all know how well he will bear that standard. He has become almost a citizen among us. He has been here a number of years, and my friends, we mean to keep him here four years from the 4th of March next. I now introduce him to you.

SPEECH OF HON. HANNIBAL HAMLIN.

Mr. Hamlin then came forward, amid great cheering, and spoke as follows: —

Fellow-Citizens: Sympathizing with you in principles which have united us, I am happy to greet you on this occasion. I am pleased to mingle my thoughts with yours in that tribute which you pay to a common cause. You have come, my friends, for the purpose of congratulating each other upon the result of the action of our friends who have met in council at Chicago, the communication of whose decision has come to us over the telegraphic wires. Unsolicited, unexpected, and undesired, the nomination has been conferred upon me. Unsolicited as it was, I accept it, with the responsibilities which attach to it,—(applause,)—in the earnest and ardent hope that the cause, which is superior to men, shall receive no detriment at my hands. (Cheers, and a voice, "some more applause.") You are here to pay a tribute to that man who is to bear your standard on to what we hope and believe a triumphant victory. (Applause.) You are here to pay a tribute to that young giant of the West, who comes from that region where the star of empire has already culminated. You come to pay a tribute to that man who is not only the representative man of your principles, but the representative man of the people—(cheers)—that man who is identified in all your interests by his early associations in life, who sympathizes justly and truly with the labor of all this broad land, himself inured to toil. (Applause.)

Capacious, comprehensive, a statesman incorruptible, a man over whom the shade of suspicion has never cast a reproach. (Continued applause.) But what is the mission, my friends, that is committed to our hands? It is to bring back your government to the position, to bring back the principles and practices of its fathers and founders, and administer in the light of their wisdom. It is to purge the government of its corruptions,—of its corruptions, compared with which those in any other administration pale into utter insignificance. (Cheers, and a voice, "three cheers for the stick and rule.") It is to maintain the integrity of the Union, with the just rights of all the States; and, while the just rights of all the States are maintained, it is also to maintain that States shall not interfere in territories outside of their own jurisdiction. (Applause.)

And it is to give new aids to commerce across the trackless ocean,—it is to foster and give new life to the industry of this broad land. What is it but the industry of our country that upholds your government? What is it but the labor of your country that spreads out your canvass on the distant sea? What is it but labor that delves in your mines, and toils in your workshops, and upholds the government under which you live? (Cheers.) Who is there that should receive the fostering care and kind regards of the government if it be not the man that toils, and adds by his industry to the wealth of the republic? This is the mission that the Republican party, under the guidance of Heaven, are to perform and discharge. (Cheers.) They are to do that, and then they will transmit to those who shall come after them our government unimpaired, and it will remain, and remain forever, the land where the oppressed of every clime and land, of every creed, may come and receive the protection of our lands and our liberty regulated by law. ("Hip, hip, hurrah," and cheers.)

SPEECH OF MR. CAMPBELL, OF PENNSYLVANIA.

After music from the band, Mr. Campbell, member of Congress, from Pennsylvania, was introduced. He said:—

I claim the right to express the sentiment of my section upon the nomination recently made at Chicago. (Cheers.) I want to say, first, my State is Union-loving and conservative to the core. She believes that the mission of this great republic, as originated by the fathers, is one of peace and liberty, but that this Democratic party now in power has been arrayed against liberty, the Revolutionary precepts, rights, and the interests of the country. (Applause and laughter.) She has therefore looked around her for some other man, and has heard of a citizen of Kentucky, born on her soil, a pioneer of the Western wilderness,—she has heard of the nomination of Abraham Lincoln with unfeigned gratification. (Applause.) She believes that Abraham Lincoln is the man for the time, and marches breast up with the advancing wave of civilization and liberty. He then went on to eulogize the platform upon which he stands, which he (Mr. Campbell) said protected the iron interests of Pennsylvania, and would build up her manufacturers, and pledged the Keystone State to the nominees of the Chicago Convention.

From the Washington House the band and the attending crowd proceeded up Pennsylvania Avenue, five hundred strong, and thence up Eighth street to the quarters of Senator Trumbull, opposite the General Post-office. About half the crowd were Democrats.

SPEECH OF SENATOR TRUMBULL.

Senator Trumbull being introduced to the meeting, addressed it in an earnest and somewhat lengthy speech in support of the great work done for the Republican party at Chicago. He had known Abraham Lincoln for twenty years. A native of Kentucky, he was brought over when an infant into Indiana. Thence, with his axe on his shoulder, he went into Illinois, where he hewed his way into distinction. He studied and for a time practised the business of a land surveyor, then he entered into the study of the law, and rapidly rose to the high distinction of the ablest lawyer in the Northwest.

They call him "Old Abe.," said Mr. Trumbull, and yet he is in the prime of life,—about fifty-one years old. He is a giant in stature, six feet three inches high, and every inch a man. (A voice—"Not high enough to be President.") Yes, high enough to be President, and he will be President. (Hurrah.) He is a giant, and without the prefix of "Little" to it. (Hurrah.) A giant in intellect as well as in stature. (A voice—"Where is Harper's Ferry.") I tell you, my friends, that the prairies of Illinois are all ablaze to-night with the fires of enthusiasm. (Cries of "Is Fred Douglas in there?" and "Abe Lincoln is the man who met Stephen A. Douglas.") Yes, and he was defeated. ("Three cheers for Douglas!" and they were given by the outsiders of the crowd, "Three groans for Lincoln," and they were given. The insiders then demanded "Three cheers for Lincoln!" and they were given with a will.)

Mr. Trumbull then explained, that in the Illinois contest of 1858, while Douglas carried the legislature, Lincoln had the popular vote by four thousand majority; and he will more than double it in November,—(Oh, gas!" "Where is John Brown?")—and I tell you he will make a clean sweep of every State west of the Alleghanies. ("How about poor old Seward?") Mr. Seward is a statesman and a patriot, and his whole heart is with our great cause.

Mr. Trumbull continued for sometime longer, amidst frequent interruptions from the outsiders, cheers for Douglas, inquiries for John Brown, &c., &c. Finally, Mr. Trumbull called for "Three cheers for Lincoln and Hamlin," which were heartily given, followed by "Three for Trumbull."

SPEECH OF MR. WASHBURNE, OF ILLINOIS—ATTACK ON THE MEETING.

Hon. Elihu Washburne, of Illinois, was next introduced to the meeting, and in a bold, clear, strong voice was entering upon a eulogistic speech of the life and character, public and private, of Mr. Lincoln, when a few stray brickbats and stones fell in among his audience, from the direction of the Patent Office, when instantly there was a general stampede in the opposite direction, the musicians of the band being among the first to take to their heels. The steadfast Republicans, immediately, about the doorstep stood their ground, and presently Major Berrett's police came up and told the speaker to go on, for that the meeting would be protected.

Mr. Washburne meantime maintained his stand upon the stoop, and in a few minutes, comparative order being restored, he resumed his speech, saying, that when the time had come that a public meeting on public affairs, could not be held in the federal capital without a riotous disturbance, it was time for a sweeping reform which would drive these lawless parasites from the footstool of power. Mr. Washburne concluded with a high eulogium of Mr. Hamlin, when the meeting, after a round or two of applause, quietly dispersed.

SPEECHES

OF

HON. ABRAHAM LINCOLN,

OF ILLINOIS.

SPEECHES.

SQUATTER SOVEREIGNTY AND ITS FALLACIES.

HON. ABRAHAM LINCOLN IN REPLY TO SENATOR DOUGLAS, CHICAGO, JULY 10, 1858.

DOUGLAS opened the senatorial canvass by a speech the evening before the delivery of the one that follows. It was in answer to the speech made by Mr. Lincoln in accepting the nomination of the Republican Convention at Springfield, June 17. Judge Douglas was not present. Mr. Lincoln was introduced by C. L. Wilson, Esq., and as he made his appearance he was greeted with a perfect storm of applause. For some moments the enthusiasm continued unabated. At last, when by a wave of his hand partial silence was restored, Mr. Lincoln said —

DOUGLAS AND HIS CRIMEAN ENEMIES.

MY FELLOW-CITIZENS: On yesterday evening, upon the occasion of the reception given to Senator Douglas, I was furnished with a seat very convenient for hearing him, and was otherwise very courteously treated by him and his friends, and for which I thank him and them. During the course of his remarks, my name was mentioned in such a way as, I suppose, renders it at least not improper that I should make some sort of reply to him. I shall not attempt to follow him in the precise order in which he addressed the assembled multitude upon that occasion, though I shall perhaps do so in the main.

There was one question to which he asked the attention of the crowd, which I deem of somewhat less importance — at least of propriety for me to dwell upon — than the others, which he brought in near the close of his speech, and which I think it would not be entirely proper for me to omit attending to; because if I were not to give some attention to it now, I should probably forget it altogether. While I am upon this subject, allow me to say that I do not intend to indulge in that inconvenient mode sometimes adopted in public speaking, of reading from documents; but I shall depart from that rule so far as to read a little scrap from his speech, which notices this first topic of which I shall speak, — that is, provided I can find it in the paper.

"I have made up my mind to appeal to the people against the combination that has been made against me! the Republican leaders having formed an alliance, an unholy and unnatural alliance, with a portion of unscrupulous federal office-holders. I intend to fight that allied army wherever I meet them. I know they deny the alliance, but yet these men who are trying to divide the Democratic party for the purpose of electing a Republican Senator in my place, are just as much the agents and tools of the supporters of Mr. Lincoln. Hence I shall deal with this allied army just as the Russians dealt with the allies at Sebastopol, — that is, the Russians did not stop to inquire, when they fired a broadside, whether it hit an Englishman, a Frenchman, or a Turk. Nor will I stop to inquire, nor shall I hesitate, whether my blows shall hit these Republican leaders or their allies, who are holding the federal offices and yet acting in concert with them."

Well, now, gentlemen, is not that very alarming? Just to think of it! right at the outset of his canvass, I, a poor, kind, amiable, intelligent gentleman, I am to be slain in this way. Why, my friend, the Judge, is not only, as it turns out, not a dead lion, nor even a living one, — he is the rugged Russian Bear!

But if they will have it, — for he says that we deny it, —

that there is any such alliance as he says there is,—and I don't propose hanging very much upon this question of veracity,—but if he will have it that there is such an alliance,—that the Administration men and we are allied, and we stand in the attitude of English, French, and Turk, he occupying the position of the Russian, in that case, I beg that he will indulge us while we barely suggest to him that these allies took Sebastopol.

THE ALLIANCE.

Gentlemen, only a few more words as to this alliance. For my part, I have to say, that whether there be such an alliance depends, so far as I know, upon what may be a right definition of the term *alliance*. If for the Republican party to see the other great party to which they are opposed divided among themselves, and not try to stop the division and rather be glad of it,—if that is an alliance, I confess I am in; but if it is meant to be said that the Republicans had formed an alliance going beyond that, by which there is contribution of money or sacrifice of principle on the one side or the other, so far as the Republican party is concerned, if there be any such thing, I protest that I neither know anything of it, nor do I believe it. I will, however, say,—as I think this branch of the argument is lugged in,—I would, before I leave it, state, for the benefit of those concerned, that one of those same Buchanan men did once tell me of an argument that he made for his opposition to Judge Douglas. He said that a friend of our Senator Douglas had been talking to him, and had, among other things, said to him: "Why, you don't want to beat Douglas?" "Yes," said he, "I do want to beat him, and I will tell you why. I believe his original Nebraska bill was right in the abstract, but it was wrong in the time that it was brought forward. It was wrong in the application to a Territory in regard to which the question had been settled; it was brought forward at a time when nobody asked him; it was tendered to the South when the South had not asked for it, but when they could not well refuse it; and for this same reason he forced that question upon our party; it has sunk the best men all over the nation, everywhere; and now, when our President, struggling with the difficulties of this man's getting up, has reached the very hardest point to turn in the case, he deserts him, and I am for putting him where he will trouble us no more."

Now, gentlemen, that is not my argument, — that is not my argument at all. I have only been stating to you the argument of a Buchanan man. You will judge if there is any force in it.

WHERE IS SQUATTER SOVEREIGNTY?

Popular sovereignty! everlasting popular sovereignty! Let us for a moment inquire into this vast matter of popular sovereignty. What is popular sovereignty? We recollect that at an early period in the history of this struggle, there was another name for the same thing, — *squatter sovereignty.* It was not exactly popular sovereignty, but squatter sovereignty. What do those terms mean? What do those terms mean when used now? And vast credit is taken by our friend, the Judge, in regard to his support of it, when he declares the last years of his life have been, and all the future years of his life shall be, devoted to this matter of popular sovereignty. What is it? Why, it is the sovereignty of the people! What was squatter sovereignty? I suppose, if it had any significance at all, it was the right of the people to govern themselves, to be sovereign in their own affairs, while they were squatted down in a country not their own, while they had squatted on a Territory that did not belong to them, in the sense that a State belongs to the people who inhabit it, — when it belonged to the nation, — such right to govern themselves was called "squatter sovereignty."

Now I wish you to mark. What has become of that squatter sovereignty? What has become of it? Can you get anybody to tell you now that the people of a Territory have any authority to govern themselves, in regard to this mooted question of slavery, before they form a State Constitution? No such thing at all, although there is a general running fire, and although there has been a hurrah made in every speech on that side, assuming that policy had given the people of a Territory the right to govern themselves upon this question; yet the point is dodged. To-day it has been decided,—no more than a year ago it was decided by the Supreme Court of the United States, and is insisted upon to-day, that the people of a Territory have no right to exclude slavery from a Territory; that if any one man chooses to take slaves into a Territory, all the rest of the people have no right to keep them out. This being so, and this decision being made one of the points that the Judge approved, and one in the approval of which he says he means to keep me down, —put me down I should not say, for I have never been up. He says he is in favor of it, and sticks to it, and expects to win his battle on that decision, which says that there is no such thing as squatter sovereignty; but that any one man may take slaves into a Territory, and all the other men in the Territory may be opposed to it, and yet by reason of the Constitution they cannot prohibit it. When that is so, how much is left of this vast matter of squatter sovereignty, I should like to know?

EFFECTS OF DRED SCOTT.

When we get back, we get to the point of the right of the people to make a constitution. Kansas was settled, for example, in 1854. It was a Territory yet, without having formed a constitution, in a very regular way, for three years. All this time negro slavery could be taken in by any few individuals, and by that decision of the Supreme Court, which the Judge approves, all the rest of the people cannot keep it out; but when they come to make a constitution they may say they will not have slavery. But it is there; they are obliged to tolerate it some way, and all experience shows it will be so,—for they will not take the negro slaves and absolutely deprive the owners of them. All experience shows this to be so. All that space of time that runs from the beginning of the settlement of the Territory until there is sufficiency of people to make a State constitution,—all that portion of time popular sovereignty is given up.

The seal is absolutely put down upon it by the court decision, and Judge Douglas puts his own upon the top of that, yet he is appealing to the people to give him vast credit for his devotion to popular sovereignty.

GENUINE POPULAR SOVEREIGNTY.

Again, when we get to the question of the right of the people to form a State constitution as they please, to form it with slavery or without slavery,—if that is anything new, I confess I don't know it. Has there ever been a time when anybody said that any other than the people of a Territory itself should form a constitution? What is now in it that Judge Douglas should have fought several years of his life, and pledge himself to fight all the remaining years of his life for? Can Judge Douglas find anybody on earth that said that anybody else should form a constitution for a people? [A voice — "Yes."] Well, I should like you to name him; I should like to know who he was. [Same voice, "John Calhoun."]

Mr. Lincoln — No, sir, I never heard of even John Calhoun saying such a thing. He insisted on the same principle as Judge Douglas; but his mode of applying it, in fact, was wrong. It is enough for my purpose to ask this crowd, when ever a Republican said anything against it? They never said anything against it, but they have constantly spoken for it; and whosoever will undertake to examine the platform, and the speeches of responsible men of the party, and of irresponsible men, too, if you please, will be unable to find one word from anybody in the Republican ranks opposed to that popular sovereignty which Judge Douglas thinks that he has invented. I suppose that Judge Douglas will claim, in a little while, that he is the inventor of the idea that the people should govern themselves; that nobody ever thought of such a thing until he brought it forward. We do not remember, that in that old Declaration of Independence, it is said that "We hold these truths to be self-evident, that all men are created equal; that they are endowed by their Creator with certain inalienable rights; that among these are life, liberty, and the pursuit of happiness; that to secure these rights, governments are instituted among men, deriving their just powers from the consent of the governed." There is the origin of popular sovereignty. Who, then, shall come in at this day and claim that he invented it?

JUDGE DOUGLAS AND THE LECOMPTON CONSTITUTION.

The Lecompton Constitution connects itself with this question, for it is in this matter of the Lecompton Constitution that our friend Judge Douglas claims such vast credit. I agree, that in opposing the Lecompton Constitution, so far as I can perceive, he was right. I do not deny that at all; and, gentlemen, you will readily see why I could not deny it even if I wanted to. But I do not wish to; for all the Republicans in the nation opposed it, and they would have opposed it just as much without Judge Douglas's aid as with it. They had all taken ground against it long before he did. Why, the reason that he urges against that Constitution, I urged against him a year before. I have the printed speech in my hand. The argument that he makes, why that Constitution should not be adopted, that the people were not fairly represented nor allowed to vote, I pointed out in a speech a year ago, which I hold in my hand now, that no fair chance was to be given to the people. [" Read it," "read it."] I shall not waste your time by trying to read it. [" Read it," "read it."] Gentlemen, reading from speeches is a very tedious business, particularly for an old man that has to put on spectacles, and more so if the man be so tall that he has to bend over to the light.

WHO DEFEATED THE LECOMPTON CONSTITUTION?

A little more, now, as to this matter of popular sovereignty and the Lecompton Constitution. The Lecompton Constitution, as the Judge tells us, was defeated. The defeat of it was a good thing or it was not. He thinks the defeat of it was a good thing, and so do I, and we agree in that. Who defeated it?

A Voice — "Judge Douglas."

Mr. Lincoln — Yes, he furnished himself, and if you suppose he controlled the other Democrats that went with him, he furnished *three* votes, while the Republicans furnished *twenty*.

That is what he did to defeat it. In the House of Representatives he and his friends furnished some twenty votes, and the Republicans furnished *ninety odd*. Now who was it that did the work."

A voice — "Douglas."

Mr. Lincoln — Why, yes, Douglas did it! To be sure he did.

Let us, however, put that proposition another way. The Republicans could not have done it without Judge Douglas. Could he have done it without them? Which could have come the nearest to doing it without the other?

A voice — "Who killed the bill?"

Another voice — "Douglas."

Mr. Lincoln — Ground was taken against it by the Republicans long before Douglas did it. The proportion of opposition to that measure is about five to one.

A voice — "Why don't they come out on it?"

Mr. Lincoln — You don't know what you are talking about, my friend. I am quite willing to answer any gentleman in the crowd who asks an *intelligent* question.

Now who, in all this country, has ever found any of our friends of Judge Douglas's way of thinking, and who have acted upon this main question, that has ever thought of uttering a word in behalf of Judge Trumbull?

A voice — "We have."

Mr. Lincoln — I defy you to show a printed resolution passed in a Democratic meeting, — I take it upon myself to defy any man to show a printed resolution of a Democratic meeting, large or small, in favor of Judge Trumbull, or any of the five to one Republicans who beat that bill. Everything must be for the Democrats! They did everything, and the five to one that really did the thing, they snub over, and they do not seem to remember that they have an existence upon the face of the earth.

THE IRREPRESSIBLE CONFLICT.

Gentlemen, I fear that I shall become tedious. I leave this branch of the subject to take hold of another. I take up that part of Judge Douglas's speech in which he respectfully attended to me.

Judge Douglas made two points upon my recent speech at Springfield. He says they are to be the issues of this campaign. The first one of these points he bases upon the language in a speech which I delivered at Springfield, which I believe I can quote correctly from memory. I said there that "we are now far into the fifth year since a policy was instituted for the avowed object, and with the confident promise, of putting an end to slavery agitation; under the operation of that policy, that agitation had only not ceased, but had constantly augmented." "I believe it will not cease until a crisis shall have been reached and passed. 'A house divided against itself cannot stand.' I believe this Government cannot endure permanently half slave and half free." "I do not expect the Union to be dissolved" — I am quoting from my speech — "I do not expect the house to fall, but I do expect it will cease to be divided. It will become all one thing or the other. Either the opponents of slavery will arrest the spread of it and place it where the public mind shall rest, in the belief that it is in the course of ultimate extinction, or its advocates will push it forward until it shall become alike lawful in all the States, North as well as South."

What is the paragraph? In this paragraph which I have quoted in your hearing, and to which I ask the attention of all, Judge Douglas thinks he discovers great political heresy. I want your attention particularly to what he has inferred from it. He says I am in favor of making all the States of this Union uniform in all their internal regulations; that in all their domestic concerns I am in favor of making them entirely uniform. He draws this inference from the language I have quoted to you. He says that I am in favor of making war by the North upon the South for the extinction of slavery; that I am also in favor of inviting (as he expresses it) the South to a war upon the North, for the purpose of nationalizing slavery. Now, it is singular enough, if you will carefully read that passage over, that I did not say that I was in favor of anything in it. I only said what I expected would take place. I made a prediction only,—it may have been a foolish one, perhaps. I did not even say that I desired that slavery should be put in course of ultimate extinction. I do say so now, however, so there need be no longer any difficulty about that. It may be written down in the great speech.

THE POPULAR MIND FOR THE EXTINCTION OF SLAVERY.

Gentlemen : Judge Douglas informed you that this speech of mine was probably carefully prepared. I admit that it was. I am not master of language; I have not a fine education; I am not capable of entering into a disquisition upon dialectics, as I believe you call it; but I do not believe the language I employed bears any such construction as Judge Douglas puts upon it. But I don't care about a quibble in regard to words. I know what I meant, and I will not leave this crowd in doubt, if I can explain it to them, what I really meant in the use of that paragraph.

I am not, in the first place, unaware that this Government has endured eighty-two years, half slave and half free. I know that. I am tolerably well acquainted with the history of the country, and I know that it has endured eighty-two years, half slave and half free. I *believe* — and that is what I meant to allude to there — I *believe* it has endured, because during all that time, until the introduction of the Nebraska Bill, the public mind did rest all the time in the belief that slavery was in course of ultimate extinction. That was what gave us the rest that we had through that period of eighty-two years; at least, so I believe. I have always hated slavery, I think, as much as any Abolitionist, — I have been an Old Line Whig, — I have always hated it, but I have always been quiet about it until this new era of the introduction of the Nebraska Bill began. I always believed that everybody was against it, and that it was in course of ultimate extinction. [Pointing to Mr. Browning, who stood near by.] Browning thought so; the great mass of the nation have rested in the belief that slavery was in course of ultimate extinction. They had reason so to believe.

The adoption of the Constitution and its attendant history led the people to believe so; and such was the belief of the framers of the Constitution itself. Why did those old men, about the time of the adoption of the Constitution, decree that slavery should not go into the new territory, where it had not already gone? Why declare that within twenty years the African slave-trade, by which slaves are supplied, might be cut off by Congress? Why were all these acts? I might enumerate more of these acts, — but enough. What were they but a clear indication that the framers of the Constitution intended and expected the ultimate extinction of that institution? And now, when I say, as I said in my speech that Judge Douglas has quoted from, when I say that I think the opponents of slavery will resist the farther spread of it, and place it where the public mind shall rest with the belief that it is in course of ultimate extinction, I only mean to say, that they will place it where the founders of this Government originally placed it.

I have said a hundred times, and I have now no inclination to take it back, that I believe there is no right, and ought to be no inclination in the people of the free States to enter into the slave States, and interfere with the question of slavery at all. I have said that always; Judge Douglas has heard me say it, — if not quite a hundred times, at least as good as a hundred times; and when it is said that I am in favor of interfering with slavery where it exists, I know it is unwarranted by anything I have ever *intended*, and, as I believe, by anything I have ever *said*. If, by any means, I have ever used language which could fairly be so construed, (as, however, I believe I never have,) I now correct it.

So much, then, for the inference that Judge Douglas draws, that I am in favor of setting the sections at war with one another. I know that I never meant any such thing, and I believe that no fair mind can infer any such thing from anything I have ever said.

LINCOLN ON CENTRALIZATION.

Now in relation to his inference that I am in favor of a general consolidation of all the local institutions of the various States. I will attend to that for a little while, and try to inquire, if I can, how on earth it could be that any man could draw such an inference from anything I said. I have said, very many times, in Judge Douglas's hearing, that no man believed more than I in the principle of self-government; that it lies at the bottom of all my ideas of just government, from beginning to end. I have denied that his use of that term applies properly. But for the thing itself, I deny that any man has ever gone ahead of me in his devotion to the principle, whatever he may have done in efficiency in advocating it. I think that I have said it in your hearing,—that I believe each individual is naturally entitled to do as he pleases with himself and the fruit of his labor, so far as it in no wise interferes with any other man's rights,—that each community, as a State, has a right to do exactly as it pleases with all the concerns within that State that interferes with the right of no other State, and that the General Government, upon principle, has no right to interfere with anything other than that general class of things that does concern the whole. I have said that at all times. I have said as illustrations, that I do not believe in the right of Illinois to interfere with the cranberry laws of Indiana, the oyster laws of Virginia, or the liquor laws of Maine. I have said these things over and over again, and I repeat them here as my sentiments.

How is it, then, that Judge Douglas infers, because I hope to see slavery put where the public mind shall rest in the belief that it is in the course of ultimate extinction, that I am in favor of Illinois going over and interfering with the cranberry laws of Indiana? What can authorize him to draw any such inference? I suppose there might be one thing that at least enabled *him* to draw such an inference that would not be true with me or many others, that is, because he looks upon all this matter of slavery as an exceedingly little thing, — this matter of keeping one sixth of the population of the whole nation in a state of oppression and tyranny unequalled in the world. He looks upon it as being an exceedingly little thing, — only equal to the question of the cranberry laws of Indiana, — as something having no moral question in it, — as something on a par with the question of whether a man shall pasture his land with cattle, or plant it with tobacco, — so little and so small a thing, that he concludes, if I could desire that if anything should be done to bring about the ultimate extinction of that little thing, I must be in favor of bringing about an amalgamation of all the other little things in the Union. Now, it so happens, — and there, I presume, is the foundation of this mistake, — that the Judge thinks thus; and it so happens that there is a vast portion of the American people that do *not* look upon that matter as being this very little thing. They look upon it as a vast moral evil; they can prove it as such by the writings of those who gave us the blessings of liberty which we enjoy, and that they so looked upon it, and not as an evil merely confining itself to the States where it is situated; and while we agree that, by the Constitution we assented to, in the States where it exists we have no right to interfere with it, because it is in the Constitution; and we are by both duty and inclination to stick by that Constitution, in all its letter and spirit, from beginning to end.

So much, then, as to my disposition, my wish, to have all the State legislatures blotted out, and to have one consolidated government, and a uniformity of domestic regulations in all the States, by which, I suppose, it is meant, if we raise corn here, we must make sugar-cane grow here too, and we must make those which grow North grow in the South. All this, I suppose, he understands I am in favor of doing. Now, so much for all this nonsense, — for I must call it so. The Judge can have no issue with me on a question of establishing uniformity in the domestic regulations of the States.

THE DRED SCOTT DECISION, AND ITS VALUE.

A little now on the other point, — the Dred Scott decision. Another of the issues, he says, that is to be made with me, is upon his devotion to the Dred Scott decision, and my opposition to it.

I have expressed heretofore, and I now repeat, my opposition to the Dred Scott decision, but I should be allowed to state the nature of that opposition, and I ask your indulgence while I do so. What is fairly implied by the term Judge Douglas has used, "Resistance to the decision?" I do not resist it. If I wanted to take Dred Scott from his master, I would be interfering with property, and that terrible difficulty that Judge Douglas speaks of, of interfering with property, would arise. But I am doing no such thing as that, but all that I am doing is refusing to obey it as a political rule. If I were in Congress, and a vote should come up on a question whether slavery should be prohibited in a new territory, in spite of the Dred Scott decision, I would vote that it should.

That is what I would do. Judge Douglas said, last night, that, before the decision, he might advance his opinion, and it might be contrary to the decision when it was made; but, after it was made, he would abide by it until it was reversed. Just so! We let this property abide by the decision, but we will try to reverse that decision. We will try to put it where Judge Douglas would not object, for he says he will obey it until it is reversed. Somebody has to reverse that decision, since it is made, and we mean to reverse it, and we mean to do it peaceably.

What are the uses of decisions of courts? They have two uses. As rules of property, they have two uses. First, they decide upon the question before the court. They decide, in this case, that Dred Scott is a slave. Nobody resists that. Not only that, but they say to everybody else that persons standing just as Dred Scott stands is as he is. That is, they say that, when a question comes up upon another person, i will be so decided again, unless the court decides in another way, unless the court overrules its decision. Well, we mean to do what we can to have the court decide the other way. That is one thing we mean to try to do.

"RESISTANCE TO THE SUPREME COURT."

The sacredness that Judge Douglas throws around this decision, is a degree of sacredness that has never been before thrown around any other decision. I have never heard of such a thing. Why, decisions apparently contrary to that decision, or that good lawyers thought were contrary to that decision, have been made by that very court before. It is the first of its kind; it is an astonisher in legal history. It is a new wonder of the world. It is based upon falsehood, in the main, as to the facts; allegations of facts upon which it stands are not facts at all, in many instances, and no decision made on any question,—the first instance of a decision made under so many unfavorable circumstances,—thus placed, has ever been held by the profession as law, and it has always needed confirmation before the lawyers regarded it as settled law. But Judge Douglas will have it that all hands must take this extraordinary decision, made under these extraordinary circumstances, and give their vote in Congress in accordance with it, yield to it, and obey it, n every possible sense. Circumstances alter cases. Do not gentlemen here remember the case of that same Supreme Court, ome twenty-five or thirty years ago, deciding that a National Bank was constitutional? I ask, if somebody does not remember that a National Bank was declared to be constitutional? uch is the truth, whether it be remembered or not. The bank harter ran out, and a recharter was granted by Congress. That echarter was laid before General Jackson. It was urged upon m, when he denied the constitutionality of the bank, that the upreme Court had decided that it was constitutional; and that eneral Jackson then said that the Supreme Court had no right lay down a rule to govern a coördinate branch of the government, the members of which had sworn to support the Constitution; that each member had sworn to support that Constitution as he understood it. I will venture here to say, that I have heard Judge Douglas say that he approved of General Jackson for that act. What has now become of all his tirade about "resistance to the Supreme Court?"

DOUGLAS VS. THE ILLINOIS REPUBLICAN PARTY.

My fellow-citizens, getting back a little, for I pass from these points, when Judge Douglas makes his threat of annihilation upon the "alliance," he is cautious to say that that warfare of his is to fall upon the leaders of the Republican party. Almost every word he utters and every distinction he makes, has its significance. He means for the Republicans who do not count themselves as leaders, to be his friends; he makes no fuss over them; it is the leaders that he is making war upon. He wants it understood that the mass of the Republican party are really his friends. It is only the leaders that are doing something, that are intolerant, and that require extermination at his hands. As this is clearly and unquestionably the light in which he presents that matter, I want to ask your attention, addressing myself to the Republicans here, that I may ask you some questions, as to where you, as the Republican party, would be placed if you sustained Judge Douglas in his present position by a re-election? I do not claim, gentlemen, to be unselfish; I do not pretend that I would not like to go to the United States Senate; I make no such hypocritical pretence, but I do say to you that in this mighty issue, it is nothing to you,—nothing to the mass of the people of the nation, whether or not Judge Douglas or myself shall ever be heard of after this night; it may be a trifle tc either of us, but in connection with this mighty question, upor which hang the destinies of the nation, perhaps, it is absolutelj nothing; but where will you be placed if you reindorse Judg Douglas? Don't you know how apt he is,—how exceedingl anxious he is at all times to seize upon anything and everythin to persuade you that something *he* has done *you* did yourselves Why, he tried to persuade you last night that our Illinois legi lature instructed him to introduce the Nebraska Bill. There was nobody in that legislature ever thought of such a thing; and when he first introduced the bill, he never thought of it; but still he fights furiously for the proposition, and that he did it because there was a standing instruction to our Senators to be always introducing Nebraska bills. He tells you he is for the Cincinnati platform, he tells you he is for the Dred Scott decision. He tells you, not in his speech last night, but substantially in a former speech, that he cares not if slavery is voted up or down, — he tells you the struggle on Lecompton is past, — it may come up again or not; and if it does, he stands where he stood when, in spite of him and his opposition, you built up the Republican party. If you indorse him, you tell him you do not care whether slavery be voted up or down, and he will close, or try to close your mouths with his declaration, repeated by the day, the week, the month, and the year. Is that what you mean? [Cries of "no," one voice "yes."] Yes, I have no doubt you who have always been for him, if you mean that. No doubt of that, soberly I have said, and I repeat it. I think, in the position in which Judge Douglas stood in opposing the Lecompton Constitution, he was right; he does not know that it will return, but if it does, we may know where to find him; and if it does not, we may know where to look for him, and that is on the Cincinnati platform. Now I could ask the Republican party, after all the hard names that Judge Douglas has called them by, — all his repeated charges of their inclination to marry with and hug negroes, — all his declarations of Black Republicanism, — by the way, we are improving, the black has got rubbed, off, — but with all that, if he be indorsed by Republican votes, where do you stand? Plainly, you stand ready saddled, bridled, and harnessed, and waiting to be driven over to the slavery extension camp of the nation, — just ready to be driven over, tied together in a lot, — to be driven over, every man with a rope around his neck, that halter being held by Judge Douglas. That is the question. If Republican men have been in earnest in what they have done, I think they had better not do it; but

I think that the Republican party is made up of those who, as far as they can peaceably, will oppose the extension of slavery, and who will hope for its ultimate extinction. If they believe it is wrong in grasping up the new lands of the continent, and keeping them from the settlement of free white laborers, who want the land to bring up their families upon; if they are in earnest, although they may make a mistake, they will grow restless, and the time will come when they will come back again and reorganize, if not by the same name, at least upon the same principles as their party now has. It is better, then, to save the work while it is begun. You have done the labor; maintain it, keep it. If men choose to serve you, go with them; but as you have made up your organization upon principle, stand by it; for, as surely as God reigns over you, and has inspired your mind, and given you a sense of propriety, and continues to give you hope, so surely will you still cling to these ideas, and you will at last come back again after your wanderings, merely to do your work over again.

A GOVERNMENT FOR WHITE MEN.

We were often — more than once at least — in the course of Judge Douglas's speech last night, reminded that this Government was made for white men, — that he believed it was made for white men. Well, that is putting it into a shape in which no one wants to deny it; but the Judge then goes into his passion for drawing inferences that are not warranted. I protest, now and forever, against that counterfeit logic which presumes that because I did not want a negro woman for a slave, I do necessarily want her for a wife. My understanding is that I need not have her for either, but, as God made us separate, we can leave one another alone, and do one another much good thereby. There are white men enough to marry all the white women, and enough black men to marry all the black women, and in God's name let them be so married. The Judge regales us with the terrible enormities that take place by the mixture of races; that the inferior race bears the superior down. Why, Judge, if we do not let them get together in the Territories, they won't mix there.

A voice — "Three cheers for Lincoln." (The cheers were given with a hearty good-will.)

Mr. Lincoln — I should say at least that that is a self-evident truth.

THE ELECTRIC CORD OF FREEDOM.

Now, it happens that we meet together once every year, sometimes about the 4th of July, for some reason or other. These 4th of July gatherings, I suppose, have their uses. If you will indulge me, I will state what I suppose to be some of them.

We are now a mighty nation; we are thirty, or about thirty millions of people, and we own and inhabit about one-fifteenth part of the dry land of the whole earth. We run our memory back over the pages of history for about eighty-two years, and we discover that we were then a very small people in point of numbers, vastly inferior to what we are now, with a vastly less extent of country, with vastly less of everything we deem desirable among men, — we look upon the change as exceedingly advantageous to us and to our posterity, and we fix upon something that happened away back, as in some way or other being connected with this rise of prosperity. We find a race of men living in that day whom we claim as our fathers and grandfathers; they were iron men; they fought for the principle that they were contending for; and we understood that by what they then did it has followed that the degree of prosperity which we now enjoy has come to us. We hold this annual celebration to remind ourselves of all the good done in this process of time, of how it was done and who did it, and how we are historically connected with it; and we go from these meetings in better humor with ourselves, — we feel more attached the one to the other, and more firmly bound to the country we inhabit. In every way we are better men in the age, and race, and country in which we live, for these celebrations. But after we have done all this we have not yet reached the whole. There is something else connected with it. We have besides these, men — descended by blood from our ancestors — among us, perhaps half our people, who are not descendants at all of these men; they are men who have come from Europe, — German, Irish, French, and Scandinavian, — men that have come from Europe themselves, or whose ancestors have come hither and settled here, finding themselves our equals in all things. If they look back through this history to trace their connection with those days by blood, they find they have none; they cannot carry themselves back into that glorious epoch, and make themselves feel that they are part of us; but when they look through that old Declaration of Independence, they find that those old men say that "we hold these truths to be self-evident, that all men are created equal," and then they feel that that moral sentiment taught in that day evidences their relation to those men, that it is the father of all moral principle in them, and that they have a right to claim it as though they were blood of the blood, and flesh of the flesh, of the men who wrote that Declaration; and so they are. That is the electric cord in that Declaration that links the hearts of patriotic and liberty-loving men together, that will link those patriotic hearts as long as the love of freedom exists in the minds of men throughout the world.

THE ARGUMENTS OF TYRANNY.

Now, sirs, for the purpose of squaring things with this idea of "don't care if slavery is voted up or voted down," for sustaining the Dred Scott decision, for holding that the Declaration of Independence did not mean anything at all, we have Judge Douglas giving his exposition of what the Declaration of Independence means, and we have him saying that the people of America are equal to the people of England. According to his construction, you Germans are not connected with it. Now, I ask you in all soberness, if all these things, if indulged in, if ratified, if confirmed and indorsed, if taught to our children, and repeated to them, do not tend to rub out the sentiment of liberty in the country, and to transform this Government into a government of some other form. Those arguments that are made, that the inferior race are to be treated with as much allowance as they are capable of enjoying; that as much is to be done for them as their condition will allow, — what are these arguments? They are the arguments that kings have made for enslaving the people in all ages of the world. You will find that all the arguments in favor of king-craft were of this class; they always bestrode the necks of the people, not that they wanted to do it, but because the people were better off for being ridden. That is their argument, and this argument of the Judge is the same old serpent that says you work and I eat, you toil and I will enjoy the fruits of it. Turn in whatever way you will, — whether it come from the mouth of a king, an excuse for enslaving the people of his country, or from the mouth of men of one race as a reason for enslaving the men of another race, — it is all the same old serpent; and I hold if that course of argumentation that is made for the purpose of convincing the public mind that we should not care about this, should be granted, it does not stop with the negro. I should like to know if, taking this old Declaration of Independence, which declares that all men are equal upon principle, and making exceptions to it, where will it stop? If one man says it does not mean a negro, why not another say it does not mean some other man? If that declaration is not the truth, let us get the statute book, in which we find it, and tear it out! Who is so bold as to do it! If it is not true, let us tear it out! [Cries of "no, no."] Let us stick to it then; let us stand firmly by it then.

THE NECESSITY.

It may be argued that there are certain conditions that make necessities, and impose them upon us; and to the extent that a necessity is imposed upon a man, he must submit to it. I think that was the condition in which we found ourselves when we established this Government. We had slavery among us; we could not get our Constitution unless we permitted them to remain in slavery; we could not secure the good we did secure if we grasped for more; and having by necessity submitted to that much, it does not destroy the principle that is the charter of our liberties. Let that charter stand as our standard.

"DO NOT LET US RETROGRESS."

My friend has said to me that I am a poor hand to quote Scripture. I will try it again, however. It is said in one of the admonitions of our Lord, "As your Father in heaven is perfect, be ye also perfect." The Saviour, I suppose, did not expect that any human creature could be perfect as the Father in heaven; but he said, "As your Father in heaven is perfect, be ye also perfect." He set that up as a standard, and he who did most toward reaching that standard, attained the highest degree of moral perfection. So I say in relation to the principle that all men are created equal, let it be as nearly reached as we can. If we cannot give freedom to every creature, let us do nothing that will impose slavery upon any other creature. Let us then turn this Government back into the channel in which the framers of the Constitution originally placed it. Let us stand firmly by each other. If we do not do so, we are turning in the contrary direction, that our friend Judge Douglas proposes — not intentionally — as working in the traces tend to make this one universal slave nation. He is one that runs in that direction, and as such I resist him.

My friends, I have detained you about as long as I desired to do; and I have only to say, let us discard all this quibbling about this man and the other man, — this race and that race, and the other race being inferior; and therefore they must be placed in an inferior position, — discarding our standard that we have left us. Let us discard all these things, and unite as one people throughout this land, until we shall once more stand up declaring that all men are created equal.

My friends, I could not, without launching off upon some

new topic, which would detain you too long, continue to-night. I thank you for this most extensive audience that you have furnished me to-night. I leave you, hoping that the lamp of liberty will burn in your bosoms until there shall no longer be a doubt that all men are created free and equal.

PRESENT POSITION OF THE SLAVERY QUESTION.

DELIVERED JULY 17, 1851, IN SPRINGFIELD.

Judge Douglas replied to the preceding speech in two elaborate arguments, at Bloomington, on the 16th of July, and at Springfield on the following day. In the evening, Mr. Lincoln replied.

THE WORK TO BE DONE — THE DEMOCRATIC APPORTIONMENT.

Fellow Citizens: Another election, which is deemed an important one, is approaching, and, as I suppose, the Republican party will, without much difficulty, elect their State ticket. But in regard to the legislature, we, the Republicans, labor under some disadvantages. In the first place, we have a legislature to elect upon an apportionment of the representation made several years ago, when the proportion of the population was far greater in the South (as compared with the North) than it now is; and inasmuch as our opponents hold almost entire sway in the South, and we a correspondingly large majority in the North, the fact that we are now to be represented as we were years ago, when the population was different, is, to us, a very great disadvantage. We had in the year 1855, according to law, a census or enumeration of the inhabitants, taken for the purpose of a new apportionment of representation. We know what a fair apportionment of representation upon that census would give us. We know that it could not, if fairly made, fail to give the Republican party from six to ten more members of the legislature than they can probably get as the law now stands.

It so happened at the last session of the legislature, that our opponents, holding the control of both branches of the legislature, steadily refused to give us such an apportionment as we were rightly entitled to have upon the census already taken. The legislature steadily refused to give us such an apportionment as we were rightfully entitled to have upon the census taken of the population of the State. The legislature would pass no bill upon that subject, except such as was at least as unfair to us as the old one, and in which, in some instances, two men in the Democratic regions were allowed to go as far toward sending a member to the legislature as three were in the Republican regions. Comparison was made at the time as to representative and senatorial districts, which completely demonstrated that such was the fact. Such a bill was passed and tendered to the Republican Governor for his signature; but principally for the reasons I have stated, he withheld his approval, and the bill fell without becoming a law.

Another disadvantage under which we labor is, that there are one or two Democratic Senators who will be members of the next legislature, and will vote for the election of Senator, who are holding over in districts in which we could, on all reasonable calculation, elect men of our own, if we only had the chance of ın election. When we consider that there are but twenty-five Senators in the Senate, taking two from the side where they ·ightfully belong and adding them to the other, is to us a disad-'antage not to be lightly regarded. Still, so it is; we have this o contend with. Perhaps there is no ground of complaint on ur part. In attending to the many things involved in the last eneral election for President, Governor, Auditor, Treasurer, ·uperintendent of Public Instruction, Members of Congress, of ıe legislature, county officers, and so on, we allowed these ıings to happen by want of sufficient attention, and we have no ıuse to complain of our adversaries, so far as this matter is con-·rned. But we have some cause to complain of the refusal to ve us a fair apportionment.

THE CANDIDATES.

There is still another disadvantage under which we labor, and to which I will ask your attention. It arises out of the relative positions of the two persons who stand before the State as candidates for the Senate. Senator Douglas is of world-wide renown. All the anxious politicians of his party, or who have been of his party for years past, have been looking upon him as certainly, at no distant day, to be the President of the United States. They have seen in his round, jolly fruitful face, post-offices, land-offices, marshalships and cabinet appointments, chargeships and foreign missions, bursting and sprouting out in wonderful exuberance, ready to be laid hold of by their greedy hands. And as they have been gazing upon this attractive picture so long, they cannot, in the little distraction that has taken place in the party, bring themselves to give up the charming hope; but with greedier anxiety they rush about him, sustain him, and give him marches, triumphal entries, and receptions beyond what even in the days of his highest prosperity they could have brought about in his favor. On the contrary, nobody has ever expected me to be President. In my poor, lean, lank face, nobody has ever seen that any cabbages were sprouting out. These are disadvantages, all taken together, that the Republicans labor under. *We* have to fight this battle upon principle, and upon principle alone. I am, in a certain sense, made the standard bearer in behalf of the Republicans. I was made so merel because there had to be some one so placed,—I being in no wis preferable to any other one of the twenty-five perhaps a hun dred we have in the Republican ranks. Then I say I wish it t be distinctly understood and borne in mind, that we have to figh this battle without many perhaps without any of the externa aids which are brought to bear against us. So I hope thos with whom I am surrounded have principle enough to nerv themselves for the task, and leave nothing undone that can b fairly done, to bring about the right result.

"THE LITTLE GIANT," AND HIS PRINCIPLES.

After Senator Douglas left Washington, as his movements were made known by the public prints, he tarried a considerable time in the city of New York; and it was heralded that, like another Napoleon, he was lying by, and framing the plan of his campaign. It was telegraphed to Washington City, and published in the *Union*, that he was framing his plan for the purpose of going to Illinois, to pounce upon, and annihilate the treasonable and disunion speech which Lincoln had made here on the 16th of June. Now, I do suppose that the Judge really spent some time in New York, maturing the plan of the campaign, as his friends heralded for him. I have been able, by noting his movements since his arrival in Illinois, to discover evidences confirmatory of that allegation. I think I have been able to see what are the material points of that plan. I will, for a little while, ask your attention to some of them. What I shall point out, though not showing the whole plan, are, neverthe-ess, the main points, as I suppose.

They are not very numerous. The first is popular sover-ignty. The second and third are attacks upon my speech made n the 16th of June. Out of these three points, — drawing ithin the range of popular sovereignty the question of the Le-ompton Constitution, — he makes his principal assault. Upon iese his successive speeches are substantially one and the same. n this matter of popular sovereignty I wish to be a little care-il. Auxiliary to these main points, to be sure, are their thun-rings of cannon, their marching and music, their fizzle-gigs, id fire-works; but I will not waste time with them. They are it the little trappings of the campaign.

Coming to the substance, — the first point, — "popular sov-eignty." It is to be labelled upon the cars in which he trav-; put upon the hacks he rides in; to be flaunted upon the hes he passes under, and the banners which wave over him. is to be dished up in as many varieties as a French cook can duce soups from potatoes. Now, as this is so great a staple of the plan of the campaign, it is worth while to examine it carefully; and if we examine only a very little, and do not allow ourselves to be misled, we shall be able to see that the whole thing is the most arrant Quixotism that was ever enacted before a community. What is the matter of popular sovereignty? The first thing, in order to understand it, is to get a good definition of what it is, and after that to see how it is applied.

THE REAL ISSUE.

I suppose almost every one knows that, in this controversy, whatever has been said has had reference to the question of negro slavery. We have not been in a controversy about the right of the people to govern themselves in the *ordinary* matters of domestic concern in the States and Territories. Mr. Buchanan, in one of his late messages, (I think when he sent up the Lecompton Constitution,) urged that the main points to which the public attention had been directed, was not in regard to the great variety of small domestic matters, but was directed to the question of negro slavery; and he asserts, that if the people had had a fair chance to vote on that question, there was no reasonable ground of objection in regard to minor questions. Now, while I think that the people had *not* had given, or offered them, a fair chance upon that slavery question; still, if there had been a fair submission to a vote upon that main question, the President's proposition would have been true to the uttermost. Hence, when hereafter I speak of popular sovereignty, I wish to be understood as applying what I say to the question of slavery only, not to other minor domestic matters of a Territory or a State.

DOUGLAS'S INCONSISTENCIES.

Does Judge Douglas, when he says that several of the past years of his life have been devoted to the question of "popular sovereignty," and that all the remainder of his life shall be devoted to it, does he mean to say that he has been devoting h life to securing to the people of the Territories the right to exclude slavery from the Territories? If he means so to say, he means to deceive; because he and every one knows that the decision of the Supreme Court, which he approves and makes especial ground of attack upon me for disapproving, forbids the people of a Territory to exclude slavery. This covers the whole ground, from the settlement of a Territory till it reaches the degree of maturity entitling it to form a State constitution. So far as all that ground is concerned, the Judge is not sustaining popular sovereignty, but absolutely opposing it. He sustains the decision which declares that the popular will of the Territories has no constitutional power to exclude slavery during their territorial existence. This being so, the period of time from the first settlement of a Territory till it reaches the point of forming a State constitution, is not the thing that the Judge has fought for or is fighting for; but on the contrary, he has fought for, and is fighting for, the thing that annihilates and crushes out that same popular sovereignty.

Well, so much being disposed of, what is left? Why, he is contending for the right of the people, when they come to make a State constitution, to make it for themselves, and precisely as best suits themselves. I say again, that is Quixotic. I defy contradiction when I declare that the Judge can find no one to oppose him on that proposition. I repeat, there is nobody opposing that proposition on *principle*. Let me not be misunderstood. I know that, with reference to the Lecompton Constitution, I may be misunderstood; but when you understand me correctly, my proposition will be true and accurate. Nobody is opposing, or has opposed, the right of the people, when they form a constitution, to form it for themselves. Mr. Buchanan and his friends have not done it; they, too, as well as the Republicans and the Anti-Lecompton Democrats, have not done it; but, on the contrary, they together have insisted on the right of the people to form a constitution for themselves. The difference between the Buchanan men on the one hand, and the Douglas men and the Republicans on the other, has not been on a question of principle, but on a question of *fact*.

WHO FORMED THE LECOMPTON CONSTITUTION?

The dispute was upon the question of fact, whether the Lecompton Constitution had been fairly formed by the people or not. Mr. Buchanan and his friends have not contended for the contrary principle any more than the Douglas men or the Republicans. They have insisted that whatever of small irregularities existed in getting up the Lecompton Constitution, were such as happen in the settlement of all new Territories. The question was, was it a fair emanation of the people? It was a question of fact, and not of principle. As to the principle, all were agreed. Judge Douglas voted with the Republicans upon that matter of fact.

He and they, by their voices and votes, denied that it was a fair emanation of the people. The Administration affirmed that it was. With respect to the evidence bearing upon that question of fact, I readily agree that Judge Douglas and the Republicans had the right on their side, and that the Administration was wrong. But I state again that, as a matter of principle, there is no dispute upon the right of a people in a Territory, merging into a State, to form a Constitution for themselves, without outside interference from any quarter. This being so, what is Judge Douglas going to spend his life for? Is he going to spend his life in maintaining a principle that nobody on earth opposes? Does he expect to stand up in majestic dignity, and go through his *apotheosis* and become a god, in the maintaining of a principle which neither man nor mouse in all God's creation is opposing? Now, something in regard to the Lecompton Constitution more especially; for I pass from this other question of popular sovereignty as the most arrant humbug that has ever been attempted on an intelligent community.

WHO KILLED THE LECOMPTON SWINDLE?

As to the Lecompton Constitution, I have already said that on the question of fact as to whether it was a fair emanation of the people or not, Judge Douglas with the Republicans and some Americans, had greatly the argument against the Administration; and while I repeat this, I wish to know what there is in the opposition of Judge Douglas to the Lecompton Constitution that entitles him to be considered the only opponent to it, —as being *par excellence* the very *quintessence* of that opposition. I agree to the rightfulness of his opposition. He in the Senate and his class of men there formed the number *three* and no more. In the House of Representatives his class of men, the Anti-Lecompton Democrats, formed a number of about twenty. It took one hundred and twenty to defeat the measure, against one hundred and twelve. Of the votes of that one hundred and twenty, Judge Douglas's friends furnished twenty, to add to which there were six Americans and ninety-four Republicans. I do not say that I am precisely accurate in their numbers, but I am sufficiently so for any use I am making of it.

Why is it that twenty shall be entitled to all the credit of doing that work, and the hundred none of it? Why, if, as Judge Douglas says, the honor is to be divided, and due credit is to be given to other parties, why is just so much given as is consonant with the wishes, the interests, and advancement of the twenty? My understanding is, when a common job is done, or a common enterprise prosecuted, if I put in five dollars to your one, I have a right to take out five dollars to your one. But he does not so understand it. He declares the dividend of credit for defeating Lecompton upon a basis which seems unprecedented and incomprehensible.

WORKS MEET FOR REPENTANCE.

Let us see. Lecompton in the raw was defeated. It afterward took a sort of cooked-up shape, and was passed in the English bill. It is said by the Judge that the defeat was a good and proper thing. If it was a good thing, why is he entitled to more credit than others, for the performance of that good act, unless there was something in the antecedents of the Republicans that might induce every one to expect them to join in that good work, and at the same time, something leading them to doubt that he would? Does he place his superior claim to credit, on the ground that he performed a good act which was never expected of him? He says I have a proneness for quoting Scripture. If I should do so now, it occurs that perhaps he places himself somewhat upon the ground of the parable of the lost sheep which went astray upon the mountains, and when the owner of the hundred sheep found the one that was lost, and threw it upon his shoulders, and came home rejoicing, it was said that there was more rejoicing over the one sheep that was lost and had been found, than over the ninety and nine in the fold. The application is made by the Saviour in this parable, thus: "Verily, I say unto you, there is more rejoicing in heaven over one sinner that repenteth, than over ninety and nine just persons that need no repentance."

And now, if the Judge claims the benefit of this parable, *let him repent.* Let him not come up here and say, "I am the only just person; and you are the ninety-nine sinners!" *Repentance* before *forgiveness* is a provision of the Christian system, and on that condition alone will the Republicans grant his forgiveness.

WHERE DOUGLAS LEARNED TO OPPOSE LECOMPTON.

How will he prove that we have ever occupied a different position in regard to the Lecompton Constitution or any principle in it? He says he did not make his opposition on the ground as to whether it was a free or slave constitution, and he would have you understand that the Republicans made their opposition because it ultimately became a slave constitution. To make proof in favor of himself on this point, he reminds us that he opposed Lecompton before the vote was taken declaring whether the State was to be free or slave. But he forgets to say that our Republican Senator, Trumbull, made a speech against Lecompton even before he did.

Why did he oppose it? Partly, as he declares, because the members of the Convention who framed it were not fairly elected by the people; that the people were not allowed to vot unless they had been registered; and that the people of whole counties, in some instances, were not registered. For these reasons he declares the constitution was not an emanation, in any true sense, from the people. He also has an additional objection as to the mode of submitting the constitution back to the people. But bearing on the question of whether the delegates were fairly elected, a speech of his, made something more than twelve months ago, from this stand, becomes important. It was made a little while before the election of the delegates who made Lecompton. In that speech he declared there was every reason to hope and believe the election would be fair; and if any one failed to vote, it would be his own culpable fault.

I, a few days after, made a sort of answer to that speech. In that answer, I made, substantially, the very argument with which he combated his Lecompton adversaries in the Senate last winter. I pointed to the facts that the people could not vote without being registered, and that the time for registering had gone by. I commented on it as wonderful that Judge Douglas could be gnorant of these facts, which every one else in the nation so vell knew.

I now pass from popular sovereignty and Lecompton. I may ave occasion to refer to one or both

HIS MISREPRESENTATIONS.

When he was preparing his plan of campaign, Napoleon-like, New York, as appears by two speeches I have heard him liver since his arrival in Illinois, he gave special attention to a eech of mine, delivered here on the 16th of June last. He s that he carefully read that speech. He told us that at icago, a week ago last night, and he repeated it at Blooming- last night. Doubtless, he repeated it again to-day, though lid not hear him. In the first two places—Chicago and omington—I heard him; to-day I did not. He said he carefully examined that speech; *when*, he did not say; but e is no reasonable doubt it was when he was in New York, preparing his plan of campaign. I am glad he did read it carefully. He says it was evidently prepared with great care. I freely admit it was prepared with care. I claim not to be more free from errors than others,—perhaps scarcely so much; but I was very careful not to put anything in that speech as a matter of fact, or make any inferences which did not appear to me to be true, and fully warrantable. If I had made any mistake, I was willing to be corrected; if I had drawn any inference in regard to Judge Douglas, or any one else, which was not warranted, I was fully prepared to modify it as soon as discovered. I planted myself upon the truth, and the truth only, so far as I knew it, or could be brought to know it.

Having made that speech with the most kindly feelings toward Judge Douglas, as manifested therein, I was gratified when I found that he had carefully examined it, and had detected no error of fact, nor any inference against him, nor any misrepresentations, of which he thought fit to complain. In neither of the two speeches I have mentioned, did he make any such complaint. I will thank any one who will inform me that he, ir his speech to-day, pointed out anything I had stated, respectin him, as being erroneous. I presume there is no such thing. have reason to be gratified that the care and caution used i that speech, left it so that he, most of all others interested i discovering error, has not been able to point out one thin against him which he could say was wrong. He seizes upc the doctrines he supposes to be included in that speech, ar declares that upon them will turn the issues of this campaig He then quotes, or attempts to quote, from my speech. I w not say that he wilfully misquotes, but he does fail to quc accurately. His attempt at quoting is from a passage whicl believe I can quote accurately from memory. I shall make t quotation now, with some comments upon it, as I have alrea said, in order that the Judge shall be left entirely without cuse for misrepresenting me. I do so now, as I hope, for last time. I do this in great caution, in order that if he rep his misrepresentation, it shall be plain to all that he does wilfully. If, after all, he still persists, I shall be compelled to reconstruct the course I have marked out for myself, and draw upon such humble resources as I have, for a new course, better suited to the real exigences of the case. I set out, in this campaign, with the intention of conducting it strictly as a gentleman, in substance at least, if not in the outside polish. The latter I shall never be, but that which constitutes the inside of a gentleman I hope I understand, and am not less inclined to practice than others. It was my purpose and expectation that this canvass would be conducted upon principle, and with fairness on both sides, and it shall not be my fault if this purpose and expectation shall be given up.

"A WAR OF SECTIONS."

He charges, in substance, that I invite a war of sections; that I propose all the local institutions of the different States shall become consolidated and uniform. What is there in the language of that speech which expresses such purpose, or bears such construction? I have again and again said that I would not enter into any of the States to disturb the institution of slavery. Judge Douglas said, at Bloomington, that I used anguage most able and ingenious for concealing what I really neant; and that, while I had protested against entering into the lave States, I nevertheless did mean to go on the banks of the)hio, and throw missiles into Kentucky, to disturb them in ıeir domestic institutions.

I said, in that speech, and I meant no more, that the institu- on of slavery ought to be placed in the very attitude where the amers of this Government placed it, and left it. I do not un- rstand that the framers of our Constitution left the people of e free States in the attitude of firing bombs or shells into the ıve States. I was not using that passage for the purpose for ıich he infers I did use it. I said, "We are now far advanced o the fifth year since a policy was created for the avowed ect, and with the confident promise, of putting an end to very agitation. Under the operation of that policy, that agitation has not only not ceased, but has constantly augmented. In my opinion, it will not cease till a crisis shall have been reached and passed. 'A house divided against itself cannot stand.' I believe that this Government cannot endure permanently half slave and half free. It will become all one thing, or all the other. Either the opponents of slavery will arrest the further spread of it, and place it where the public mind shall rest in the belief that it is in the course of ultimate extinction, or its advocates will push it forward till it shall become alike lawful in all the States, old as well as new, North as well as South."

Now you all see, from that quotation, I did not express my *wish* on anything. In that passage, I indicated no wish or purpose of my own; I simply expressed my *expectation*. Cannot the Judge perceive a distinction between a *purpose* and an *expectation?* I have often expressed an expectation to die, but I have never expressed a *wish* to die. I said at Chicago, and now repeat, that I am quite aware this Government has endured, half slave and half free, for eighty-two years. I understand that little bit of history. I expressed the opinion I did, because I perceived, or thought I perceived, a new set of causes introduced. I did say at Chicago, in my speech there, that I do wish to see the spread of slavery arrested, and to see it placed where the public mind shall rest in the belief that it is in th course of ultimate extinction. I said that, because I supposed when the public mind shall rest in that belief, we shall hav peace on the slavery question. I have believed, and no believe, the public mind did rest on that belief up to the intr tion of the Nebraska Bill.

THE NATIONALIZATION OF SLAVERY.

Although I have ever been opposed to slavery, so far I rest in the hope and belief that it was in the course of ultimate e tinction. For that reason, it had been a minor question wi me. I might have been mistaken; but I had believed, a now believe, that the whole public mind, that is, the mind the great majority, had rested in that belief up to the repeal of the Missouri Compromise. But upon that event, I became convinced that either I had been resting in a delusion, or the institution was being placed on a new basis,—a basis for making it perpetual, national, and universal. Subsequent events have greatly confirmed me in that belief. I believe that bill to be the beginning of a conspiracy for that purpose. So believing, I have since then considered that question a paramount one. So believing, I think the public mind will never rest till the power of Congress to restrict the spread of it shall again be acknowledged and exercised on the one hand, or, on the other, all resistance be entirely crushed out. I have expressed that opinion, and I entertain it to-night. It is denied that there is any tendency to the nationalization of slavery in these States.

CAROLINIAN AND VIRGINIAN TESTIMONY.

Mr. Brooks, of South Carolina, in one of his speeches, when they were presenting him canes, silver plate, gold pitchers, and the like, for assaulting Senator Sumner, distinctly affirmed his opinion that when this Constitution was formed, it was the belief of no man that slavery would last to the present day.

He said, what I think, that the framers of our Constitution placed the institution of slavery where the public mind rested in the hope that it was in the course of ultimate extinction. But he went on to say that the men of the present age, by their experience, have become wiser than the framers of the Constitution; and the invention of the cotton-gin had made the perpetuity of slavery a necessity in this country.

As another piece of evidence tending to this same point: Quite recently in Virginia, a man—the owner of slaves—made a will providing that after his death certain of his slaves would have their freedom if they should so choose, and go to iberia, rather than remain in slavery. They chose to be berated. But the persons to whom they would descend as operty, claimed them as slaves. A suit was instituted, which ally came to the Supreme Court of Virginia, and was therein decided against the sláves, upon the ground that a negro cannot make a choice, — that they had no legal power to choose, — could not perform the condition upon which their freedom depended.

I do not mention this with any purpose of criticising it, but to connect it with the arguments as affording additional evidence of the change of sentiment upon this question of slavery in the direction of making it perpetual and national. I argue now as I did before, that there is such a tendency; and I am backed, not merely by the facts, but by the open confession in the slave States.

THE RULE OF THE FATHERS AND ITS EFFECTS.

And now, as to the Judge's inference, that because I wish to see slavery placed in the course of ultimate extinction, — placed where our fathers originally placed it,—I wish to annihilate the State legislatures, — to force cotton to grow upon the tops of the Green Mountains, — to freeze ice in Florida, — to cut lumber on the broad Illinois prairies, — that I am in favor of all these ridiculous and impossible things.

It seems to me it is a complete answer to all this to ask, if, when Congress did have the fashion of restricting slavery from free territory; when courts did have the fashion of deciding that taking a slave into a free country made him free, — I say it is a sufficient answer to ask, if any of this ridiculous nonsense about consolidation and uniformity, did actually follow? Who heard of any such thing, because of the ordinance of '87? because of the Missouri Restriction? because of the numerous court decisions of that character?

JUDICIAL AUTHORITY.

Now, as to the Dred Scott decision; for upon that he make his last point at me. He boldly takes ground in favor of the decision.

This is one half of the onslaught, and one third of the enti plan of the campaign. I am opposed to that decision in a ce tain sense, but not in the sense which he puts on it. I say that in so far as it decided in favor of Dred Scott's master, and against Dred Scott and his family, I do not propose to disturb or resist the decision.

I never have proposed to do any such thing. I think, that in respect for judicial authority, my humble history would not suffer in comparison with that of Judge Douglas. He would have the citizen conform his vote to that decision; the member of Congress, his; the President his use of the veto power. He would make it a rule of political action for the people and all the departments of the Government. I would not. By resisting it as a political rule, I disturb no right of property, create no disorder, excite no mobs.

When he spoke at Chicago, on Friday evening of last week, he made this same point upon me. On Saturday evening I replied, and reminded him of a Supreme Court decision, which he opposed for at least several years. Last night, at Bloomington, he took some notice of that reply, but entirely forgot to remember that part of it.

He renews his onslaught upon me, forgetting to remember that I have turned the tables against himself on that very point. I renew the effort to draw his attention to it. I wish to stand erect before the country, as well as Judge Douglas, on this question of judicial authority; and therefore I add something to the authority, in favor of my own position. I wish to show hat I am sustained by authority, in addition to that heretofore resented. I do not expect to convince the Judge. It is part f the plan of his campaign, and he will cling to it with a des-erate gripe. Even turn it upon him,— the sharp point against im, and gaff him through, — he will still cling to it till he can nvent some new dodge to take the place of it.

DANGERS OF JUDICIAL ENCROACHMENTS.

In public speaking it is tedious reading from documents; but must beg to indulge the practice to a limited extent. I shall ad from a letter written by Mr. Jefferson in 1820, and now to be found in the seventh volume of his correspondence, at page 177. It seems he had been presented, by a gentleman of the name of Jarvis, with a book, or essay, or periodical, called the "Republican," and he was writing in acknowledgment of the present, and noting some of its contents. After expressing the hope that the work will produce a favorable effect upon the minds of the young, he proceeds to say: —

"That it will have this tendency may be expected, and for that reason I feel an urgency to note what I deem an error in it, the more requiring notice as your opinion is strengthened by that of many others. You seem, in pages 84 and 148, to consider the judges as the ultimate arbiters of all constitutional questions,—a very dangerous doctrine indeed, and one which would place us under the despotism of an oligarchy. Our judges are as honest as other men, and not more so. They have, with others, the same passions for party, for power, and the privilege of their corps. Their maxim is, '*boni judicis est ampliare jurisdictionem;*' and their power is the more dangerous as they are in office for life, and not responsible, as the other functionaries are, to the elective control. The Constitution has erected no such single tribunal, knowing that, to whatever hands confided, with the corruptions of time and party, its members would become despots. It has more wisely made all the departments coequal and co-sovereign with themselves."

Thus we see the power claimed for the Supreme Court by Judge Douglas, Mr. Jefferson holds, would reduce us to the despotism of an oligarchy.

Now, I have said no more than this,—in fact, never quite so much as this · at least I am sustained by Mr. Jefferson.

WHY DOUGLAS SUPPORTS THE DECISION.

Let us go a little further. You remember we once had : National Bank. Some one owed the bank a debt; he was sue and sought to avoid payment, on the ground that the bank wa unconstitutional. The case went to the Supreme Court, an therein it was decided that the bank was constitutional. Tl whole Democratic party revolted against that decision. General Jackson himself asserted, that he, as President, would not be bound to hold a National Bank to be constitutional, even though the Court had decided it to be so. He fell in precisely with the view of Mr. Jefferson, and acted upon it under his official oath, in vetoing a charter for a National Bank. The declaration that Congress does not possess this constitutional power to charter a bank, has gone into the Democratic platform, at their National Conventions, and was brought forward and reaffirmed in their last Convention at Cincinnati. They have contended for that declaration, in the very teeth of the Supreme Court, for more than a quarter of a century. In fact, they have reduced the decision to an absolute nullity. That decision, I repeat, is repudiated in the Cincinnati platform; and still, as if to show that effrontery can go no farther, Judge Douglas vaunts in the very speeches in which he denounces me for opposing the Dred Scott decision, that he stands on the Cincinnati platform.

Now, I wish to know what the Judge can charge upon me, with respect to decisions of the Supreme Court, which does not lie, in all its length, breadth, and proportions, at his own door. The plain truth is simply this: Judge Douglas is *for* Supreme Court decisions when he likes, and against them when he does not like them. He is for the Dred Scott decision because it tends to nationalize slavery, — because it is part of the original combination for that object. It so happens, singularly enough, that I never stood opposed to a decision of the Supreme Court till this. On the contrary, I have no recollection that he was ever particularly in favor of one till this. He never was in favor of any, nor opposed to any, till the present one, which helps to nationalize slavery.

Free men of Sangamon, — free men of Illinois, — free men everywhere, — judge ye between him and me, upon this issue.

THE PARALLELS OF HISTORY.

He says this Dred Scott case is a very small matter at most, that it has no practical effect; that at best, or rather, I suppose, at worst, it is but an abstraction. I submit that the proposition that the thing which determines whether a man is free or a slave, is rather *concrete* than *abstract.* I think you would conclude that it was, if your liberty depended upon it, and so would Judge Douglas if his liberty depended upon it. But suppose it was on the question of spreading slavery over the new Territories that he considers it as being merely an abstract matter, one of no practical importance. How has the planting of slavery in new countries always been effected? It has now been decided that slavery cannot be kept out of our new Territories by any legal means. In what do our new Territories now differ in this respect from the old Colonies when slavery was first planted within them? It was planted, as Mr. Clay once declared, and as history proves true, by individual men, in spite of the wishes of the people; the mother Government refusing to prohibit it, and withholding from the people of the Colonies the authority to prohibit it for themselves. Mr. Clay says this was one of the great and just causes of complaint against Great Britain by the Colonies, and the best apology we can now make for having the institution amongst us. In that precise condition our Nebraska politicians have at last succeeded in placing our own new Territories; the Government will not prohibit slavery within them, nor allow the people to prohibit it.

I defy any man to find any difference between the policy which originally planted slavery in these Colonies and that policy which now prevails in our new Territories. If it does not go into them, it is only because no individual wishes it to go. The Judge indulged himself, doubtless to-day, with the question as to what I am going to do with or about the Dred Scott decision. Well, Judge, will you please tell me what you did about the bank decision? Will you not graciously allow us to do with the Dred Scott decision precisely as you did with the bank decision? You succeeded in breaking down the moral effect of that decision; did you find it necessary to amend the Constitution? or to set up a court of negroes in order to do it?

Clay — Webster — Douglas.

There is one other point. Judge Douglas has a very affectionate leaning toward the Americans and Old Whigs. Last evening, in a sort of weeping tone, he described to us a deathbed scene. He had been called to the side of Mr. Clay, in his last moments, in order that the genius of "popular sovereignty" might duly descend from the dying man and settle upon him, the living and most worthy successor. He could do no less than promise that he would devote the remainder of his life to "popular sovereignty;" and then the great statesman departs in peace. By this part of the "plan of the campaign," the Judge has evidently promised himself that tears shall be drawn down the cheeks of all Old Whigs, as large as half-grown apples.

Mr. Webster, too, was mentioned; but it did not quite come to a death-bed scene, as to him. It would be amusing, if it were not disgusting, to see how quick these compromise-breakers administer on the political effects of their dead adversaries, trumping up claims never before heard of, and dividing the assets among themselves. If I should be found dead to-morrow morning, nothing but my insignificance could prevent a speech being made on my authority, before the end of next week. It so happens that in that "popular sovereignty" with which Mr. Clay was identified, the Missouri Compromise was expressly reserved; and it was a little singular if Mr. Clay cast his manle upon Judge Douglas on purpose to have that compromise epealed.

Again, the Judge did not keep faith with Mr. Clay when he rst brought in his Nebraska Bill. He left the Missouri Comromise unrepealed; and in his report accompanying the bill, e told the world he did it on purpose. The manes of Mr. lay must have been in great agony, till thirty days later, when popular sovereignty" stood forth in all its glory.

AMENDING THE DECLARATION OF INDEPENDENCE.

One more thing. Last night Judge Douglas tormented himf with horrors about my disposition to make negroes perfectly equal with white men in social and political relations. He did not stop to show that I have said any such thing, or that it legitimately follows from anything I have said; but he rushes on with his assertions. I adhere to the Declaration of Independence. If Judge Douglas and his friends are not willing to stand by it, let them come up and amend it. Let them make it read that all men are created equal, except negroes. Let us have it decided, whether the Declaration of Independence, in this blessed year of 1858, shall be thus amended. In his construction of the Declaration last year, he said it only meant that Americans in America were equal to Englishmen in England. Then, when I pointed out to him that by that rule he excludes the Germans, the Irish, the Portuguese, and all the other people who have come amongst us since the Revolution, he reconstructs his construction. In his last speech he tells us it meant Europeans.

I press him a little further, and ask if it meant to include the Russians in Asia? Or does he mean to exclude that vast population from the principles of our Declaration of Independence? I expect ere long he will introduce another amendment to his definition. He is not at all particular. He is satisfied with anything which does not endanger the nationalizing of negro slavery. It may draw white men down; but it must not lift negroes up. Who shall say, "I am the superior, and yor are the inferior?"

THE EQUAL RIGHT TO LABOR.

My declarations upon this subject of negro slavery may b misrepresented, but cannot be misunderstood. I have said th I do not understand the declaration to mean that all men we created equal in all respects. They are not our equal in colo but I suppose that it does mean to declare that all men a equal in some respect; they are equal in their right to "lif liberty, and the pursuit of happiness." Certainly the negro not our equal in color, — perhaps not in many other respect still, in the right to put into his mouth the bread that his o hands have earned, he is the equal of every other man, white or black. In pointing out that more has been given you, you cannot be justified in taking away the little which has been given him. All I ask for the negro is, that if you do not like him, let him alone. If God gave him but little, that little let him enjoy.

WHAT THE FRAMERS OF THE CONSTITUTION MEANT AND DID.

When our Government was established, we had the institution of slavery among us. We were in a certain sense compelled to tolerate its existence. It was a sort of necessity. We had gone through our struggle and secured our own independence. The framers of the Constitution found the institution of slavery amongst their other institutions at the time. They found that by an effort to eradicate it, they might lose much of what they had already gained. They were obliged to bow to the necessity. They gave power to Congress to abolish the slave-trade at the end of twenty years. They also prohibited it in the territories where it did not exist. They did what they could and yielded to the necessity for the rest. I also yield to all which follows from that necessity. What I would most desire would be the separation of the white and black races.

CONSPIRACY TO MAKE SLAVERY NATIONAL.

One more point on this Springfield speech, which Judge Douglas says he has read so carefully. I expressed my belief in the existence of a conspiracy to perpetuate and nationalize slavery. I did not profess to know it, nor do I now. I showed the part Judge Douglas had played in the string of facts, constituting to my mind the proof of that conspiracy. I showed the parts played by others.

I charged that the people had been deceived into carrying the last presidential election, by the impression that the people of the Territories might exclude slavery if they chose, when it was known in advance by the conspirators, that the court was to decide that neither Congress nor the people could so exclude slavery. These charges are more distinctly made than anything else in the speech.

Judge Douglas has carefully read and re-read that speech. He has not, so far as I know, contradicted those charges. In the two speeches which I heard, he certainly did not. On his own tacit admission I renew that charge. I charge him with having been a party to that conspiracy, and to that deception, for the sole purpose of nationalizing slavery.

GOVERNMENTAL CONTROL OF THE TERRITORIES vs. SQUATTER SOVEREIGNTY.

DELIVERED AT COLUMBUS, OHIO, SEPTEMBER, 1859.

Mr. Lincoln spoke twice during the Ohio gubernatorial campaign of 1859, in response to an invitation from the Republicans, and replying to Judge Douglas. He spoke first at the capital of the State, as follows.

DEMOCRATIC MISREPRESENTATIONS CORRECTED.

Fellow-citizens of the State of Ohio: I cannot fail to remember that I appear for the first time before an audience in this now great State, — an audience that is accustomed to hear such speakers as Corwin, and Chase, and Wade, and many other renowned men; and remembering this, I feel that it will be well for you as for me, that you should not raise your expectations to that standard to which you would have been justified in raising them, had one of these distinguished men appeared before you. You would, perhaps, be only preparing a disappointment for yourselves, and, as a consequence of your disappointment, mortification to me. I hope, therefore, that you will commence with very moderate expectations; and, perhaps, if you will give me your attention, I shall be able to interest you to a moderate degree.

Appearing here for the first time in my life, I have been somewhat embarrassed for a topic by way of introduction to my speech; but I have been relieved from that embarrassment by an introduction which the *Ohio Statesman* newspaper gave me this morning. In this paper I have read an article, in which, among other statements, I find the following: —

"In debating with Senator Douglas during the memorable contest last fall, Mr. Lincoln declared in favor of negro suffrage, and attempted to defend that vile conception against the Little Giant."

I mention this now, at the opening of my remarks, for the purpose of making three comments upon it. The first I have already announced, — it furnishes me an introductory topic; the second is to show that the gentleman is mistaken; thirdly, to give him an opportunity to correct it.

In the first place, in regard to this matter being a mistake. I have found that it is not entirely safe, when one is misrepresented under his very nose, to allow the misrepresentation to go uncontradicted. I therefore propose, here, at the outset, not only to say that this is a misrepresentation, but to show conclusively that it is so; and you will bear with me while I read a couple of extracts from that very "memorable" debate with Judge Douglas last year, to which this newspaper refers. In the first pitched battle which Senator Douglas and myself had, at the town of Ottawa, I used the language which I will now read. Having been previously reading an extract, I continued as follows: —

"Now, gentlemen, I don't want to read at any greater length, but this is the true complexion of all I have ever said in regard to the institution of slavery, and the black race. This is the whole of it, and anything that argues me into his idea of perfect social and political equality with the negro, is but a specious and fantastic arrangement of words, by which a man can prove a horse-chestnut to be a chestnut horse. I will say here, while upon this subject, that I have no purpose directly or indirectly to interfere with the institution of slavery in the States where it exists. I believe I have no lawful right to do so, and I have no inclination to do so. I have no purpose to introduce political and social equality between the white and the black races. There is a physical difference between the two, which, in my judgment, will probably forbid their ever living together upon the footing of perfect equality, and inasmuch as it becomes a necessity that there must be a difference, I, as well as Judge Douglas, am in favor of the race to which I belong having the superior position. I have never said anything to the contrary, but I hold that, notwithstanding all this, there is no reason in the world why the negro is not entitled to all the natural rights enumerated in the Declaration of Independence, the right to life, liberty, and the pursuit of happiness. I hold that he is as much entitled to these as the white man. I agree with Judge Douglas, he is not my equal in many respects, — certainly not in color, perhaps not in moral or intellectual endowments. But in the right to eat the bread, without leave of anybody else, which his own hand earns, *he is my equal, and the equal of Judge Douglas, and the equal of every living man.*"

Upon a subsequent occasion, when the reason for making a statement like this recurred, I said: —

"While I was at the hotel to-day, an elderly gentleman called upon me to know whether I was really in favor of producing perfect equality between the negroes and white people. While I had not proposed to myself, on this occasion, to say much on that subject, yet, as the question was asked me, I thought I would occupy perhaps five minutes in saying something in regard to it. I will say, then, that I am not, nor ever have been, in favor of bringing about, in any way, the social and political equality of the white and black races; that I am not, nor ever have been, in favor of making voters or jurors of negroes, nor of qualifying them to hold office, or intermarry with the white people; and I will say, in addition to this, that there is a physical difference between the white and black races, which I believe will forever forbid the two races living together on terms of social and political equality. And, inasmuch as they cannot so live, while they do remain together, there must be the position of superior and inferior, and I, as much as any other man, am in favor of having the superior position assigned to the white race. I say, upon this occasion, I do not perceive that, because the white man is to have the superior position, the negro should be denied everything. I do not understand that, because I do not want a negro woman for a slave, I must necessarily want her for a wife. My understanding is that I can just let her alone. I am now in my fiftieth year, and I certainly never have had a black woman for either a slave or a wife. So, it seems to me quite possible for us to get along without making either slaves or wives of negroes. I will add to this, that I have never seen, to my knowledge, a man, woman, or child, who was in favor of producing perfect equality, social and political, between negroes and white men. I recollect of but one distinguished instance that I ever heard of so frequently as to be satisfied of its correctness, and that is the case of Judge Douglas's old friend, Col. Richard M. Johnson. I will also add to the remarks I have made, (for I am not going to enter at large upon this subject,) that I have never had the least apprehension that I or my friends would marry negroes, if there was no law to keep them from it; but, as Judge Douglas and his friends seem to be in great apprehension that they might, if there were no law to keep them from it, I give him the most solemn pledge that I will, to the very last, stand by the law of the State, which forbids the marrying of white people with negroes."

There, my friends, you have briefly what I have, upon former occasions, said upon the subject to which this newspaper, to the extent of its ability, has drawn the public attention. In it you not only perceive, as a probability, that in that contest I did not at any time say I was in favor of negro suffrage; but the absolute proof that twice, — once substantially, and once expressly, — I declared against it. Having shown you this, there remains but a word of comment upon that newspaper article. It is this: that I presume the editor of that paper is an honest and truth-loving man, and that he will be greatly obliged to me for furnishing him thus early an opportunity to correct the misrepresentation he has made, before it has run so long that malicious people can call him a liar.

DOUGLAS AND THE EXTENSION OF SLAVERY.

The Giant himself has been here recently. I have seen a brief report of his speech. If it were otherwise unpleasant to me to introduce the subject of the negro as a topic for discussion, I might be somewhat relieved by the fact that he dealt exclusively in that subject while he was here. I shall, therefore, without much hesitation or diffidence, enter upon this subject.

The American people, on the first day of January, 1854, found the African slave-trade prohibited by a law of Congress. In a majority of the States of this Union, they found African slavery, or any other sort of slavery, prohibited by State constitutions. They also found a law existing, supposed to be valid, by which slavery was excluded from almost all the territory the United States then owned. This was the condition of the country, with reference to the institution of slavery, on the first of January, 1854. A few days after that, a bill was introduced into Congress, which ran through its regular course in the two branches of the national legislature, and finally passed into a law in the month of May, by which the act of Congress prohibiting slavery from going into the Territories of the United States was repealed. In connection with the law itself, and, in fact, in the terms of the law, the then existing prohibition was not only repealed, but there was a declaration of a purpose on the part of Congress never thereafter to exercise any power that they might have, real or supposed, to prohibit the extension or spread of slavery. This was a very great change; for the law thus repealed was of more than thirty years' standing. Following rapidly upon the heels of this action of Congress, a decision of the Supreme Court is made, by which it is declared that Congress, if it desires to prohibit the spread of slavery into the Territories, has no constitutional power to do so. Not only so, but that decision lays down principles, which, if pushed to their logical conclusion,—I say, pushed to their logical conclusion,—would decide that the constitutions of free States, forbidding slavery, are themselves unconstitutional. Mark me, I do not say the Judge said this, and let no man say I affirm the Judge used these words; but I only say it is my opinion that what he did say, if pressed to its logical conclusion, would inevitably result thus.

THE REPUBLICAN PARTY — ITS PURPOSE.

Looking at these things, the Republican party, as I understand its principles and policy, believe that there is great danger of the institution of slavery being spread out and extended, until it is ultimately made alike lawful in all the States of this Union; so believing, to prevent that incidental and ultimate consummation, is the original and chief purpose of the Republican organization. I say, "chief purpose" of the Republican organization; for it is certainly true that if the national house shall fall into the hands of the Republicans, they will have to attend to all the other matters of national house-keeping, as well as this. The chief and real purpose of the Republican party is eminently conservative. It proposes nothing save and except to restore this Government to its original tone in regard to this element of slavery, and there to maintain it, looking for no further change in reference to it, than that which the original framers of the Government themselves expected and looked forward to.

ITS DANGER.

The chief danger to this purpose of the Republican party is not just now the revival of the African slave-trade, or the passage of a congressional slave code, or the declaring of a second Dred Scott decision, making slavery lawful in all the States. These are not pressing us just now. They are not quite ready yet. The authors of these measures know that we are too strong for them; but they will be upon us in due time, and we shall be grappling with them hand to hand, if they are not now headed off. They are not now the chief danger to the purpose of the Republican organization; but the most imminent danger that now threatens that purpose is that insidious Douglas popular sovereignty. This is the miner and sapper. While it does not propose to revive the African slave-trade, nor to pass a slave code, nor to make a second Dred Scott decision, it is preparing us for the onslaught and charge of these ultimate enemies when they shall be ready to come on, and the word of command for them to advance shall be given. I say this Douglas popular sovereignty, — for there is a broad distinction, as I now understand it, between that article and a genuine popular sovereignty.

GENUINE POPULAR SOVEREIGNTY.

I believe there is a genuine popular sovereignty. I think a definition of genuine popular sovereignty, in the abstract, would be about this: That each man shall do precisely as he pleases with himself, and with all those things which exclusively concern him. Applied to government, this principle would be, that a general government shall do all those things which pertain to it, and all the local governments shall do precisely as they please, in respect to those matters which exclusively concern them. I understand that this government of the United States, under which we live, is based upon this principle; and I am misunderstood if it is supposed that I have any war to make upon that priinciple.

DOUGLAS'S BOGUS ARTICLE.

Now, what is Judge Douglas's popular sovereignty? It is, as a principle, no other than that, if one man chooses to make a slave of another man, neither that other man nor anybody else has a right to object. Applied in government, as he seeks to apply it, it is this: If, in a new territory into which a few people are beginning to enter for the purpose of making their homes, they choose to either exclude slavery from their limits, or to establish it there, however one or the other may affect the persons to be enslaved, or the infinitely greater number of persons who are afterward to inhabit that territory, or the other members of the families of communities, of which they are but an incipient member, or the general head of the family of States as parent of all, — however their action may affect one or the other of these, there is no power or right to interfere. That is Douglas's popular sovereignty applied.

THE HARPER ESSAY.

He has a good deal of trouble with popular sovereignty. His explanations explanatory of explanations explained are interminable. The most lengthy, and, as I suppose, the most maturely considered of his long series of explanations is his great essay in Harper's Magazine. I will not attempt to entèr on any very thorough investigation of his argument, as there made and presented. I will nevertheless occupy a good portion of your time here in drawing your attention to certain points in it. Such of you as may have read this document, will have perceived that the Judge, early in the document, quotes from two persons as belonging to the Republican party, without naming them, but who can readily be recognized as being Gov. Seward, of New York, and myself. It is true that, exactly fifteen months ago this day, I believe, I, for the first time, expressed a sentiment upon this subject, and in such a manner that it should get into print, that the public might see it beyond the circle of my hearers; and my expression of it, at that time, is the quotation that Judge Douglas makes. He has not made the quotation with accuracy, but justice to him requires me to say that it is sufficiently accurate not to change its sense.

The sense of that quotation condensed, is this, — that this slavery element is a durable element of discord among us, and that we shall probably not have perfect peace, in this country, with it, until it either masters the free principle in our government, or is so far mastered by the free principle as for the public mind to rest in the belief that it is going to its end. This sentiment, which I now express in this way, was, at no great distance of time, perhaps in different language, and in connection with some collateral ideas, expressed by Gov. Seward.

Judge Douglas has been so much annoyed by the expression of that sentiment, that he has constantly, I believe, in almost all his speeches since it was uttered, been referring to it. I find he alluded to it in his speech here, as well as in the copy-right essay. I do not now enter upon this for the purpose of making an elaborate argument to show that we were right in the expression of that sentiment. In other words, I shall not stop to say all that might properly be said upon this point; but I only ask your attention to it for the purpose of making one or two points upon it.

THE ELEMENT OF DISCORD.

If you will read the copy-right essay, you will discover that Judge Douglas himself says a controversy between the American Colonies and the Government of Great Britain began on the slavery question, in 1699, and continued from that time until the Revolution; and, while he did not say so, we all know that it has continued with more or less violence ever since the Revolution.

Then we need not appeal to history, to the declarations of the framers of the Government, but we know from Judge Douglas himself, that slavery began to be an element of discord among the white people of this country as far back as 1699, or one hundred and sixty years ago, or five generations of men, — counting thirty years to a generation. Now, it would seem to me that it might have occurred to Judge Douglas, or anybody who had turned his attention to these facts, that there was something in the nature of that thing, slavery, somewhat durable for mischief and discord.

THE TRUE VIEW OF IT.

There is another point I desire to make in regard to this matter, before I leave it. From the adoption of the Constitution down to 1820, is the precise period of our history, when we had comparative peace upon this question, — the precise period of time when we came nearer to having peace about it than any other time of that entire one hundred and sixty years, in which he says it began, or of the eighty years of our own Constitution. Then it would be worth our while to stop and examine into the probable reason of our coming nearer to having peace then than at any other time. This was the precise period of time in which our fathers adopted, and during which they followed a policy restricting the spread of slavery, and the whole Union was acquiescing in it. The whole country looked forward to the ultimate extinction of the institution. It was when a policy had been adopted, and was prevailing, which led all just and rightminded men to suppose that slavery was gradually coming to an end, and that they might be quiet about it, watching it as it expired. I think Judge Douglas might have perceived that, too; and whether he did or not, it is worth the attention of fair-minded men, here and elsewhere, to consider whether that is not the truth of the case. If he had looked at these two facts, that this matter has been an element of discord for one hundred and sixty years among this people, and that the only comparative peace we have had about it was when that policy prevailed in this Government, which he now wars upon, he might then, perhaps, have been brought to a more just appreciation of what I said fifteen months ago, — that "a house divided against itself cannot stand. I believe that this Government cannot endure permanently, half slave and half free. I do not expect the house to fall. I do not expect the Union to dissolve; but I do expect it will cease to be divided. It will become all one thing, or all the other. Either the opponents of slavery will arrest the further spread of it, and place it where the public mind will rest in the belief that it is in the course of ultimate extinction; or its advocates will push it forward, until it shall become alike lawful in all the States, old as well as new, North as well as South." That was my sentiment at that time. In connection with it, I said, "We are now far into the fifth year since a policy was inaugurated, with the avowed object and confident promise of putting an end to slavery agitation. Under the operation of the policy, that agitation has not only not ceased, but has constantly augmented." I now say to you here, that we are advanced still farther into the sixth year since that policy of Judge Douglas, — that popular sovereignty of his, for quieting the slavery question, — was made the national policy. Fifteen months more have been added since I uttered that sentiment, and I call upon you, and all other rightminded men, to say whether that fifteen months have belied or corroborated my words.

CHEERS FOR JOHN HICKMAN.

While I am here upon this subject, I cannot but express gratitude that this true view of this element of discord among us,— as I believe it is, — is attracting more and more attention. I do not believe that Governor Seward uttered that sentiment because I had done so before, but because he reflected upon this subject, and saw the truth of it. Nor do I believe, because Gov. Seward or I uttered it, that Mr. Hickman, of Pennsylvania, in different language, since that time, has declared his belief in the antagonism which exists between the principles of liberty and slavery. You see we are multiplying. Now, while I am speaking of Hickman, let me say, I know but little about him. I have never seen him, and know scarcely anything about the man; but I will say this much of him: Of all the anti-Lecompton Democracy that have been brought to my notice, he alone has the true, genuine ring of the metal. And now, without indorsing anything else he has said, I will ask this audience to give three cheers for Hickman. [The audience responded with three rousing cheers for Hickman.]

DOUGLAS'S ASSUMPTION.

Another point in the copy-right essay to which I would ask your attention, is rather a feature to be extracted from the whole thing, than from any express declaration of it at any point. It is a general feature of that document, and indeed, of all of Judge Douglas's discussions of this question, that the Territories of the

United States and the States of this Union are exactly alike,— that there is no difference between them at all, — that the Constitution applies to the Territories precisely as it does to the States, — and that the United States Government, under the Constitution, may not do in a State what it may not do in a Territory, and what it must do in a State, it must do in a Territory. Gentlemen, is that a true view of the case? It is necessary for this squatter sovereignty; but is it true?

Let us consider. What does it depend upon? It depends altogether upon the proposition that the States must, without the interference of the General Government, do all those things that pertain *exclusively* to themselves, — that are local in their nature, — that have no connection with the General Government. After Judge Douglas has established this proposition, which nobody disputes or ever has disputed, he proceeds to assume, without proving it, that slavery is one of those little, unimportant, trivial matters which are of just about as much consequence as the question would be to me, whether my neighbor should raise horned cattle or plant tobacco; that there is no moral question about it, but that it is altogether a matter of dollars and cents; that when a new Territory is opened for settlement, the first man who goes into it may plant there a thing which, like the Canada thistle or some other of those pests of the soil, cannot be dug out by the millions of men who will come thereafter; that it is one of those little things that is so trivial in its nature that it has no effect upon anybody save the few men who first plant upon the soil; that it is not a thing which in any way affects the family of communities composing these States, nor any way endangers the General Government. Judge Douglas ignores altogether the very well-known fact, that we never had a serious menace to our political existence, except it sprang from this thing, which he chooses to regard as only upon a par with onions and potatoes.

A CONSTITUTIONAL DIFFICULTY IN THIS LOGIC.

Turn it, and contemplate it in another view. He says, that according to his popular sovereignty, the General Government may give to the Territories governors, judges, marshals, secretaries, and all the other chief men to govern them, but they must not touch upon this other question. Why? The question of who shall be governor of a Territory for a year or two, and pass away, without his track being left upon the soil, or an act which he did for good or for evil being left behind, is a question of vast national magnitude. It is so much opposed in its nature to locality, that the nation itself must decide it; while this other matter of planting slavery upon a soil, — a thing which once planted cannot be eradicated by the succeeding millions who have as much right there as the first comers, or, if eradicated, not without infinite difficulty and a long struggle,—he considers the power to prohibit it as one of these little, local, trivial things that the nation ought not to say a word about; that it affects nobody save the few men who are there.

Take these two things and consider them together, present the question of planting a State with the institution of slavery by the side of a question of who shall be governor of Kansas for a year or two, and is there a man here, — is there a man on earth, — who would not say the governor question is the little one, and the slavery question is the great one? I ask any honest Democrat if the small, the local, and the trivial and temporary question is not, Who shall be Governor? While the durable, the important, and the mischievous one is, Shall this soil be planted with slavery?

This is an idea, I suppose, which has arisen in Judge Douglas's mind from his peculiar structure. I suppose the institution of slavery really looks small to him. He is so put up by nature that a lash upon his back would hurt him, but a lash upon anybody else's back does not hurt him. That is the build of the man, and consequently he looks upon the matter of slavery in this unimportant light.

THE CHOICE OF DEMOCRATIC AUTHORITIES.

Judge Douglas ought to remember, when he is endeavoring to force this policy upon the American people, that while he is put up in that way a good many are not. He ought to remember that there was once in this country a man by the name of Thomas Jefferson, supposed to be a Democrat, — a man whose principles and policy are not very prevalent amongst Democrats to-day, it is true; — but that man did not take exactly this view of the insignificance of the element of slavery which our friend Judge Douglas does. In contemplation of this thing, we all know he was led to exclaim, "I tremble for my country when I remember that God is just!" We know he looked upon it when he thus expressed himself. There was danger to this country,— danger of the avenging justice of God in that little unimportant popular sovereignty question of Judge Douglas. He supposed there was a question of God's eternal justice wrapped up in the enslaving of any race of men, or any man, and that those who did so braved the arm of Jehovah; that when a nation thus dared the Almighty, every friend of that nation had cause to dread his wrath. Choose ye between Jefferson and Douglas as to what is the true view of this element among us.

KANSAS AND ADMISSION TO THE UNION.

There is another little difficulty about this matter of treating the territories and States alike in all things, to which I ask your attention, and I shall leave this branch of the case. If there is no difference between them, why not make the territories States at once? What is the reason that Kansas was not fit to come into the Union when it was organized into a Territory, in Judge Douglas's view? Can any of you tell any reason why it should not have come into the Union at once? They are fit, as he thinks, to decide upon the slavery question, — the largest and most important with which they could possibly deal, — what could they do by coming into the Union that they are not fit to do, according to his view, by staying out of it? Oh, they are not fit to sit in Congress and decide upon the rates of postage, or questions of *ad valorem*, or specific duties on foreign goods, or live-oak timber contracts; they are not fit to decide these vastly important matters, which are rational in their import, but they are fit, "from the jump," to decide this little negro question. But, gentlemen, the case is too plain; I occupy too much time on this head, and I pass on.

"KICKING THE FAT INTO THE FIRE."

Near the close of the copy-right essay, the Judge, I think, comes very near kicking his own fat into the fire. I did not think, when I commenced these remarks, that I should read from that article, but I now believe I will.

"This exposition of the history of these measures shows conclusively that the authors of the compromise measures of 1850, and of the Kansas-Nebraska act of 1854, as well as the members of the Continental Congress of 1774, and the founders of our system of government subsequent to the Revolution, regarded the people of the Territories and Colonies as political communities which were entitled to a free and exclusive power of legislation in their provisional legislatures, where their representation could alone be preserved, in all cases of taxation and internal polity."

When the Judge saw that putting in the word "slavery" would contradict his own history, he put in what he knew would pass as synonymous with it, "internal polity." Whenever we find *that* in one of his speeches, the substitute is used in this mannner; and I can tell you the reason. It would be too bald a contradiction to say slavery, but "internal polity" is a general phrase which would pass in some quarters, and which he hopes will pass with the reading community for the same thing: —

"This right pertains to the people collectively, as a law-abiding and peaceful community, and not in the isolated individuals who may wander upon the public domain in violation of the law. It can only be exercised where there are inhabitants sufficient to constitute a government, and capable of performing its various functions and duties, a fact to be ascertained and determined by" — who do you think? Judge Douglas says, "by Congress?"

"Whether the number shall be fixed at ten, fifteen, or twenty thousand inhabitants, does not affect the principle."

THE FOLLY OF IT.

Now I have only a few comments to make. Popular sovereignty, by his own words, does not pertain to the few persons who wander upon the public domain in violation of law. We have his words for that. When it does pertain to them, is when they are sufficient to be formed into an organized political community, and he fixes the minimum for that at 10,000, and the maximum at 20,000. Now I would like to know what is to be done with the 9,000? Are they all to be treated, until they are large enough to be organized into a political community, as wanderers upon the public land in violation of law? And if so treated and driven out, at what point of time would there ever be ten thousand? If they were not driven out, but remained there as trespassers upon the public land in violation of the law can they establish slavery there? No, the Judge says popular sovereignty don't pertain to them then. Can they exclude it then? No, popular sovereignty don't pertain to them then. I would like to know, in the case covered by the essay, what condition the people of the Territory are in before they reach the number of ten thousand?

WHERE THE JUDGE REACHES.

But the main point I wish to ask attention to is, that the question as to when they shall have reached a sufficient number to be formed into a regular organized community, is to be decided "by Congress." Judge Douglas says so. Well, gentlemen, that is about all we want. No, that is all the Southerners want. That is what all those who are for slavery want. They do not want Congress to prohibit slavery from coming into the new Territories, and they do not want popular sovereignty to hinder it; and as Congress is to say when they are ready to be organized, all that the South has to do is to get Congress to hold off. Let Congress hold off until they are ready to be admitted as a State, and the South has all it wants in taking slavery into and planting it in all the Territories that we now have, or hereafter may have. In a word, the whole thing, at a dash of the pen, is at last put in the power of Congress; for if they do not have this popular sovereignty until Congress organizes them, I ask if it at last does not come from Congress? If, at last, it amounts to anything at all, Congress gives it to them. I submit this rather for your reflection than for comment. After all that is said, at last, by a dash of the pen, everything that has gone before is undone, and he puts the whole question under the control of Congress. After fighting through more than three hours, if you undertake to read it, he at last places the whole matter under the control of that power which he had been contending against, and arrives at a result directly contrary to what he had been laboring to do. He at last leaves the whole matter to the control of Congress.

THE OBJECTS OF THE HARPER ARTICLE.

There are two main objects, as I understand it, of this Harper's Magazine essay. One was to show, if possible, that the men of our revolutionary times were in favor of his popular sovereignty; and the other was to show that the Dred Scott decision had not entirely squelched out this popular sovereignty. I do not propose, in regard to this argument drawn from the history of former times, to enter into a detailed examination of the historical statements he has made. I have the impression that they are inaccurate in a great many instances. Sometimes in positive statement, but very much more inaccurate by the suppression of statements that really belong to the history. But I do not propose to affirm that this is so to any very great extent; or to enter into a very minute examination of his historical statements. I avoid doing so upon this principle, — that if it were important for me to pass out of this lot in the least period of time possible, and I came to that fence and saw by a calculation of my known strength and agility that I could clear it at a bound, it would be folly to stop and consider whether I could or not crawl through a crack. So I say of the whole history, contained in his essay. where he endeavored to link the men of the Revolution to popular sovereignty. It only requires an effort to leap out of it,—a single bound, to be entirely successful. If you read it over you will find that he quotes here and there from documents of the revolutionary times, tending to show that the people of the Colonies were desirous of regulating their own concerns in their own way, that the British Government should not interfere; that at one time they struggled with the British Government to be permitted to exclude the African slave-trade; if not directly, to be permitted to exclude it indirectly by taxation sufficient to discourage and destroy it. From these and many things of this sort, Judge Douglas argues that they were in favor of the people of our own Territories excluding slavery if they wanted to, or planting it there if they wanted to, doing just as they pleased from the time they settled upon the Territory. Now, however his history may apply, and whatever of his argument there may be that is sound and accurate or unsound and inaccurate, if we can find out what these men did themselves do upon this very question of slavery in the Territories, does it not end the whole thing? If, after all this labor and effort to show that the men of the Revolution were in favor of his popular sovereignty and his mode of dealing with slavery in the Territories, we can show that these very men took hold of that subject, and dealt with it, we can see for ourselves *how* they dealt with it. It is not a matter of argument or inference, but we know what they thought about it.

OMISSIONS OF THE AUTHOR.

It is precisely upon that part of the history of the country that one important omission is made by Judge Douglas. He selects parts of the history of the United States upon the subject of slavery, and treats it as the whole, omitting from his historical sketch the legislation of Congress in regard to the admission of Missouri, by which the Missouri Compromise was established, and slavery excluded from a country half as large as the present United States. All this is left out of his history, and in no wise alluded to by him, so far as I can remember, save once, when he makes a remark, that upon his principle the Supreme Court were authorized to pronounce a decision that the act called the Missouri Compromise was unconstitutional. All that history has been left out. But this part of the history of the country was not made by the men of the Revolution.

ORDINANCE OF 1787.

There was another part of our political history made by the very men who were the actors in the Revolution, which has taken the name of the Ordinance of '87. Let me bring that history to your attention. In 1784, I believe, this same Mr. Jefferson drew up an ordinance for the government of the country upon which we now stand; or rather a frame or draft of an ordinance for the government of this country, here in Ohio, our neighbors in Indiana, us who live in Illinois, our neighbors in Wisconsin and Michigan. In that ordinance, drawn up not only for the government of that territory, but for the territories South of the Ohio River, Mr. Jefferson expressly provided for the prohibition of slavery. Judge Douglas says, and perhaps is right, that that provision was lost from that ordinance. I believe that is true. When the vote was taken upon it, a majority of all present in the Congress of the confederation voted for it; but there were so many absentees that those voting for it did not make a clear majority necessary, and it was lost. But three years after that the Congress of the confederation were together again, and they adopted a new ordinance for the government of this Northwest Territory, not contemplating territory South of the river, for the States owning that Territory had hitherto refrained from giving it to the General Government; hence they made the ordinance to apply only to what the Government owned. In that, the provision excluding slavery *was inserted and passed unanimously*, or at any rate it passed and became a part of the law of the land. Under that ordinance we live. First here in Ohio you were a Territory, then an enabling act was passed, authorizing you to form a constitution and State government, provided it was republican and not in conflict with the Ordinance of '87. When you framed your constitution and presented it for admission, I think you will find the legislation upon the subject will show that, "whereas you had formed a constitution that was republican, and not in conflict with the Ordinance of '87," therefore you were admitted upon equal footing with the original States. The same process in a few years was gone through with in Indiana, and so with Illinois, and the same substantially with Michigan and Wisconsin.

ADMISSION OF NEW STATES.

Not only did that ordinance prevail, but it was constantly looked to whenever a step was taken by a new Territory to become a State. Congress always turned their attention to it, and in all their movements upon this subject, they traced their course by that Ordinance of '87. When they admitted new States, they advertised them of this ordinance as a part of the legislation of this country. They did so because they had traced the Ordinance of '87 throughout the history of this country. Begin with the men of the Revolution, and go down for sixty entire years, and until the last scrap of that Territory comes into the Union in the form of the State of Wisconsin, — every thing was made to conform with the Ordinance of '87, excluding slavery from that vast extent of country.

I omitted to mention in the right place that the Constitution of the United States was in process of being framed when that

Ordinance was made by the Congress of the Confederation; and one of the first acts of Congress itself, under the new Constitution itself, was to give force to that ordinance by putting power to carry it out in the hands of the new officers under the Constitution, in the place of the old ones, who had been legislated out of existence by the change in the Government from the Confederation to the Constitution. Not only so, but I believe Indiana once or twice, if not Ohio, petitioned the General Government for the privilege of suspending that provision and allowing them to have slaves. A report made by Mr. Randolph of Virginia, himself a slaveholder, was directly against it, and the action was to refuse them the privilege of violating the Ordinance of '87.

AN EXTRAORDINARY SPECTACLE.

This period of history, which I have run over briefly, is, I presume, as familiar to most of this assembly as any other part of the history of our country. I suppose that few of my hearers are not as familiar with that part of history as I am, and I only mention it to recall your attention to it at this time. And hence I ask how extraordinary a thing it is that a man who has occupied a position upon the floor of the Senate of the United States, who is now in his third term, and who looks to see the government of this whole country fall into his own hands, pretending to give a truthful and accurate history of the slavery question in this country, should so entirely ignore the whole of that portion of our history, — the most important of all. Is it not a most extraordinary spectacle, that a man should stand up and ask for any confidence in his statements, who sets out as he does with portions of history, calling upon the people to believe that it is a true and fair representation, when the leading part and controlling feature of the whole history is carefully suppressed?

But the mere leaving out is not the most remarkable feature of this most remarkable essay. His proposition is to establish that the leading men of the Revolution were for his great principle of non-intervention by the Government in the question of slavery in the Territories; while history shows that they decided in the cases actually brought before them, in exactly the contrary way, and he knows it. Not only did they so decide at that time, but they stuck to it during sixty years, through thick and thin, as long as there was one of the revolutionary heroes upon the stage of political action. Through their whole course, from first to last, they clung to freedom. And now he asks the community to believe that the men of the Revolution were in favor of his great principle, when we have the naked history that they themselves dealt with this very subject-matter of his principle, and utterly repudiated his principle, acting upon a precisely contrary ground. It is as impudent and absurd as if a prosecuting attorney should stand up before a jury, and ask them to convict A as the murderer of B, while B was walking alive before them.

"STEALING THE LIVERY OF HEAVEN TO SERVE THE DEVIL IN."

I say again, if Judge Douglas asserts that the men of the Revolution acted upon principles by which, to be consistent with themselves, they ought to have adopted his popular sovereignty, then, upon a consideration of his own argument, he had a right to make you believe that they understood the principles of government, but misapplied them, — that he has arisen to enlighten the world as to the just application of this principle. He has a right to try to persuade you that he understands their principles better than they did, and, therefore, he will apply them now, not as they did, but as they ought to have done. He has a right to go before the community, and try to convince them of this; but he has no right to attempt to impose upon any one the belief that these men themselves approved of his great principle. There are two ways of establishing a proposition. One is by trying to demonstrate it upon reason; and the other is, to show that great men in former times have thought so and so, and thus to pass it by the weight of pure authority. Now, if Judge Douglas will demonstrate somehow that this is popular sovereignty, — the right of one man to make a slave of another, without any right in that other, or any one else to object, — demonstrate it as Euclid demonstrated propositions, — there is no objection. But when he comes forward, seeking to carry a principle by bringing to it the authority of men who themselves utterly repudiate that principle, I ask that he shall not be permitted to do it.

"STICK TO THE FATHERS, JUDGE."

I see, in the Judge's speech here, a short sentence in these words: "Our fathers, when they formed this Government under which we live, understood this question just as well and even better than we do now." That is true; I stick to that. I will stand by Judge Douglas in that to the bitter end. And now, Judge Douglas, come and stand by me, and truthfully show how they acted, understanding it better than we do. All I ask of you, Judge Douglas, is to stick to the proposition that the men of the Revolution understood this subject better than we do now, *and with that better understanding they acted better than you are trying to act now.*

DRED SCOTT DECISION.

I wish to say something now in regard to the Dred Scott decision, as dealt with by Judge Douglas. In that "memorable debate" between Judge Douglas and myself, last year, the Judge thought fit to commence a process of catechizing me, and at Freeport I answered his questions, and propounded some to him. Among others propounded to him was one that I have here now. The substance, as I remember it, is, "Can the people of a United States Territory, under the Dred Scott decision, in any lawful way, against the wish of any citizen of the United States, exclude slavery from its limits, prior to the formation of a State constitution?" He answered that they could lawfully exclude slavery from the United States Territories, notwithstanding the Dred Scott decision. There was something about that answer that has probably been a trouble to the Judge ever since.

WHICH HORN OF THE DILEMMA?

The Dred Scott decision expressly gives every citizen of the United States a right to carry his slaves into the United States Territories. And now there was some inconsistency in saying that the decision was right, and saying, too, that the people of the Territory could lawfully drive slavery out again. When all the trash, the words, the collateral matter, was cleared away from it, — all the chaff was fanned out of it, — it was a bare absurdity, — *no less than that a thing may be lawfully driven away from where it has a lawful right to be.* Clear it of all the verbiage, and that is the naked truth of his proposition, — that a thing may be lawfully driven from the place where it has a lawful right to stay. Well, it was because the Judge couldn't help seeing this, that he has had so much trouble with it; and what I want to ask your special attention to, just now, is to remind you, if you have not noticed the fact, that the Judge does not any longer say that the people can exclude slavery. He does not say so in the copy-right essay; he did not say so in the speech that he made here; and, so far as I know, since his re-election to the Senate, he has never said, as he did at Freeport, that the people of the Territories can exclude slavery. He desires that you, who wish the Territories to remain free, should believe that he stands by that position; but he does not say it himself. He escapes, to some extent, the absurd position I have stated, by changing his language entirely. What he says now is something different in language, and we will consider whether it is not different in sense too. It is now that the Dred Scott decision, or rather the Constitution under that decision, does not carry slavery into the Territories beyond the power of the people of the Territories *to control it as other property.* He does not say the people can drive it out, but they can control it as other property. The language is different; we should consider whether the sense is different. Driving a horse out of this lot is too plain a proposition to be mistaken about; it is putting him on the other side of the fence. Or it might be a sort of exclusion of him from the lot if you were to kill him, and let the worms devour him; but neither of these things is the same as "controlling him as other property." That would be to feed him, to pamper him, to ride him, to use and abuse him, to make the most money out of him "as other property;" but please you, what do the men who are in favor of slavery want more than this? What do they really want, other than that slavery, being in the Territories, shall be controlled as other property?

If they want anything else, I do not comprehend it. I ask your attention to this, first, for the purpose of pointing out the change of ground the Judge has made; and, in the second place, the importance of the change, — that that change is not such as to give you gentlemen who want his popular sovereignty the power to exclude the institution or drive it out at all. I know the Judge sometimes squints at the argument that in controlling it as other property by unfriendly legislation, they may control it to death, — as you might in the case of a horse, perhaps, feed him so lightly, and ride him so much, that he would die. But when you come to legislative control, there is something more to be attended to. I have no doubt, myself, that if the Territories should undertake to control slave property as other property,—that is, control it in such a way that it would be the most valuable as property, and make it bear its just proportion in the way of burdens as property—really deal with it as property, —the Supreme Court of the United States will say, "God speed you, and amen." But I undertake to give the opinion, at least, that if the Territories attempt, by any direct legislation, to drive the man with his slave out of the Territory, or to decide that his slave is free because of his being taken in there, or to tax him to such an extent that he cannot keep him there, the Supreme Court will unhesitatingly decide all such legislation unconstitutional, as long as that Supreme Court is constructed as the Dred Scott Supreme Court is. The first two things they have already decided, except that there is a little quibble among lawyers between the words *dicta* and decision. They have already decided a negro cannot be made free by territorial legislation.

UNFRIENDLY LEGISLATION.

What is that Dred Scott decision? Judge Douglas labors to show that it is one thing, while I think it is altogether different. It is a long opinion, but it is all embodied in this short statement: "The Constitution of the United States forbids Congress to deprive a man of his property, without due process of law; the right of property in slaves is distinctly and expressly affirmed in that Constitution; therefore if Congress shall undertake to say that a man's slave is no longer his slave, when he crosses a certain line into a Territory, that is depriving him of his property without due process of law, and is unconstitutional." There is the whole Dred Scott decision. They add that if Congress cannot do so itself, Congress cannot confer any power to do so, and hence any effort by the Territorial legislature to do either of these things is absolutely decided against. It is a foregone conclusion by that court.

Now, as to this indirect mode by "unfriendly legislation," all lawyers here will readily understand that such a proposition cannot be tolerated for a moment, because a legislature cannot indirectly do that which it cannot accomplish directly. Then I say any legislation to control this property, as property, for its benefit as property, would be hailed by this Dred Scott Supreme Court, and fully sustained; but any legislation driving slave property out, or destroying it as property, directly or indirectly, will most assuredly, by that court, be held unconstitutional.

MR. LINCOLN'S MODESTY.

Judge Douglas says if the Constitution carries slavery into the Territories, beyond the power of the people of the Territories to control it as other property, then it follows logically that every one who swears to support the Constitution of the United States, must give that support to that property which it needs. And if the Constitution carries slavery into the Territories, beyond the power of the people to control it as other property, then it also carries it into the States, because the Constitution is the supreme law of the land. Now, gentlemen, if it were not for my excessive modesty, I would say that I told that very thing to Judge Douglas quite a year ago. This argument is here in print, and if it were not for my modesty, as I said, I might call your attention to it. If you read it, you will find that I not only made that argument, but made it better than he has made it since.

There is, however, this difference. I say now, and said then, there is no sort of question that the Supreme Court *has* decided that it is the right of the slaveholder to take his slave and hold him in the Territory; and saying this, Judge Douglas himself admits the conclusion. He says if that is so, this consequence will follow; and because this consequence would follow, his argument is, the decision cannot, therefore, be that way, — "that would spoil my popular sovereignty, and it cannot be possible that this great principle has been squelched out in this extraordinary way. It might be, if it were not for the extraordinary consequences of spoiling my humbug."

NEGATIVE DECLARATIONS.

Another feature of the Judge's argument about the Dred Scott case, is an effort to show that that decision deals altogether in declarations of negatives; that the Constitution does not affirm anything as expounded by the Dred Scott decision, but it only declares a want of power, a total absence of power, in reference to the Territories. It seems to be his purpose to make the whole of that decision to result in a mere negative declaration of a want of power in Congress to do anything in relation to this matter in the Territories. I know the opinion of the judges states that there is a total absence of power; but that is, unfortunately, not all it states; for the judges add that the right of property in a slave is distinctly and expressly affirmed in the Constitution. It does not stop at saying that the right of property in a slave is recognized in the Constitution, is declared to exist somewhere in the Constitution, but says it is *affirmed* in the Constitution. Its language is equivalent to saying that it is embodied and so woven into that instrument that it cannot be detached without breaking the Constitution itself. In a word, it is part of the Constitution.

Douglas is singularly unfortunate in his effort to make out that decision to be altogether negative, when the express language at the vital part is that this is distinctly affirmed in the Constitution. I think myself, and I repeat it here, that this decision does not merely carry slavery into the Territories, but, by its logical conclusion, it carries it into the States in which we live. One provision of that Constitution is, that it shall be the supreme law of the land, — I do not quote the language, — any constitution or law of any State to the contrary notwithstanding. This Dred Scott decision says that the right of property in a slave is affirmed in that Constitution, which is the supreme law of the land, any State constitution or law notwithstanding. Then I say that to destroy a thing which is distinctly affirmed and supported by the supreme law of the land, even by a State constitution or law, is a violation of that supreme law, and there is no escape from it. In my judgment, there is no avoiding that result, save that the American people shall see that constitutions are better construed than our Constitution is construed in that decision. They must take care that it is more faithfully and truly carried out than it is there expounded.

DOUGLAS AND THE AFRICAN SLAVE-TRADE.

I must hasten to a conclusion. Near the beginning of my remarks, I said that this insidious Douglas popular sovereignty is the measure that now threatens the purpose of the Republican party to prevent slavery from being nationalized in the United States. I propose to ask your attention for a little while to some propositions in affirmance of that statement. Take it just as it stands, and apply it as a principle; extend and apply that principle elsewhere, and consider where it will lead you. I now put this proposition, that Judge Douglas's popular sovereignty applied will reopen the African slave-trade; and I will demonstrate it by any variety of ways in which you can turn the subject, or look at it.

The Judge says that the people of the Territories have the right, by his principle, to have slaves if they want them. Then I say that the people in Georgia have the right to buy slaves in Africa if they want them, and I defy any man on earth to show any distinction between the two things; to show that the one is either more wicked or more unlawful; to show, on original principles, that one is better or worse than the other; or to show, by the Constitution, that one differs a whit from the other. He will tell me, doubtless, that there is no constitutional provision against people taking slaves into the new Territories, and I tell him that there is equally no constitutional provision against buying slaves in Africa. He will tell you that a people, in the exercise of popular sovereignty, ought to do as they please about that thing, and have slaves if they want them; and I tell you that the people of Georgia are as much entitled to popular sovereignty, and to buy slaves in Africa if they want them, as the people of the Territory are to have slaves if they want them. I ask any man, dealing honestly with himself, to point out a distinction.

I have recently seen a letter of Judge Douglas, in which, without stating that to be the object, he doubtless endeavors to make a distinction between the two. He says he is unalterably opposed to the repeal of the laws against the African slave-trade. And why? He then seeks to give a reason that would not apply to his popular sovereignty in the Territories. What is that reason? "The abolition of the African slave-trade is a compromise of the Constitution!" I deny it. There is no truth in the proposition that the abolition of the African slave-trade is a compromise of the Constitution, and there is nothing in that instrument which bears out the statement. It is made for the purpose of getting up a distinction between the revival of the African slave-trade and his "great principle."

At the time the Constitution of the United States was adopted it was expected that the slave-trade would be abolished. I should assert, and insist upon that, if Judge Douglas denied it. But I know that it was equally expected that slavery would be excluded from the Territories, and I can show by history, that in regard to these two things, public opinion was exactly alike, while in regard to positive action, there was more done in the Ordinance of '87 to resist the spread of slavery than was ever done to abolish the foreign slave-trade. Lest I be misunderstood, I say again that at the time of the formation of the Constitution, public expectation was that the slave-trade would be abolished, but no more so than the spread of slavery in the Territories should be restrained. They stand alike, except that in the Ordinance of '87 there was a mark left by public opinion, showing that it was more committed against the spread of slavery in the Territories than against the foreign slave-trade.

NO SUCH THING AS COMPROMISE.

Compromise! What word of compromise was there about it. Why, the public sense was then in favor of the abolition of the slave-trade; but there was at the time a very great commercial interest involved in it and extensive capital in that branch of trade. There were doubtless the incipient stages of improvement in the South in the way of farming, dependent on the slave-trade, and they made a proposition to Congress to abolish the trade after allowing it twenty years, a sufficient time for the capital and commerce engaged in it to be transferred to other channels. They made no provision that it should be abolished in twenty years; I do not doubt that they expected it would be; but they made no bargain about it. The public sentiment left no doubt in the minds of any that it would be done away. I repeat, there is nothing in the history of those times in favor of that matter being a *compromise* of the Constitution. It was the public expectation at the time, manifested in a thousand ways, that the spread of slavery should also be restricted.

NEGRO OR CROCODILE.

Then I say, if this principle is established, that there is no wrong in slavery, and whoever wants it has a right to have it, is a matter of dollars and cents, a sort of question as to how they shall deal with brutes; that between us and the negro here there is no sort of question, but that at the South the question is between the negro and the crocodile. That is all. It is a mere matter of policy; there is a perfect right according to interest to do just as you please; when this is done, where this doctrine prevails, the miners and sappers will have formed public opinion for the slave-trade. They will be ready for Jeff. Davis and Stephens, and other leaders of that company, to sound the bugle for the revival of the slave-trade, for the second Dred Scott decision, for the flood of slavery to be poured over the free States, while we shall be here tied down and helpless and run over like sheep.

It is to be a part and parcel of this same idea, to say to men who want to adhere to the Democratic party, who have always belonged to that party, and are only looking about for some excuse to stick to it, but nevertheless hate slavery, that Douglas's popular sovereignty is as good a way as any to oppose slavery. They allow themselves to be persuaded easily, in accordance with their previous dispositions, into this belief, that it is about as good a way of opposing slavery as any, and we can do that without straining our old party ties or breaking up old political associations. We can do so without being called negro worshippers. We can do that without being subjected to the gibes and sneers that are so readily thrown out in place of argument where no argument can be found. So let us stick to this popular sovereignty,— this insidious popular sovereignty. Now let me call your attention to one thing that has really happened, which shows this gradual and steady debauching of public opinion, this course of preparation for the revival of the slave-trade, for the territorial slave code, and the new Dred Scott decision that is to carry slavery into the free States. Did you ever, five years ago, hear of anybody in the world saying that the negro had no share in the Declaration of National Independence; that it did not mean negroes at all; and when "all men" were spoken of, negroes were not included?

I am satisfied that five years ago that proposition was not put upon paper by any living being anywhere. I have been unable at any time to find a man in an audience who would declare that he had ever known of anybody saying so five years ago. But last year there was not a Douglas popular sovereign in Illinois who did not say it. Is there one in Ohio but declares his firm belief that the Declaration of Independence did not mean negroes at all? I do not know how this is; I have not been here much; but I presume you are very much alike everywhere. Then I suppose that all now express the belief that the Declaration of Independence never did mean negroes. I call upon one of them to say that he said it five years ago.

If you think that now, and did not think it then, the next thing that strikes me is to remark that there has been a *change* wrought in you, and a very significant change it is, being no less than changing the negro, in your estimation, from the rank of a man to that of a brute. They are taking him down, and placing him, when spoken of, among reptiles and crocodiles, as Judge Douglas himself expresses it.

Is not this change wrought in your minds a very important change? Public opinion in this country is everything. In a nation like ours this popular sovereignty and squatter sovereignty have already wrought a change in the public mind to the extent I have stated. There is no man in this crowd who can contradict it.

WHAT ALL THIS IS TENDING TO.

Now, if you are opposed to slavery honestly, as much as anybody, I ask you to note that fact, and the like of which is to follow, to be plastered on, layer after layer, until very soon you are prepared to deal with the negro everywhere as with the brute. If public sentiment has not been debauched already to this point, a new turn of the screw in that direction is all that is wanting; and this is constantly being done by the teachers of this insidious popular sovereignty. You need but one or two turns further until your minds, now ripening under these teachings, will be ready for all these things, and you will receive and support, or submit to, the slave-trade, revived with all its horrors, a slave code enforced in our Territories, and a new Dred Scott decision to bring slavery up into the very heart of the free North. This, I must say, is but carrying out those words prophetically spoken by Mr. Clay, many, many years ago,—I believe more than thirty years,—which he told an audience that if they would repress all tendencies to liberty and ultimate emancipation, they must go back to the era of our independence and muzzle the cannon which thundered its annual joyous return on the Fourth of July; they must blow out the moral lights around us; they must penetrate the human soul and eradicate the love of liberty; but until they did these things, and others eloquently enumerated by him, they could not repress all tendencies to ultimate emancipation.

I ask attention to the fact that in a pre-eminent degree these popular sovereigns are at this work; blowing out the moral lights around us; teaching that the negro is no longer a man, but a brute; that the Declaration has nothing to do with him; that he ranks with the crocodile and the reptile; that man, with body and soul, is a matter of dollars and cents. I suggest to this portion of the Ohio Republicans, or Democrats, if there be any present, the serious consideration of this fact, that there is now going on among you a steady process of debauching public opinion on this subject. With this, my friends, I bid you adieu.

OHIO AND KENTUCKY, OR THE TWO SYSTEMS.

Mr. Lincoln spoke in Cincinnati, for the first time, September, 1859, during the same canvass.

JUDGE DOUGLAS'S CHARGE.

My fellow-citizens of the State of Ohio: This is the first time in my life that I have appeared before an audience in so great a city as this. I therefore, though I am no longer a young man, make this appearance under some degree of embarrassment. But I have found that when one is embarrassed, usually the shortest way to get through with it is to quit talking or thinking about it, and go at something else.

I understand that you have had recently with you my very distinguished friend, Judge Douglas, of Illinois; and I understand, without having had an opportunity (not greatly sought, to be sure) of seeing a report of the speech that he made here, that he did me the honor to mention my humble name. I suppose that he did so for the purpose of making some objection to some sentiment at some time expressed by me. I should expect, it is true, that Judge Douglas had reminded you, or informed you, if you had never before heard it, that I had once in my life declared it as my opinion, that this Government cannot "endure permanently, half slave and half free; that 'a house divided against itself cannot stand,'" and, as I had expressed it, I did not expect the house to fall; that I did not expect the Union to be dissolved,—but that I did expect it would cease to be divided; that it would become all one thing or all the other; that either the opposition of slavery would arrest the further spread of it, and place it where the public mind would rest in the belief that it was in the course of ultimate extinction; or the friends of slavery will push it forward until it becomes alike lawful in all the States, old or new, free as well as slave. I did, fifteen months ago, express that opinion; and upon many occasions Judge Douglas has denounced it; and has greatly, intentionally or unintentionally, misrepresented my purpose in the expression of that opinion.

I presume, without having seen a report of his speech, that he did so here. I presume that he alluded also to that opinion in different language, — having been expressed at a subsequent time by Governor Seward of New York, — and that he took the two in a lump and denounced them; that he tried to point out that there was something couched in this opinion which led to the making of an entire uniformity of the local institutions of the various States of the Union, in utter disregard of the different States, which in their nature would seem to require a variety of institutions and a variety of laws, conforming to the differences in the nature of the different States.

Not only so,—I presume he insisted that this was a declaration of war between the free and slave States, — that it was the sounding to the onset of continual war between the different States, — the slave and free States.

A SAFE DISTANCE.

This charge, in this form, was made by Judge Douglas, on, I believe, the 9th of July, 1858, in Chicago, in my hearing. On the next evening, I made some reply to it. I informed him that many of the inferences he drew from that expression of mine were altogether foreign to any purpose entertained by me, and in so far as he should ascribe those inferences to me, as my purpose, he was entirely mistaken; and in so far as he might argue that whatever might be my purpose, actions, conforming to my views, would lead to these results, he might argue and establish if he could; but, so far as purposes were concerned, he was totally mistaken as to me.

When I made that reply to him, — when I told him, on the question of declaring war between the different States of the Union, that I had not said that I did not expect any peace upon this question until slavery was exterminated; that I had only said I expected peace when that institution was put where the public mind should rest in the belief that it was in course of ultimate extinction; that I believed from the organization of our government, until a very recent period of time, the institution had been placed and continued upon such a basis; that we had had comparative peace upon that question through a portion of that period of time, only because the public mind rested in that belief in regard to it, and that when we returned to that position in relation to that matter, I supposed we should again have peace as we previously had. I assured him, as I now assure you, that I neither then had, nor have, or ever had, any purpose in any way of interfering with the institution of slavery, where it exists. I believe we have no power, under the Constitution of the United States, or rather under the form of Government under which we live, to interfere with the institution of slavery, or any other of the institutions of our sister States, be they free or slave States. I declared then, and I now re-declare, that I have as little inclination to interfere with the institution of slavery where it now exists, through the instrumentality of the General Government, or any other instrumentality, as I believe we have no power to do so. I accidentally used this expression: I had no purpose of entering into the slave States to disturb the institution of slavery! So, upon the first occasion that Judge Douglas got an opportunity to reply to me, he passed by the whole body of what I had said upon that subject, and seized upon the particular expression of mine, that I had no purpose of entering into the slave States to disturb the institution of slavery. "Oh, no," said he, "he (Lincoln) won't enter into the slave States to disturb the institution of slavery; he is too prudent a man to do such a thing as that; he only means that he will go on to the line between the free and slave States, and shoot over at them. This is all he means to do. He means to do them all the harm he can, to disturb them all he can, in such a way as to keep his own hide in perfect safety."

Well, now, I did not think, at that time, that that was either a very dignified or very logical argument; but so it was, I had to get along with it as well as I could.

SHOOTING OVER THE LINE.

It has occurred to me here to-night, that if I ever do shoot over the line at the people on the other side of the line into a slave State, and purpose to do so, keeping my skin safe, that I have now about the best chance I shall ever have. I should not wonder that there are some Kentuckians about this audience; we are close to Kentucky; and whether that be so or not, we are on elevated ground, and by speaking distinctly, I should not wonder if some of the Kentuckians would hear me on the other side of the river. For that reason I propose to address a portion of what I have to say to the Kentuckians.

A PLEA FOR THE "LITTLE GIANT."

I say, then, in the first place, to the Kentuckians, that I am what they call, as I understand it, a "Black Republican." I think slavery is wrong, morally and politically. I desire that it should be no further spread in these United States, and I should not object if it should gradually terminate in the whole Union. While I say this for myself, I say to you, Kentuckians, that I understand you differ radically with me upon this proposition; that you believe slavery is a good thing; that slavery is right; that it ought to be extended and perpetuated in this Union. Now, there being this broad difference between us, I do not pretend, in addressing myself to you, Kentuckians, to attempt proselyting you; that would be a vain effort. I do not enter upon it. I only propose to try to show you that you ought to nominate for the next Presidency, at Charleston, my distinguished friend, Judge Douglas. In all that there is a difference between you and him, I understand he is sincerely for you, and more wisely for you, than you are for yourselves. I will try to demonstrate that proposition. Understand, now, I say that I believe he is as sincerely for you, and more wisely for you, than you are for yourselves.

WHAT DO YOU WANT?

What do you want more than anything else to make successful your views of slavery; to advance the outspread of it, and to secure and perpetuate the nationality of it? What do you want more than anything else? What is needed absolutely? What is indispensable to you? Why! if I may be allowed to answer the question, it is to retain a hold upon the North; it is to retain support and strength from the free States. If you can get this support and strength from the free States, you can succeed. If you do not get this support and this strength from the free States, you are in the minority, and you are beaten at once.

If that proposition be admitted, — and it is undeniable, — then the next thing I say to you is, that Douglas, of all the men in this nation, is the only man that affords you any hold upon the free States; that no other man can give you any strength in the free States. This being so, if you doubt the other branch of the proposition, whether he is for you, whether he is really for you, as I have expressed it, I propose asking your attention for a while to a few facts.

THE DIFFERENCE.

The issue between you and me, understand, is, that I think slavery is wrong, and ought not to be outspread, and you think it is right, and ought to be extended and perpetuated. [A voice, "O Lord!"] That is my Kentuckian I am talking to now.

I now proceed to try to show you that Douglas is as sincerely for you, and more wisely for you, than you are for yourselves.

MOULDING PUBLIC OPINION.

In the first place, we know that in a Government like this,—in a Government of the people, where the voice of all the men of that country, substantially, enters into the execution or administration, rather of the Government,—in such a Government, what lies at the bottom of all of it, is public opinion. I lay down the proposition, that Judge Douglas is not only the man that promises you, in advance, a hold upon the North, and support in the North, but that he constantly moulds public opinion to your ends; that in every possible way he can, he constantly moulds the public opinion of the North to your ends; and if there are a few things in which he seems to be against you,—a few things which he says that appear to be against you, and a few that he forbears to say, which you would like to have him say,—you ought to remember that the saying of the one, or the forbearing to say the other, would lose his hold upon the North, and, by consequence, would lose his capacity to serve you.

Upon this subject of moulding public opinion, I call your attention to the fact,—for a well-established fact it is,—that the Judge never says your institution of slavery is wrong; he never says it is right, to be sure; but he never says it is wrong. There is not a public man in the United States, I believe, with the exception of Senator Douglas, who has not, at some time in his life, declared his opinion whether the thing is right or wrong; but Senator Douglas never declares it is wrong. He leaves himself at perfect liberty to do all in your favor, which he would be hindered from doing if he were to declare the thing to be wrong. On the contrary, he takes all the chances that he has for inveigling the sentiment of the North, opposed to slavery, into your support, by never saying it is right. This you ought to set down to his credit. You ought to give him full credit for this much, little though it be, in comparison to the whole which he does for you.

DOUGLAS'S SEESAW.

Some other things I will ask your attention to. He said upon the floor of the United States Senate, and he has repeated it, as I understand, a great many times, that he does not care whether slavery is "voted up or voted down." This again shows you, or ought to show you, if you would reason upon it, that he does not believe it to be wrong, — for a man may say, when he sees nothing wrong in a thing, that he does not care whether it be voted up or voted down; but no man can logically say that he cares not whether a thing goes up or goes down, which to him appears to be wrong. You therefore have a demonstration in this, that, to Judge Douglas's mind, your favorite institution, which you would have spread out and made perpetual, is no wrong.

THE ISOTHERMAL LINE, — WHERE IS IT?

Another thing he tells you, in a speech made at Memphis, in Tennessee, shortly after the canvass in Illinois, last year. He there distinctly told the people, that there was a "line drawn by the Almighty across this continent, on the one side of which the soil must always be cultivated by slaves;" that he did not pretend to know exactly where that line was, but that there was such a line. I want to ask your attention to that proposition again, — that there is one portion of this continent where the Almighty has designed the soil shall always be cultivated by slaves; that its being cultivated by slaves at that place is right; that it has the direct sympathy and authority of the Almighty. Whenever you can get these Northern audiences to adopt the opinion that slavery is right on the other side of the Ohio,—whenever you can get them, in pursuance of Douglas's views, to adopt that sentiment, — they will very readily make the other argument, which is perfectly logical, that that which is right on that side of the Ohio, cannot be wrong on this; and that if you have that property on that side of the Ohio, under the seal and stamp of the Almighty, when by any means it escapes over here, it is wrong to have constitutions and laws "to devil" you about it. So Douglas 's moulding the public opinion of the North, first to say that the thing is right in your State over the Ohio River, and hence to say that that which is right there is not wrong here, and that all laws and constitutions here, recognizing it as being wrong, are themselves wrong, and ought to be repealed and abrogated. He will tell you, men of Ohio, that if you choose here to have laws against slavery, it is in conformity to the idea that your climate is not suited to it, — that your climate is not suited to slave labor, — and therefore you have constitutions and laws against it.

THE SUGAR-CANE ARGUMENT.

Let us attend to that argument for a little while and see if it be sound. You do not raise sugar-cane (except the new-fashioned sugar-cane, and you won't raise that long), but they do raise it in Louisiana. You don't raise it in Ohio, because you can't raise it profitably, because the climate don't suit. They do raise it in Louisiana because there it is profitable. Now, Douglas will tell you that is precisely the slavery question. That they do have slaves there because they are profitable, and you don't have them here because they are not profitable. If that is so, then it leads to dealing with the one precisely as with the other. Is there then anything in the constitution or laws of Ohio against raising sugar-cane? Have you found it necessary to put any such provision in your law? Surely not! No man desires to raise sugar-cane in Ohio; but, if any man did desire to do so, you would say it was a tyrannical law that forbids his doing so; and whenever you shall agree with Douglas, whenever your minds are brought to adopt his argument, as surely you will have reached the conclusion, that although slavery is not profitable in Ohio, if any man wants it, it is wrong to him not to let him have it.

In this matter Judge Douglas is preparing the public mind for you of Kentucky, to make perpetual that good thing in your estimation, about which you and I differ.

THE NEGRO A BRUTE—A DEMOCRATIC PRINCIPLE.

In this connection let me ask your attention to another thing. I believe it is safe to assert that five years ago, no living man had expressed the opinion that the negro had no share in the Declaration of Independence. Let me state that again: five years ago no living man had expressed the opinion that the negro had no share in the Declaration of Independence. If there is in this large audience any man who ever knew of that opinion being put upon paper as much as five years ago, I will be obliged to him now or at a subsequent time to show it.

If that be true, I wish you then to note the next fact; that within the space of five years Senator Douglas, in the argument of this question, has got his entire party, so far as I know, without exception, to join in saying that the negro has no share in the Declaration of Independence. If there be now in all these United States one Douglas man that does not say this, I have been unable upon any occasion to scare him up. Now if none of you said this five years ago, and all of you say it now, that is a matter that you Kentuckians ought to note. That is a vast change in the Northern public sentiment upon that question.

Of what tendency is that change? The tendency of that change is to bring the public mind to the conclusion that when men are spoken of, the negro is not meant; that when negroes are spoken of, brutes alone are contemplated. That change in public sentiment has already degraded the black man in the estimation of Douglas and his followers from the condition of a man of some sort, and assigned him to the condition of a brute. Now, you Kentuckians ought to give Douglas credit for this. That is the largest possible stride that can be made in regard to the perpetuation of your thing of slavery.

A voice—"Speak to Ohio men, and not to Kentuckians."

Mr. Lincoln—I beg permission to speak as I please.

THE BIBLE ARGUMENT AND DOUGLAS.

In Kentucky perhaps, in many of the slave States certainly, you are trying to establish the rightfulness of slavery by reference to the Bible. You are trying to show that slavery existed in the Bible times by divine ordinance. Now, Douglas is wiser than you, for your own benefit, upon that subject. Douglas knows that whenever you establish that slavery was right by the Bible, it will occur that that slavery was the slavery of the *white* man, — of men without reference to color, — and he knows very well that you may entertain that idea in Kentucky as much as you please, but you will never win any Northern support upon it. He makes a wiser argument for you; he makes the argument that the slavery of the *black* man, the slavery of the man who has a skin of a different color from your own, is right. He thereby brings to your support Northern voters who could not for a moment be brought by your own argument of the Bible-right of slavery. Will you not give him credit for that? Will you not say that in this matter he is more wisely for you than you are for yourselves?

THE CROCODILE PLEA.

Now, having established with his entire party this doctrine,— having been entirely successful in that branch of his efforts in your behalf, he is ready for another.

At this same meeting at Memphis, he declared that, while in all contests between the negro and the white man, he was for the white man, but that in all questions between the negro and the crocodile, he was for the negro. He did not make that declaration accidentally at Memphis. He made it a great many times in the canvass in Illinois last year (though I don't know that it was reported in any of his speeches there), but he frequently made it. I believe he repeated it at Columbus, and I should not wonder if he repeated it here. It is, then, a deliberate way of expressing himself upon that subject. It is a matter of mature deliberation with him thus to express himself upon that point of his case. It therefore requires some deliberate attention.

The first inference seems to be that if you do not enslave the negro, you are wronging the white man in some way or other; and that whoever is opposed to the negro being enslaved, is, in some way or other, against the white man. Is not that a falsehood? If there was a necessary conflict between the white man and the negro, I should be for the white man as much as Judge Douglas; but I say there is no such necessary conflict. I say that there is room enough for us all to be free, and that it not only does not wrong the white man that the negro should be free, but it positively wrongs the mass of the white men that the negro should be enslaved; that the mass of white men are really injured by the effects of slave labor in the vicinity of the fields of their own labor.

But I do not desire to dwell upon this branch of the question more than to say that this assumption of his is false, and I do hope that that fallacy will not long prevail in the minds of intelligent white men. At all events, you ought to thank Judge Douglas for it. It is for your benefit it is made.

The other branch of it is, that in a struggle between the negro and the crocodile, he is for the negro. Well, I don't know that there is any struggle between the negro and the crocodile, either. I suppose that if a crocodile (or as we old river boatmen used to call them, alligators) should come across a white man, he would kill him if he could, and so he would a negro. But what, at last, is this proposition? I believe that it is a sort of a proposition in proportion, which may be stated thus: "As the negro is to the white man, so is the crocodile to the negro; and as the negro may rightfully treat the crocodile as a beast or a reptile, so the white man may rightfully treat the negro as a beast or a reptile. That is really the "knip" of all that argument of his.

Now, my brother Kentuckians, who believe in this, you ought to thank Judge Douglas for having put that in a much more taking way than any of yourselves have done.

WHERE IS THE DISTINCTION?

Again, Douglas's *great principle*, "popular sovereignty," as he calls it, gives you, by natural consequence, the revival of the slave-trade whenever you want it. If you question this, listen awhile, consider awhile, what I shall advance in support of that proposition.

He says that it is the sacred right of the man who goes into the territories, to have slavery if he wants it. Grant that, for argument's sake. Is it not the sacred right of the man who don't go there equally to buy slaves in Africa, if he wants them? Can you point out the difference? The man who goes into the territories of Kansas and Nebraska, or any other new territory, with the sacred right of taking a slave there which belongs to him, would certainly have no more right to take one there than I would, who own no slave, but who would desire to buy one and take him there. You will not say, — you, the friends of Judge Douglas, — but that the man who does not own a slave, has an equal right to buy one and take him to the Territory, as the other does?

A voice — "I want to ask a question. Don't foreign nations interfere with the slave-trade?"

Mr. Lincoln — Well! I understand it to be a principle of Democracy to whip foreign nations whenever they interfere with us.

Voice — "I only asked for information. I am a Republican myself."

Mr. Lincoln — You and I will be on the best terms in the world, but I do not wish to be diverted from the point I was trying to press.

THE LOGIC OF IT.

I say that Douglas's popular sovereignty, establishing his sacred right in the people, if you please, if carried to its logical conclusion, gives equally the sacred right to the people of the States or the Territories themselves to buy slaves, wherever they can buy them cheapest; and if any man can show a distinction, I should like to hear him try it. If any man can show how the people of Kansas have a better right to slaves because they want them, than the people of Georgia have to buy them in Africa, I want him to do it. I think it cannot be done. If it is "popular sovereignty" for the people to have slaves because they want them, it is popular sovereignty for them to buy them in Africa, because they desire to do so.

REPEAL OF THE AFRICAN SLAVE-TRADE LAWS.

I know that Douglas has recently made a little effort,—not seeming to notice that he had a different theory,—has made an effort to get rid of that. He has written a letter, addressed to somebody, I believe, who resides in Iowa, declaring his opposition to the repeal of the laws that prohibit the African slave-trade. He bases his opposition to such repeal upon the ground that these laws are themselves one of the compromises of the Constitution of the United States. Now it would be very interesting to see Judge Douglas or any of his friends turn to the Constitution of the United States and point out that compromise, to show where there is any compromise in the Constitution, or provision in the Constitution, express or implied, by which the administrators of that Constitution are under any obligation to repeal the African slave-trade. I know, or at least I think I know, that the framers of that Constitution did expect that the African slave-trade would be abolished at the end of twenty years, to which time their prohibition against its being abolished extended. I think there is abundant contemporaneous history to show that the framers of the Constitution expected it to be abolished. But while they so expected, they gave nothing for that expectation, and they put no provision in the Constitution requiring it should be so abolished. The migration or importation of such persons as the States shall see fit to admit shall not be prohibited, but a certain tax might be levied upon such importation. But what was to be done after that time? The Contitution is as silent about that as it is silent, personally, about myself. There is absolutely nothing in it about that subject,—there is only the expectation of the framers of the Constitution that the slave-trade would be abolished at the end of that time, and they expected it would be abolished, owing to public sentiment, before that time, and they put that provision in, in order that it should not be abolished before that time, for reasons which I suppose they thought to be sound ones, but which I will not now try to enumerate before you.

WHAT THE FRAMERS OF THE CONSTITUTION EXPECTED.

But while they expected the slave-trade would be abolished at that time, they expected that the spread of slavery into the new territories should also be restricted. It is as easy to prove that the framers of the Constitution of the United States expected that slavery should be prohibited from extending into the new territories, as it is to prove that it was expected that the slave-trade should be abolished. Both these things were expected. One was no more expected than the other, and one was no more a compromise of the Constitution than the other. There was nothing said in the Constitution in regard to the spread of slavery into the territory. I grant that; but there was something very important said about it by the same generation of men in the adoption of the old Ordinance of '87, through the influence of which you here in Ohio, our neighbors in Indiana, we in Illinois, our neighbors in Michigan and Wisconsin are happy, prosperous, teeming millions of free men. That generation of men, though not to the full extent members of the Convention that framed the Constitution, were to some extent members of that Convention, holding seats at the same time in one body and the other, so that if there was any compromise on either of these subjects, the strong evidence is that that compromise was in favor of the restriction of slavery from the new territories.

A SHREWD GAME.

But Douglas says that he is unalterably opposed to the repeal of those laws; because, in his view, it is a compromise of the Constitution. You Kentuckians, no doubt, are somewhat offended with that! You ought not to be! You ought to be patient! You ought to know that if he said less than that, he would lose the power of "lugging" the Northern States to your support. Really, what you would push him to do would take from him his entire power to serve you. And you ought to remember how long, by precedent, Judge Douglas holds himself obliged to stick by compromises. You ought to remember that by the time you yourselves think you are ready to inaugurate measures for the revival of the African slave-trade, that sufficient time will have arrived, by precedent, for Judge Douglas to break through that compromise. He says now nothing more strong than he said in 1849, when he declared in favor of the Missouri Compromise, — that precisely four years and a quarter after he declared that compromise to be a sacred thing, which "no ruthless hand would ever dare to touch," he, himself, brought forward the measure, ruthlessly to destroy it. By a mere calculation of time, it will only be four years more until he is ready to take back his profession about the sacredness of of the compromise abolishing the slave-trade. Precisely as soon as you are ready to have his services in that direction, by fair calculation, you may be sure of having them.

THE "UNFRIENDLY LEGISLATION" DODGE.

But you remember and set down to Judge Douglas's debt, or discredit, that he, last year, said the people of Territories can, in spite of the Dred Scott decision, exclude your slaves from those territories; that he declared by "unfriendly legislation," the extension of your property into the new territories may be cut off in the teeth of the decision of the Supreme Court of the United States.

He assumed that position at Freeport on the 27th of August,

1858. He said that the people of the territories can exclude slavery, in so many words. You ought, however, to bear in mind that he has never said it since. You may hunt in every speech that he has since made, and he has never used that expression once. He has never seemed to notice that he is stating his views differently from what he did then; but, by some sort of accident, he has always really stated it differently. He has always since then declared that "the Constitution does not carry slavery into the Territories of the United States beyond the power of the people legally to control it, as other property." Now, there is a difference in the language used upon that former occasion and in this latter day. There may or may not be a difference in the meaning, but it is worth while considering whether there is not also a difference in meaning.

HOW THE SUPREME COURT WOULD REGARD IT.

What is it to exclude? Why, it is to drive it out. It is in some way to put it out of the territory. It is to force it across the line, or change its character, so that as property it is out of existence. But what is the controlling of it "as other property?" Is controlling it as other property the same thing as destroying it, or driving it away? I should think not. I should think the controlling of it as other property would be just about what you in Kentucky should want. I understand the controlling of property means the controlling of it for the benefit of the owner of it. While I have no doubt the Supreme Court of the United States would say "God speed" to any of the territorial legislatures that should thus control slave property, they would sing quite a different tune, if by the pretence of controlling it they were to undertake to pass laws which virtually excluded it, and that upon a very well known principle to all lawyers, that what a legislature cannot directly do, it cannot do by indirection; that as the legislature has not the power to drive slaves out, they have no power by indirection, by tax, or by imposing burdens in any way upon that property, to effect the same end, and that any attempt to do so would be held by the Dred Scott court unconstitutional.

THE ABSURDITY.

Douglas is not willing to stand by his first proposition, that they can exclude it, because we have seen that that proposition amounts to nothing more nor less than the naked absurdity, that you may lawfully drive out that which has a lawful right to remain. He admitted at first that the slave might be lawfully taken into the territories under the Constitution of the United States, and yet asserted that he might be lawfully driven out. That being the proposition, it is the absurdity I have stated. He is not willing to stand in the face of that direct, naked, and impudent absurdity; he has, therefore, modified his language into that of being "*controlled as other property.*"

The Kentuckians don't like this in Douglas! I will tell you where it will go. He now swears by the court. He was once a leading man in Illinois to break down a court, because it had made a decision he did not like. But he now not only swears by the court, the courts having got to working for you, but he denounces all men that do not swear by the courts, as unpatriotic, as bad citizens. When one of these acts of unfriendly legislation shall impose such heavy burdens as to, in effect, destroy property in slaves in a territory and show plainly enough that there can be no mistake in the purpose of the legislature to make them so burdensome, this same Supreme Court will decide that law to be unconstitutional, and he will be ready to say for your benefit, "I swear by the court; I give it up;" and while that is going on he has been getting all his men to swear by the courts, and to give it up with him. In this again he serves you faithfully, and as I say, more wisely than you serve yourselves.

AUTHORSHIP OF "THE IRREPRESSIBLE CONFLICT" DOCTRINE.

Again; I have alluded in the beginning of these remarks to

the fact, that Judge Douglas has made great complaint of my having expressed the opinion that this Government "cannot endure permanently half slave and half free." He has complained of Seward for using different language, and declaring that there is an "irrepressible conflict" between the principles of free and slave labor. [A voice — "He says it is not original with Seward. That is original with Lincoln."] I will attend to that immediately, sir. Since that time, Hickman, of Pennsylvania, expressed the same sentiment. He has never denounced Mr. Hickman: why? There is a little chance, notwithstanding that opinion in the mouth of Hickman, that he may yet be a Douglas man. That is the difference! It is not unpatriotic to hold that opinion, if a man is a Douglas man.

But neither I, nor Seward, nor Hickman, is entitled to the enviable or unenviable distinction of having first expressed that idea. That same idea was expressed by the Richmond *Enquirer* in Virginia, in 1856; quite two years before it was expressed by the first of us. And while Douglas was pluming himself, that in his conflict with my humble self, last year, he had "squelched out" that fatal heresy, as he delighted to call it, and suggested that if he only had had a chance to be in New York and meet Seward he would have "squelched" it there also, it never occurred to him to breathe a word against Pryor. I don't think that you can discover that Douglas ever talked of going to Virginia to "squelch" out that idea there. No. More than that. That same Roger A. Pryor was brought to Washington City and made the editor of the *par excellence* Douglas paper, after making use of that expression, which, in us, is so unpatriotic and heretical. From all this, my Kentucky friends may see that this opinion is heretical in his view only when it is expressed by men suspected of a desire that the country shall all become free, and not when expressed by those fairly known to entertain the desire that the whole country shall become slave. When expressed by that class of men, it is in nowise offensive to him. In this again, my friends of Kentucky, you have Judge Douglas with you.

WHO WORKED FOR DOUGLAS'S ELECTION.

There is another reason why you Southern people ought to nominate Douglas at your Convention at Charleston. That reason is the wonderful capacity of the man; the power he has of doing what would seem to be impossible. Let me call your attention to one of these apparently impossible things.

Douglas had three or four very distinguished men of the most extreme anti-slavery views of any men in the Republican party, expressing their desire for his re-election to the Senate last year. That would, of itself, have seemed to be a little wonderful, but that wonder is heightened when we see that Wise of Virginia, a man exactly opposed to them, a man who believes in the Divine right of slavery, was also expressing his desire that Douglas should be re-elected; that another man, that may be said to be kindred to Wise, Mr. Breckinridge, the Vice-President, and of your own State, was also agreeing with the anti-slavery men in the North, that Douglas ought to be re-elected. Still, to heighten the wonder, a Senator from Kentucky, whom I have always loved with an affection as tender and endearing as I have ever loved any man; who was opposed to the anti-slavery men for reasons which seemed sufficient to him, and equally opposed to Wise and Breckinridge, was writing letters into Illinois to secure the re-election of Douglas. Now that all these conflicting elements should be brought, while at daggers' points, with one another, to support him, is a feat that is worthy for you to note and consider. It is quite probable that each of these classes of men thought, by the re-election of Douglas, their peculiar views would gain something; it is probable that the anti-slavery men thought their views would gain something; that Wise and Breckinridge thought so too, as regards their opinions; that Mr. Crittenden thought that his views would gain something, although he was opposed to both these other men. It is probable that each and all of them thought that they were using Douglas, and it is yet an unsolved problem whether he was not using them all. If he was, then it is for you to consider whether that power to perform wonders, is one for you lightly to throw away.

NO CHARGE FOR THE OPINION.

There is one other thing that I will say to you in this relation. It is but my opinion, I give it to you without a fee. It is my opinion that it is for you to take him or be defeated; and that if you do take him you may be beaten. You will surely be beaten if you do not take him. We, the Republicans and others forming the opposition of the country, intend to "stand by our guns," to be patient and firm, and in the long run to beat you whether you take him or not. We know that before we fairly beat you we have to beat you both together. We know that you are "all of a feather," and that we have to beat you altogether, and we expect to do it. We don't intend to be very impatient about it. We mean to be as deliberate and calm about it as it is possible to be, but as firm and resolved as it is possible for men to be. When we do as we say, beat you, you perhaps want to know what we will do with you.

WHAT WE MEAN TO DO.

I will tell you, so far as I am authorized to speak for the opposition, what we mean to do with you. We mean to treat you, as near as we possibly can, as Washington, Jefferson, and Madison treated you. We mean to leave you alone, and in no way to interfere with your institution; to abide by all and every compromise of the Constitution, and, in a word, coming back to the original proposition, to treat you, so far as degenerated men (if we have degenerated) may, according to the examples of those noble fathers, — Washington, Jefferson, and Madison. We mean to remember that you are as good as we; that there is no difference between us other than the difference of circumstances. We mean to recognize and bear in mind always that you have as good hearts in your bosoms as other people, or as we claim to have, and treat you accordingly. We mean to marry your girls when we have a chance, — the white ones, I mean, — and I have the honor to inform you that I once did have a chance in that way.

WHAT WILL THE SOUTH DO?

I have told you what we mean to do. I want to know, now, when that thing takes place, what do you mean to do? I often hear it intimated that you mean to divide the Union whenever a Republican, or anything like it, is elected President of the United States. [A voice, "That is so."] "That is so," one of them says; I wonder if he is a Kentuckian? [A voice, "He is a Douglas man."] Well, then, I want to know what you are going to do with your half of it. Are you going to split the Ohio down through, and push your half off a piece? Or are you going to keep it right alongside of us outrageous fellows? Or are you going to build up a wall some way between your country and ours, by which that movable property of yours can't come over here any more, to the danger of your losing it? Do you think you can better yourselves on that subject by leaving us here under no obligation whatever to return those specimens of your movable property that come hither? You have divided the Union because we would not do right with you, as you think, upon that subject; when we cease to be under obligations to do anything for you, how much better off do you think you will be? Will you make war upon us, and kill us all? Why, gentlemen, I think you are as gallant and as brave men as live; that you can fight as bravely in a good cause, man for man, as any other people living; that you have shown yourselves capable of this upon various occasions; but, man for man, you are not better than we are, and there are not so many of you as there are of us. You will never make much of a hand at whipping us. If we were fewer in numbers than you, I think that you could whip us; if we were equal, it would likely be a drawn battle; but, being inferior in numbers, you will make nothing by attempting to master us.

But perhaps I have addressed myself as long, or longer, to the Kentuckians, than I ought to have done, inasmuch as I have said that, whatever course you take, we intend, in the end, to beat you. I propose to address a few remarks to our friends, by way of discussing with them the best means of keeping that promise that I have in good faith made.

THE FALLACY OF THE DOUGLAS ARGUMENT — HISTORICAL STATEMENT.

It may appear a little episodical for me to mention the topic of which I shall speak now. It is a favorable proposition of Douglas's that the interference of the General Government, through the Ordinance of '87, or through any other act of the General Government, never has made, nor ever can make, a free State; that the Ordinance of '87 did not make free States of Ohio, Indiana, or Illinois. That these States are free upon his "great principle" of popular sovereignty, because the people of those several States have chosen to make them so. At Columbus, and probably here, he undertook to compliment the people that they themselves have made the State of Ohio free, and that the Ordinance of '87 was not entitled in any degree to divide the honor with them. I have no doubt that the people of the State of Ohio did make her free according to their own will and judgment, but let the facts be remembered.

In 1802, I believe, it was you who made your first constitution with the clause prohibiting slavery, and you did it, I suppose, very nearly unanimously; but you should bear in mind that you, — speaking of you as one people, — that you did so unembarrassed by the actual presence of the institution amongst you; that you made it a free State, not with the embarrassment upon you of already having among you many slaves, which, if they had been here, and you had sought to make a free State, you would not know what to do with. If they had been among you, embarrassing difficulties, most probably, would have induced you to tolerate a slave constitution instead of a free one, as indeed these very difficulties have constrained every people on this continent who have adopted slavery.

Pray, what was it that made you free? What kept you free?

Did you not find your country free when you came to decide that Ohio should be a free State? It is important to inquire by what reason you found it so? Let us take an illustration between the States of Ohio and Kentucky. Kentucky is separated by this River Ohio, not a mile wide. A portion of Kentucky, by reason of the course of the Ohio, is further north than this portion of Ohio in which we now stand. Kentucky is entirely covered with slavery; Ohio is entirely free from it. What made that difference? Was it climate? No! A portion of Kentucky was further north than this portion of Ohio. Was it soil? No! There is nothing in the soil of the one more favorable to slave labor than the other. It was not climate or soil that caused one side of the line to be entirely covered with slavery, and the other side free of it. What was it? Study over it. Tell us, if you can, in all the range of conjecture, if there be anything you can conceive of that made that difference, other than that there was no law of any sort keeping it out of Kentucky? while the Ordinance of '87 kept it out of Ohio. If there is any other reason than this, I confess that it is wholly beyond my power to conceive of it. This, then, I offer to combat the idea that that Ordinance has never made any State free.

INDIANA.

I don't stop at this illustration. I come to the State of Indiana; and what I have said as between Kentucky and Ohio, I repeat as between Indiana and Kentucky; it is equally applicable. One additional argument is applicable also to Indiana. In her territorial condition she more than once petitioned Congress to abrogate the Ordinance entirely, or at least so far as to suspend its operation for a time, in order that they should exercise the "popular sovereignty" of having slaves if they wanted them. The men then controlling the General Government, imitating the men of the Revolution, refused Indiana that privilege. And so we have the evidence that Indiana supposed she could have slaves, if it were not for that Ordinance; that she besought

Congress to put that barrier out of the way; that Congress refused to do so, and it all ended at last in Indiana being a free State. Tell me not then that the Ordinance of '87 had nothing to do with making Indiana a free State, when we find some men chafing against and only restrained by that barrier.

ILLINOIS — MISSOURI.

Come down again to our State of Illinois. The great Northwest Territory, including Ohio, Indiana, Illinois, Michigan, and Wisconsin, was acquired first, I believe, by the British Government, in part at least from the French. Before the establishment of our independence, it became a part of Virginia; enabling Virginia afterward to transfer it to the General Government. There were French settlements in what is now Illinois, and at the same time there were French settlements in what is now Missouri, in the tract of country that was not purchased till about 1803. In these French settlements negro slavery had existed for many years, — perhaps more than a hundred, if not as much as two hundred years, — at Kaskaskia, in Illinois, and at St. Genevieve, or Cape Girardeau, perhaps, in Missouri. The number of slaves was not very great, but there was about the same number in each place. They were there when we acquired the territory. There was no effort made to break up the relation of master and slave. and even the Ordinance of 1787 was not so enforced as to destroy that slavery in Illinois; nor did the Ordinance apply to Missouri at all.

What I want to ask your attention to, at this point, is that Illinois and Missouri came into the Union about the same time; Illinois in the latter part of 1818, and Missouri, after a struggle, I believe sometime in 1820. They had been filling up with American people about the same period of time; their progress enabling them to come into the Union about the same. At the end of that ten years, in which they had been so preparing (for it was about that period of time), the number of slaves in Illinois had actually decreased; while in Missouri, beginning with very few, at the end of that ten years, there were about ten thousand. This being so, and it being remembered that Missouri and Illinois are, to a certain extent, in the same parallel of latitude, — that the northern half of Missouri and the southern half of Illinois are in the same parallel of latitude, — so that climate would have the same effect upon one as upon the other, and that in the soil there is no material difference, so far as bears upon the question of slavery being settled upon one or the other, — there being none of those natural causes to produce a difference in filling them, and yet there being a broad difference in their filling up, we are led again to inquire what was the cause of that difference?

It is most natural to say that in Missouri there was no law to keep that country from filling up with slaves, while in Illinois there was the Ordinance of '87. The Ordinance being there, slavery decreased during that ten years; the Ordinance not being in the other, it increased from a few to ten thousand. Can anybody doubt the reason of the difference?

I think all these facts most abundantly prove that my friend Judge Douglas's proposition, that the Ordinance of '87, or the national restriction of slavery, never had a tendency to make a free State, is a fallacy—a proposition without the shadow or substance of truth about it.

SLAVERY IN ILLINOIS.

Douglas sometimes says that all the States (and it is part of this same proposition I have been discussing) that have become free, have become so upon his "great principle;" that the State of Illinois itself came into the Union as a slave State, and that the people, upon the "great principle" of popular sovereignty, have since made it a free State. Allow me but a little while to state to you what facts there are to justify him in saying that Illinois came into the Union as a slave State.

I have mentioned to you that there were a few old French slaves there. They numbered, I think, one or two hundred. Besides that, there had been a territorial law for indenturing black persons. Under that law, in violation of the Ordinance of '87, but without any enforcement of the Ordinance to overthrow the system, there had been a small number of slaves introduced as indentured persons. Owing to this the clause for the prohibition of slavery was slightly modified. Instead of running like yours, that neither slavery nor involuntary servitude, except for crime, of which the party shall have been duly convicted, should exist in the State, they said that neither slavery nor involuntary servitude should thereafter be introduced, and that the children of indentured servants should be born free; and nothing was said about the few old French slaves. Out of this fact, that the clause for prohibiting slavery was modified because of the actual presence of it, Douglas asserts again and again that Illinois came into the Union as a slave State. How far the facts sustain the conclusion that he draws, it is for intelligent and impartial men to decide. I leave it with you with these remarks, worthy of being remembered, that that little thing, those few indentured servants being there, was of itself sufficient to modify a constitution made by a people ardently desiring to have a free constitution; showing the power of the actual presence of the institution of slavery to prevent any people, however anxious to make a free State, from making it perfectly so.

I have been detaining you longer perhaps than I ought to do.

BOGUS VS. GENUINE POPULAR SOVEREIGNTY.

I am in some doubt whether to introduce another topic upon which I could talk awhile. [Cries of "Go on," and "Give us it."] It is this, then: Douglas's popular sovereignty, as a principle, is simply this. If one man chooses to make a slave of another man, neither that man nor anybody else has a right to object. Apply it to government, as he seeks to apply it, and it is this: If, in a new territory, into which a few people are beginning to enter for the purpose of making their homes, they choose to either exclude slavery from their limits, or to establish it there, however one or the other may affect the persons to be enslaved, or the infinitely greater number of persons who are afterward to inhabit that territory, or the other members of the family of communities, of which they are but an incipient member, or the general head of the family of States as parent of all, — however their action may affect one or the other of these, there is no power or right to interfere. That is Douglas's popular sovereignty applied. Now I think that there is a real popular sovereignty in the world. I think a definition of popular sovereignty, in the abstract, would be about this — that each man shall do precisely as he pleases with himself, and with all those things which exclusively concern him. Applied in government, this principle would be, that a general government shall do all those things which pertain to it, and all the local governments shall do precisely as they please in respect to these matters which exclusively concern them.

Douglas looks upon slavery as so insignificant that the people must decide that question for themselves, and yet they are not fit to decide who shall be their governor, judge, or secretary, or who shall be any of their officers. These are vast national matters, in his estimation, but the little matter in his estimation is that of planting slavery there. That is purely of local interest, which nobody should be allowed to say a word about.

FALSE AND TRUE IDEAS OF LABOR.

Labor is the great source from which nearly all, if not all, human comforts and necessities are drawn. There is a difference in opinion about the elements of labor in society. Some men assume that there is a necessary connection between capital and labor, and that connection draws within it the whole of the labor of the community. They assume that nobody works unless capital excites them to work. They begin next to consider what is the best way. They say there are but two ways; one is to hire men and to allure them to labor by their consent; the other is to buy the men and drive them to it, and that is slavery. Having assumed that, they proceed to discuss the question of whether the laborers themselves are better off in the condition of slaves or of hired laborers, and they usually decide that they are better off in the condition of slaves.

In the first place, I say that the whole thing is a mistake. That there is a certain relation between capital and labor, I admit. That it does exist, and rightfully exists, I think is true. That men who are industrious, and sober, and honest in the pursuit of their own interests should after awhile accumulate capital, and after that should be allowed to enjoy it in peace, and also if they should choose, when they have accumulated it, to use it to save themselves from actual labor, and hire other people to labor for them, is right. In doing so they do not wrong the man they employ, for they find men who have not of their own land to work upon, or shops to work in, and who are benefited by working for others, hired laborers, receiving their capital for it. Thus a few men that own capital, hire a few others, and these establish the relation of capital and labor rightfully. A relation of which I make no complaint. But I insist that that relation, after all, does not embrace more than one eighth of the labor of the country.

. . . .

Mr. Lincoln then proceeded to argue that the laborer owning himself, should have precedence over him who is forced to labor by an owner. He continued.

HOW FREE LABOR PRINCIPLES WILL TRIUMPH.

I have taken upon myself, in the name of some of you to say, that we expect upon these principles to ultimately beat them. In order to do so, I think we want and must have a national policy in regard to the institution of slavery, that acknowledges and deals with that institution as being wrong. Whoever desires the prevention of the spread of slavery and the nationalization of that institution, yields all, when he yields to any policy that either recognizes slavery as being right, or as being an indifferent thing. Nothing will make you successful but setting up a policy which shall treat the thing as being wrong. When I say this, I do not mean to say that this General Government is charged with the duty of redressing or preventing all the wrongs in the world; but I do think that it is charged w preventing and redressing all wrongs which are wrongs to itself. This Government is expressly charged with the duty of providing for the general welfare. We believe that the spreading out and perpetuity of the institution of slavery impairs the general welfare. We believe,—nay, we know, that that is the only thing that has ever threatened the perpetuity of the Union itself. The only thing which has ever menaced the destruction of the Government under which we live, is this very thing. To repress this thing, we think, is providing for the general welfare. Our friends in Kentucky differ from us. We need not make our argument for them, but we who think it is wrong in all its relations, or in some of them at least, must decide as to our own actions, and our own course, upon our own judgment.

WHAT WE MAY DO, AND WHAT NOT.

I say that we must not interfere with the institution of slavery in the States where it exists, because the Constitution forbids it, and the general welfare does not require us to do so. We must not withhold an efficient Fugitive Slave Law because the Constitution requires us, as I understand it, not to withhold such a law. But we must prevent the outspreading of the institution, because neither the Constitution nor general welfare requires us to extend it. We must prevent the revival of the African slave-trade, and the enacting by Congress of a territorial slave code. We must prevent each of these things being done by either congresses or courts. The people of these United States are the rightful masters of both congresses and courts, not to overthrow the Constitution, but to overthrow the men who pervert the Constitution.

To do these things we must employ instrumentalities. We must hold conventions; we must adopt platforms, if we conform to ordinary custom; we must nominate candidates, and we must carry elections. In all these things, I think that we ought to keep in view our real purpose, and in none do anything that stands adverse to our purpose. If we shall adopt a platform that fails to recognize or express our purpose, or elect a man that declares himself inimical to our purpose, we not only take nothing by our success, but we tacitly admit that we act upon no other principle than a desire to have "the loaves and fishes," by which, in the end, our apparent success is really an injury to us.

WHO SHOULD BE THE CANDIDATE.

I know that this is very desirable with me, as with everybody else, that all the elements of the Opposition shall unite in the next presidential election and in all future time. I am anxious that that should be, but there are things seriously to be considered in relation to that matter. If the terms can be arranged, I am in favor of the Union. But suppose we shall take up some man and put him upon one end or the other of the ticket, who declares himself against us in regard to the prevention of the spread of slavery; who turns up his nose and says he is tired of hearing anything more about it; who is more against us than against the enemy,—what will be the issue? Why, he will get no slave States, after all, — he has tried that already, until being beat is the rule for him. If we nominate him upon that ground, he will not carry a slave State, and not only so, but that portion of our men who are high-strung upon the principle we really fight for, will not go for him, and he won't get a single electoral vote anywhere, except, perhaps, in the State of Maryland. There is no use in saying to us that we are stubborn and obstinate, because we won't do some such thing as this. We cannot do it. We cannot get our men to vote it. I speak by the card, that we cannot give the State of Illinois in such case by fifty thousand. We should be flatter down than the "Negro Democracy" themselves have the heart to wish to see us.

"HE WHO GATHERETH NOT WITH US, SCATTERETH."

After saying this much, let me say a little on the other side. There are plenty of men in the slave States that are altogether good enough for me to be either President or Vice-President, provided they will profess their sympathy with our purpose, and will place themselves on the ground that our men, upon principle, can vote for them. There are scores of them, good men in their character for intelligence and talent and integrity. If such a one will place himself upon the right ground, I am for his occupying one place upon the next Republican or Opposition ticket. I will heartily go for him. But unless he does so place himself, I think it a matter of perfect nonsense to attempt to bring about a union upon any other basis, — that if a union be made, the elements will scatter so that there can be no success for such a ticket, nor anything like success. The good old maxims of the Bible are applicable, and truly applicable, to human affairs; and in this, as in other things, we may say here, that he who is not for us, is against us, — he who gathereth not with us, scattereth. I should be glad to have some of the many good, and able, and noble men of the South to place themselves where we can confer upon them the high honor of an election upon one or the other end of our ticket. It would do my soul good to do that thing. It would enable us to teach them that, inasmuch as we select one of their own number to carry out our principles, we are free from the charge that we mean more than we say.

But, my friends, I have detained you much longer than I expected to do. I believe I may do myself the compliment to say that you have stayed and heard me with great patience; for which I return you my most sincere thanks.

NATIONAL POLITICS AND THE REPUBLICAN PLATFORM.

DELIVERED AT THE COOPER INSTITUTE, NEW YORK, FEBRUARY 28, 1860.

THE SPEAKER'S PREMISES.

Mr. President and Fellow Citizens of New York: The facts with which I shall deal this evening are mainly old and familiar; nor is there anything new in the general use I shall make of them. If there shall be any novelty, it will be in the mode of presenting the facts, and the inferences and observations following that presentation. In his speech, last autumn, at Columbus, Ohio, as reported in the New York Times, Senator Douglas said: —

"Our fathers, when they framed the Government under which we live, understood this question just as well, and even better, than we do now."

I fully indorse this, and I adopt it as a text for this discourse. [Applause.] I so adopt it because it furnishes a precise and an agreed starting-point for a discussion between the Republicans and that wing of the Democracy headed by Senator Douglas. It simply leaves the inquiry, — What was the understanding those fathers had of the question mentioned? What is the frame of government under which we live? The answer must be, the Constitution of the United States. That Constitution consists of the original, framed in 1787, (and under which the present Government first went into operation,) and twelve subsequently framed amendments, the first ten of which were framed in 1789.

THE FATHERS OF THE CONSTITUTION.

Who were our fathers that framed the Constitution? The "thirty-nine" who signed the original instrument may be fairly called our fathers who framed that part of the present Government. It is almost exactly true to say they framed it, and it is altogether true to say they fairly represented the opinion and sentiment of the whole nation at that time. Their names being familiar to nearly all, and accessible to quite all, need not now be repeated. I take these "thirty-nine," for the present, as being "our fathers who framed the Government under which we live." What is the question which, according to the text, those fathers understood as well and even better than we do now? It is this: "Does the proper division of local from federal authority, or anything in the Constitution, forbid our Federal Government to control as to slavery in our federal territories?"

DOUGLAS AND LINCOLN.

Upon this Douglas held the affirmative, and Republicans the negative. The affirmative and denial form an issue; and this issue, this question, is precisely what the text declares our fathers understood better than we. [Cheers.] Let us now inquire whether the "thirty-nine," or any of them, ever acted upon this question; and if they did, how they acted upon it, — how they expressed that better understanding. In 1784, three years before the Constitution, the United States then owning the Northwestern Territory, and no other, the Congress of the Confederation had before them the question of prohibiting slavery in that territory; and four of the "thirty-nine" who afterwards framed the Constitution were in that Congress, and voted on that question. Of these, Roger Sherman, Thomas Mifflin, and Hugh Williamson voted for the prohibition, thus showing that, in their understanding, no line dividing local from federal authority, nor anything else, properly forbade the Federal Government to control as to slavery in federal territory.

The other of the four, James McHenry, voted against the

prohibition, showing that for some cause he thought it improper to vote for it. In 1787, still before the Constitution, but while the Convention was in session framing it, and while the Northwestern Territory still was the only territory owned by the United States, — the same question of prohibiting slavery in the territory again came before the Congress of the Confederation, and three more of the "thirty-nine" who afterwards signed the Constitution were in that Congress, and voted on that question. They were William Blount, William Few, and Abraham Baldwin, and they all voted for the prohibition, thus showing that, in their understanding, no line dividing local from federal authority, nor anything else, properly forbade the Federal Government to control as to slavery in federal territory.

THE ORDINANCE OF 1787.

This time the prohibition became a law, being a part of what is now well known as the Ordinance of 1787. The question of federal control of slavery in the territories seems not to have been directly before the Convention which framed the original Constitution; and hence it is not recorded that the "thirty-nine," or any of them, while engaged on that instrument, expressed any opinion on that precise question. In 1790, by the first Congress which sat under the Constitution, an act was passed to enforce the Ordinance of 1787, including the prohibition of slavery in the Northwestern Territory. The bill for this act was reported by one of the "thirty-nine," Thomas Fitzsimmons, then a member of the House of Representatives, from Pennsylvania. It went through all its stages without a word of opposition, and finally passed both branches without yeas and nays, which is equivalent to a unanimous passage. [Cheers.] In this Congress there were sixteen of the "thirty-nine" fathers who framed the original Constitution. They were

John Langdon, Thomas Fitzsimmons, Richard Bassett, Nicholas Gilman, Wm. Few, George Read, Wm. S. Johnson, Abraham Baldwin, Pierce Butler, Roger Sherman, Rufus King, Daniel Carroll, Robert Morris, Wm. Patterson, James Madison, George Clymer.

This shows that, in their understanding, no line dividing local from federal authority, nor anything in the Constitution, properly forbade Congress to prohibit slavery in the federal territory, else both their fidelity to correct principle, and their oath to support the Constitution would have constrained them to oppose the prohibition.

OPINION OF GEORGE WASHINGTON.

Again, George Washington, another of the "thirty-nine," was then the President of the United States, and, as such, approved and signed the bill, thus completing its validity as a law, and thus showing that, in his understanding, no line dividing local from federal authority, nor anything in the Constitution, forbade the Federal Government to control as to slavery in federal territory. [Loud applause.] No great while after the adoption of the original Constitution, North Carolina ceded to the Federal Government the country now constituting the State of Tennessee; and a few years later, Georgia ceded that which now constitutes the States of Mississippi and Alabama. In both deeds of session, it was made a condition by the ceding States, that the Federal Government should not prohibit slavery in the ceded country. Under these circumstances, Congress, on taking charge of these countries, did not absolutely prohibit slavery within them.

CONGRESS DID INTERFERE.

But they did interfere with it, — take control of it, — even there, to a certain extent. In 1798 Congress organized the Territory of Mississippi. In the act of organization they prohibited the bringing of slaves into the territory, from any place without the United States, by fine, and giving freedom to slaves so brought. This act passed both branches of Congress without yeas and nays. In that Congress were three of the "thirty-nine" who framed the original Constitution. They were John Langdon, George Read, and Abraham Baldwin. They all probably voted for it. Certainly they would have placed their opposition to it upon record, if, in their understanding, any line dividing local and federal authority, or anything in the Constitution, properly forbade the Federal Government to control as to slavery in federal territory. [Applause.]

In 1803, the Federal Government purchased the Louisiana country. Our former territorial acquisitions came from certain of our own States, but this Louisiana country was acquired from a foreign nation. In 1804, Congress gave a territorial organization to that part of it which now constitutes the State of Louisiana. New Orleans, lying within that part, was an old and comparatively large city. There were other considerable towns and settlements, and slavery was extensively and thoroughly intermingled with the people. Congress did not, in the territorial act, prohibit slavery; but they did interfere with it, take control of it, in a more marked and extensive way than they did in the case of Mississippi.

THE LOUISIANA PROVISO.

The substance of the provision therein made, in relation to slaves, was this: —

First. That no slave should be imported into the territory from foreign parts.

Second. That no slave should be carried into it who had been imported into the States since the first day of May, 1798.

Third. That no slave should be carried into it, except by the owner, and for his own use as a settler; the penalty, in all the cases, being a fine upon the violator of the law, and the freedom to the slave. [Prolonged cheers.]

This act also was passed without yeas or nays. In the Congress which passed it, there were two of the "thirty-nine." They were Abraham Baldwin and Jonathan Dayton. As stated in the case of Mississippi, it is probable they both voted for it. They would not have allowed it to pass without recording their opposition to it, if, in their understanding, it violated either the line properly dividing local from federal authority, or any provision of the Constitution. Many votes were taken, by yeas and nays, in both branches of Congress, upon the various phases of the general question. Two of the "thirty-nine," Rufus King and Charles Pinckney, were members of that Congress. Mr. King steadily voted for slavery prohibition, and against all compromises, while Mr. Pinckney has steadily voted against slavery prohibition, and against all compromises. [Cheers.] By this, Mr. King showed that, in his understanding, no line dividing local from federal authority, nor anything in the Constitution, was violated by Congress prohibiting slavery in federal territory, while Mr. Pinckney, by his votes, showed that, in his understanding, there was some sufficient reason for opposing such prohibition in that case.

THE FATHERS ON RECORD.

The cases I have mentioned are the only acts of the "thirty-nine," or any of them, upon the direct issue, which I have been able to discover. To enumerate the persons who thus acted, as being four in 1784, three in 1787, seventeen in 1789, three in 1798, two in 1804, and two in 1819–20, there would be thirty-one of them. But this would be counting John Langdon, Roger Sherman, William Few, Rufus King, and George Read, each twice, and Abraham Baldwin four times. [Applause.] He was a Georgian, too. [Renewed applause and laughter.] The true number of those of the "thirty-nine" whom I have shown to have acted upon the question, which, by the text, they understood better than we, is twenty-three, leaving sixteen not to have acted upon it in any way. Here, then, we have twenty-three of our "thirty-nine" fathers, who framed the Government under which we live, who have, upon their official responsibility and their corporal oaths, acted upon the very question which the text affirms they "understood just as well, and even better than we do now," and twenty-one of them — a clear majority of the whole thirty-nine — so acting upon it as to make them guilty of gross political impropriety and wilful perjury, if, in their understanding, any proper division between local and federal authority, or anything in the Constitution they had made themselves, and sworn to support, forbade the Federal Government to control as to slavery in the federal territories. [Cheers.] Thus the twenty-one acted; and as actions speak louder than words, so actions under such responsibility speak still louder. Two of the twenty-three voted against the congressional prohibition of slavery in the federal territories, in the instances in which they acted upon the question. But for what reason they so voted is not known. They may have done so because they thought a proper division of local from federal authority, or some provision or principle of the Constitution, stood in the way; or they may, without any such question, have voted against the prohibition, or what appeared to them to be sufficient grounds of expediency.

THE RESPONSIBILITY OF THE OATH TO SUPPORT THE CONSTITUTION.

No one who has sworn to support the Constitution can conscientiously vote for what he understands to be an unconstitutional measure, however expedient he may think it; but one may and ought to vote against a measure which he deems constitutional, if, at the same time, he deems it inexpedient. It therefore would be unsafe to set down even the two who voted against the prohibition, as having done so because, in their understanding, any proper division of local from federal authority, or anything in the Constitution, forbade the Federal Government to control as to slavery in federal territory. [Laughter and prolonged applause.] The remaining sixteen of the "thirty-nine," so far as I have discovered, have left no record of their understanding upon the direct question of federal control of slavery in the federal territories.

But there is much reason to believe that their understanding upon that question would not have appeared different from that of their twenty-three compeers, had it been manifested at all.

For the purpose of adhering rigidly to the text, I have purposely omitted whatever understanding may have been manifested by any person, however distinguished, other than the thirty-nine fathers who framed the original Constitution; and, for the same reason, I have also admitted whatever understanding may have been manifested by any of the "thirty-nine" even, on any other phase of the general question of slavery. If we should look into their acts and declarations on those other phases, as the foreign slave-trade, and the morality and policy of slavery generally, it would appear to us, that on the direct question of federal control of slavery in the federal territories, the sixteen, if they had acted at all, would probably have acted just as the twenty-three did.

ANTI-SLAVERY MEN OF THE LAST CENTURY.

Among that sixteen were several of the most noted anti-slavery men of those times, — as Dr. Franklin, Alexander Hamilton, and Gouverneur Morris,—while there was not one now known to have been otherwise, unless it may be John Rutledge, of South Carolina. [Applause.] The sum of the whole is, that of our "thirty-nine" fathers who framed the original Constitution, twenty-one, — a clear majority of the whole, — certainly understood that no proper division of local from federal authority, nor any part of the Constitution, forbade the Federal Government to control slavery in the federal territories, while all the rest, probably, had the same understanding. Such, unquestionably, was the understanding of our fathers who framed the original Constitution; and the text affirms that they understood the question better than we. [Laughter and cheers.]

But, so far, I have been considering the understanding of the question manifested by the framers of the original Constitution. In and by the original instrument, a mode was provided for amending it; and, as I have already stated, the present frame of government under which we live consists of that original, and twelve amendatory articles framed and adopted since. Those who now insist that federal control of slavery in federal territories violates the Constitution, point us to the provisions which they suppose it thus violates; and, as I understand, they all fix upon provisions in these amendatory articles, and not in that instrument.

THE SUPREME COURT IN THE DRED SCOTT CASE.

The Supreme Court in the Dred Scott case plant themselves upon the first amendment, which provides that "no person shall be deprived of property, without due process of law;" while Senator Douglas, and his peculiar adherents, plant themselves upon the tenth amendment, providing that "the powers not granted by the Constitution are reserved to the States respectively and to the people." Now, it so happens that these amendments were framed by the first Congress which sat under the Constitution,—the identical Congress which passed the act already mentioned, enforcing the prohibition of slavery in the Northwestern Territory. [Applause.] Not only was it the same Congress, but they were the identical same individual men who, at the same session, at the same time within the session, had under consideration, and in progress towards maturity, these constitutional amendments, and this act prohibiting slavery in all the territory the nation then owned.

The constitutional amendments were introduced before and passed after the act of enforcing the Ordinance of '87; so that during the whole pendency of the act to enforce the ordinance, the constitutional amendments were also pending. That Congress, consisting in all of seventy-six members, including sixteen of the framers of the original Constitution, as before stated, were pre-eminently our fathers who framed that part of the Government under which we live, which is now claimed as forbidding the Federal Government to control slavery in the federal territories. Is it not a little presumptuous in any one at this day to affirm that the two things which that Congress deliberately framed, and carried to maturity at the same time, are absolutely inconsistent with each other?

THE ABSURDITY OF CHARGING INCONSISTENCY UPON THE FATHERS.

And does not such affirmation become impudently absurd when coupled with the other affirmation, from the same mouth, that those who did the things alleged to be inconsistent understood whether they really were inconsistent better than we, — better than he who affirms that they are inconsistent? [Applause and great merriment.] It is surely safe to assume that the "thirty-nine" framers of the original Constitution, and the seventy-six members of the Congress which framed the amendments thereto, taken altogether, do certainly include those who may be fairly called "our fathers who framed the government under which we live." And so assuming, I defy any man to show that any one of them ever in his whole life declared that, in his understanding, any proper division of local from federal authority, or any part of the Constitution, forbade the Federal Government to control as to slavery in the federal territories. [Loud applause.]

I go a step further. I defy any one to show that any living man in the whole world, ever did, prior to the beginning of the present century, (and I might almost say prior to the beginning of the last half of the present century,) declare that, in his understanding, any proper division of local from federal authority, or any part of the Constitution, forbade the Federal Government to control as to slavery in the federal territories. To those who so now declare, I give, not only "our fathers who framed the government under which we live," but with them all other living men within the century in which it was framed, among them to search, and they shall not be able to find the evidence of a single man agreeing with them. Now and here, let me guard a little against being misunderstood.

MODERN DOCTRINES FALSE AND DECEPTIVE.

I do not mean to say we are bound to follow implicity in whatever our fathers did. To do so would be to discard all the lights of current experience, — to reject all progress, all improvement.

What I do say is, that if we would supplant the opinions and policy of our fathers, in any case, we should do so upon evidence so conclusive, and argument so clear, that even their great authority, fairly considered and weighed, cannot stand; and most surely not in a case whereof we ourselves declare they understood the question better than we. [Laughter.] If any man, at this day, sincerely believes that a proper division of local from federal authority, or any part of the Constitution, forbids the Federal Government to control as to slavery in the federal territories, he is right to say so, and to enforce his position by all truthful evidence and fair argument which he can. But he has no right to mislead others, who have less access to history and less leisure to study it, into the false belief that "our fathers, who framed the government under which we live," were of the same opinion, — thus substituting falsehood and deception for truthful evidence and fair argument. [Applause.] If any man at this day sincerely believes "our fathers who framed the government under which we live," used and applied principles, in other cases, which ought to have led them to understand that a proper division of local from federal authority, or some part of the Constitution, forbids the federal government to control as to slavery in the federal territories, he is right to say so. But he should, at the same time, brave the responsibility of declaring that, in his opinion, he understands their principles better than they did themselves, — [great laughter,] — and especially should he not shirk that responsibility by asserting that they "understood the question just as well, and even better, than we do now." [Applause.]

WHAT REPUBLICANS ASK AND DESIRE.

But enough. Let all who believe that our "fathers, who framed the government under which we live, understood this question just as well, and even better than we do now," speak as they spoke, and act as they acted upon it. This is all Republicans ask, — all Republicans desire in relation to slavery. As those fathers marked it, so let it be again marked, as an evil not to be extended, but to be tolerated, and protected only because of and so far as its actual presence among us make that toleration and protection a necessity. [Loud applause.] Let all the guarantees those fathers gave it, be not grudgingly, but fully and fairly maintained. For this Republicans contend, and with this, so far as I know or believe, they will be content. [Applause.]

And now, if they would listen — as I suppose they will not — I would address a few words to the Southern people. [Laughter.] I would say to them: You consider yourselves a reasonable and a just people, and I consider that in the general qualities of reason and justice you are not inferior to any other people; still, when you speak of us Republicans, you do so only to denounce us as reptiles, or, at the best, as no better than outlaws. You will grant a hearing to pirates or murderers, but nothing like it to "Black Republicans." [Laughter.]

THE REPUBLICAN PARTY NOT SECTIONAL

In all your contentions with one another, each of you deem an unconditional condemnation of "Black Republicanism" as the first thing to be attended to. [Laughter.] Indeed, such condemnation of us seems to be an indispensable prerequisite— license, so to speak —among you to be admitted or permitted to speak at all. Now, can you or not be prevailed upon to pause and to consider whether this is quite just to us, or even to yourselves? Bring forward your charges and specifications, and then be patient long enough to hear us deny or justify. You say we are sectional. We deny it. [Loud applause.] That makes an issue, and the burden of proof is upon you. [Laughter and applause.] You produce your proof: and what is it? Why, that our party has no existence in your section, — gets no votes in your section. The fact is substantially true; but does it prove the issue? If it does, then, in case we should, without change of principle, begin to get votes in your section, we should thereby cease to be sectional. [Great merriment.] You cannot escape this conclusion; and yet, are you willing to abide by it? If you are, you will probably soon find that we have ceased to be sectional, for we shall get votes in your section this very year. [Loud cheers.] You will then begin to discover, as the truth plainly is, that your proof does not touch the issue. The fact that we get no votes in your section is a fact of your making, and not ours. As if there be fault in that fact, that fault is primarily yours, and remains until you show that we repel you by some wrong principle or practice. If we do repel you by any wrong principle, the fault is ours; but this brings you to where you ought to have started, — to a discussion of the right or wrong of our principle. [Loud applause.]

WASHINGTON'S FAREWELL ADDRESS.

If our principle, put in practice, would wrong your section for the benefit of ours, or for any other object, then our principle, and we with it, are sectional, and are justly opposed and denounced as such. Meet us, then, on the question of whether our principle, put in practice, would wrong your section; and so meet it as if it were possible that something may be said on our side. [Laughter.] Do you accept the challenge? No. Then you really believe that the principle which our fathers, who framed the government under which we live, thought so clearly right as to adopt it, and indorse it again and again, upon their official oaths, is, in fact, so clearly wrong as to demand your condemnation without a moment's consideration. [Applause.]

Some of you delight to flaunt in our faces the warning against sectional parties given by Washington in his Farewell Address. Less than eight years before Washington gave that warning, he had, as President of the United States, approved and signed an act of Congress, enforcing the prohibition of slavery in the Northwestern Territory, which act embodied the policy of the Government upon that subject, up to and at the very moment he penned that warning; and about one year after he penned it, he wrote to Lafayette that he considered that prohibition a wise measure, expressing in the same connection his hope that we should some time have a confederacy of free States. [Applause.] Bearing this in mind, and seeing that sectionalism has since arisen upon this same subject, is that warning a weapon in your hands against us, or in our hands against you? Could Washington himself speak, would he cast the blame of that sectionalism upon us who sustain his policy, or upon you who repudiate it? [Applause.] We respect that warning of Washington, and we commend it to you, together with his example, pointing to the right application of it. [Applause.] But you say you are conservative,—eminently conservative,—while we are revolutionary, destructive, or something of the sort.

POLITICAL CONSERVATISM.

What is conservatism? Is it not adherence to the old and tried, against the new and untried? We stick to, contend for, the identical old policy, on the point in controversy, which was adopted by our fathers who framed the government under which we live; while you with one accord reject, and scout, and spit upon the old policy, and insist upon substituting something new. True, you disagree among yourselves as of what that substitute shall be. You have a variety of new propositions and plans, but you are unanimous in rejecting and denouncing the old policy of the fathers. Some of you are for reviving the foreign slave-trade; some for a congressional slave code for the territories; some for Congress forbidding the territories from prohibiting slavery within their limits; some for maintaining slavery in the territories through the judiciary; some for the "gur-reat pur-rinciple" — [laughter] — that "if one man would enslave another, no third man should object," fantastically called "popular sovereignty," — [renewed laughter and applause,] — but never a man among you in favor of federal prohibition of slavery in federal territories, according to the practice of our fathers, who framed the government under which we live.

Not one of your various plans can show a precedent or an advocate in the century within which our Government originated.

Consider, then, whether your claim of conservatism for yourselves, and your charge of destructiveness against us, are based on the most clear and stable foundations. Again, you say we have made the slavery question more prominent than formerly. We deny it. We admit that it is more prominent, but we deny that we made it so. It was not we, but you, who discarded the old policy of the fathers. We resisted, and still resist, your innovation, your want of conservatism, and thence comes the greater prominence of the question. Would you have that question reduced to its former proportions? Go back to that old policy. What has been, will be again, under the same conditions. If you would have the peace of the old times, readopt the precepts and policy of the old times. [Applause.]

JOHN BROWN AND HARPER'S FERRY.

You charge that we stir up insurrection among your slaves. We deny it; and what is your proof? Harper's Ferry! [Great laughter.] John Brown! [Renewed laughter.] John Brown was no Republican, and you have failed to implicate a single Republican in his Harper's Ferry enterprise. [Loud applause.] If any member of our party is guilty in that matter, you know it, or you do not know it. If you do know it, you are inexcusable to not designate the man, and prove the fact. If you do not know it, you are inexcusable to assert it, and especially to persist in the assertion after you have tried and failed to make the proof. [Great applause.] You need not be told that persisting in a charge which one does not know to be true is simply a malicious slander. [Applause.] Some of you generously admit that no Republican designedly aided or encouraged the Harper's Ferry affair, but still insist that our doctrines and declarations necessarily lead to such results. We know we hold no doctrines, and make no declarations, which were not held to and made by our fathers, who framed the government under which we live. [Applause.] You never dealt fairly by us in relation to this affair.

EFFECTS OF THE INVASION ON LATE ELECTIONS.

When it occurred, some important State elections were near at hand, and you were in evident glee with the belief that, by charging the blame upon us, you could get an advantage of us in those elections. The elections came, and your expectations were not quite fulfilled. [Laughter.] You did not sweep New York, and New Jersey, and Wisconsin, and Minnesota, precisely like fire sweeps over the prairie in high wind. [Laughter.] You are still drumming at this idea. Go on with it. If you think you can, by slandering a woman, make her love you, or by vilifying a man make him vote with you, go on and try it. [Boisterous laughter, and prolonged applause.] Every Republican man knew that, as to himself, at least, your charge was a slander, and he was not much inclined by it to cast his vote in your favor.

Republican doctrines and declarations are accompanied with a continual protest against any interference whatever with your slaves, or with you about your slaves. Surely, this does not encourage them to revolt. True, we do, in common with our fathers, who framed the government under which we live, declare our belief that slavery is wrong; [applause ;] but the slaves do not hear us declare even this; for everything we say or do, the slaves would scarcely know there is a Republican party. I believe they would not, in fact, generally know it but for your misrepresentation of us in their hearing. In your political contests among yourselves, each faction charged the other with sympathy for the Black Republicans; and then, to give point to the charge, define Black Republicanism to be simply insurrection, blood and thunder among the slaves. [Boisterous laughter and applause.]

SLAVE INSURRECTIONS.

Slave insurrections are no more common now than they were before the Republican party was organized. What induced the Southampton insurrection, twenty years ago, in which, at least, three times as many lives were lost as at Harper's Ferry? You can scarcely stretch your very elastic fancy to the conclusion that Southampton was got up by Black Republicanism. [Laughter.] In the present state of things in the United States, I do not think a general or even a very extensive slave insurrection, is possible. The indispensable concert of action cannot be obtained. The slaves have no means of rapid communication; nor can incendiary free men, black or white, supply it. The explosive materials are everywhere in parcels, but there neither are nor can be supplied the indispensable connecting trains.

Much is said by Southern people about the affection of slaves for their masters and mistresses, and a part of it, at least, is true. A plot for an uprising could scarcely be devised and communicated to twenty individuals, before some one of them, to save the life of a favorite master or mistress, would divulge it. This is the rule; and the slave revolution in Hayti was not an exception to it, but a case occurring under peculiar circumstances. The gunpowder plot of British history, though not connected with slaves, was more in point. In this case, only about twenty were admitted to the secret, and yet one of them, in his anxiety to save a friend, betrayed the plot to that friend, and, by consequence, averted the calamity. Occasional poisonings from the kitchen, and open or stealthy assassinations in the field, and local revolts extending to a score or so, will continue to occur as the natural results of slavery; but no general insurrection of slaves, as I think, can happen in this country for a long time. Whoever much fears, or much hopes, for such an event, will be alike disappointed.

THE NATIONAL JUDGMENT AND FEELING.

There is a judgment and feeling against slavery in this nation which cast, at least, a million and a half of votes. You cannot destroy that judgment and feeling, that sentiment, by breaking up the political organization which rallies around it. You can scarcely scatter and disperse an army which has been formed into order in the heaviest fire, but, if you could, how much would you gain by forcing the sentiment which created it out of the peaceful channel of the ballot-box into some other channel? What would that other channel probably be? Would the number of John Browns be lessened or enlarged by the operation? But you will break up the Union, rather than submit to a denial of your constitutional rights. That has a somewhat reckless sound; but it would be palliated, if not fully justified, were we proposing, by mere force of numbers, to deprive you of some right plainly written down in the Constitution. But we are proposing no such thing. When you make these declarations, you have a specific and well-understood allusion to an assumed constitutional right of yours to take slaves into the federal territories, and to hold them there as property.

SILENCE OF THE CONSTITUTION AS TO THE RIGHT OF TAKING SLAVES INTO THE TERRITORIES.

But no such right is specifically written in this Constitution. That instrument is literally silent about any such right. We, on the contrary, deny that such a right has any existence in the Constitution, even by implication. [Applause.] Your purpose, then, plainly stated, is, that you will destroy the Government, unless you be allowed to construe and enforce the Constitution as you please, on all points in dispute between you and us. You will ruin or rule in all events. This, plainly stated, is your language to us. Perhaps you will say the Supreme Court has decided the disputed constitutional question in your favor. Not quite so. But waving the lawyers' distinction between dictum and decision, the Court have decided the question for you in a sort of way. The Court substantially said, it is your constitutional right to take slaves into the federal territories, and to hold them there as property. When I say the decision was made in a sort of a way, I mean it was made in a divided court by a bare majority of the judges, and they not quite agreeing with one another in the reasons for making it; that it is so made as that its avowed supporters disagree with one another about its meaning; and that was mainly based upon a mistaken statement of fact, — the statement in the opinion that "the right of property in a slave is distinctly and expressly affirmed in the Constitution."

SLAVES CONSIDERED AS PERSONS AND NOT AS PROPERTY.

An inspection of the Constitution will show that the right of property in a slave is not distinctly and expressly affirmed in it. [Applause.] Bear in mind, the judges do not pledge their judicial opinion that such a right is impliedly affirmed in the Constitution, but they pledge their veracity that it is distinctly and expressly affirmed there — "distinctly" — that it is not mingled with anything else — expressly, that is, in words meaning just that without the aid of any inference, and susceptible of no other meaning. If they had only pledged their judicial opinion that such right is affirmed in the instrument by implication, it would be open to others to show that neither the word "slave" nor "slavery" is to be found in the Constitution, nor the word "property" even, in any connection with language alluding to the things, slave or slavery, [applause,] and that wherever in that instrument the slave is alluded to, he is called a "person," and wherever his master's legal right in relation to him is alluded to, it is spoken of as "service or labor due," as a "debt" payable in service and labor. Also, it would be open to show, by contemporaneous history, that this mode of alluding to slaves and slavery, instead of speaking of them, was employed on purpose to exclude from the Constitution the idea that there could be property in man.

THE SUPREME COURT TO RECONSIDER THEIR DECISION.

To show all this is easy and certain. When this obvious mistake of the judges shall be brought to their notice, is it not reasonable to expect that they will withdraw the mistaken statement, and reconsider the conclusion based upon it? And then it is to be remembered that "our fathers, who framed the government under which we live,"—the men who made the Constitution,—decided this same constitutional question in our favor long ago,—decided it without a division among themselves, when making the decision; without division among themselves about the meaning of it after it was made; and, so far as any evidence is left, without basing it upon any mistaken statement of facts. Under all these circumstances, do you really feel yourselves justified to break up this Government, unless such a court decision of yours is, shall be at once submitted to as a conclusive and final rule of political action?

DISSOLUTION OF THE UNION.

But you will not abide the election of a Republican President. In that supposed event, you say you will destroy the Union; and then, you say, the great crime of having destroyed it will be upon us! [Laughter.] That is cool. [Great laughter.] A highwayman holds a pistol to my ear, and mutters through his teeth, "Stand and deliver, or I shall kill you, and you will be a murderer!" [Continued laughter.] To be sure, what the robber demanded of me—my money—was my own, and I had a clear right to keep it; but it was no more my own than my vote is my own,—["That's so," and applause,]—and the threat of death to me, to extort my money, and the threat of destruction to the Union, to extort my vote, can scarcely be distinguished in principle.

A few words now to Republicans. It is exceedingly desirable that all parts of this great confederacy shall be at peace and harmony one with another. Let us Republicans do our part to have it so. ["We will," and applause.] Even though much provoked, let us do nothing through passion and ill-temper. Even though the Southern people will not so much as listen to us, let us calmly consider their demands, and yield to them, if in our deliberate view of our duty we possibly can. Judging by all they say and do, and by the subject and nature of their controversy with us, let us determine, if we can, what will satisfy them. Will they be satisfied if the territories be unconditionally surrendered to them? We know they will not. In all their present complaints against us, the territories are scarcely mentioned. Invasions and insurrections are the rage now. Will it satisfy them if, in the future, we have nothing to do with invasions and insurrections? We know it will not. We so know because we know we never had anything to do with invasions and insurrections; and yet this total abstaining does not exempt us from the charge and the denunciation.

THE DIFFERENCE OF OPINION.

The question recurs, What will satisfy them? Simply this: We must not only let them alone, but, we trust, somehow convince them that we do let them alone. This, we know by experience, is no easy task. We have been trying to so convince them from the very beginning of our organization, but with no success. In all our platforms and speeches, we have constantly protested our purpose to let them alone; but this has had no tendency to convince them. Alike unavailing to convince them, is the fact that they have never detected a man of us in any attempt to disturb them. These natural and apparently adequate means all failing, what will convince them? This, and this only: Cease to call slavery wrong, and join them in calling it right. And this must be done thoroughly, — done in acts as well as in words. Silence will not be tolerated,—we must place ourselves avowedly with them. Douglas's new sedition law must be enacted and enforced, suppressing all declarations that slavery is wrong, whether made in politics, in presses, in pulpits, or in private. We must arrest and return their fugitive slaves with greedy pleasure; we must pull down our free State constitutions; the whole atmosphere must be disinfected from all taint of opposition to slavery, before they will cease to believe that all their troubles proceed from us. I am quite aware they do not state their case precisely in this way. Most of them would probably say to us, "Let us alone, do nothing to us, and say what you please about slavery." But we do let them alone, — have never disturbed them, — so that, after all, it is what we say which dissatisfies them. They will continue to accuse us of doing, until we cease saying. I am also aware they have not as yet, in terms, demanded the overthrow of our free State constitutions.

THE GIST OF THE CONTROVERSY.

Yet those constitutions declare the wrong of slavery with more solemn emphasis than do all sayings against it; and, when all these other sayings shall have been silenced, the overthrow of these constitutions will be demanded, and nothing be left to resist the demand. It is nothing to the contrary that they do not demand the whole of this just now. Demanding what they do, and for the reason they do, they can voluntarily stop nowhere short of this consummation. Holding as they do, that slavery is morally right and socially elevating, they cannot cease to demand a full national recognition of it as a legal right and a social blessing. [Applause.] Nor can we justifiably withhold this on any ground save our conviction that slavery is wrong.

If slavery is right, all words, acts, laws, and constitutions against it are themselves wrong, and should be silenced and swept away. If it is right, we cannot justly object to its nationality, — its universality; if it is wrong, they cannot justly insist upon its extension, — its enlargement. All they ask we could readily grant, if we thought slavery right; all we ask, they could as readily grant, if they thought it wrong. Their thinking it right, and our thinking it wrong, is the precise fact upon which depends the whole controversy. Thinking it right, as they do, they are not to blame for desiring its full recognition, as being right; but thinking it wrong, as we do, can we yield to them? Can we cast our votes with this view, and against our own? In view of our moral, social, and political responsibilities, can we do this? [" No, no," and applause.]

SLAVERY NOT TO BE INTERFERED WITH WHERE IT ALREADY EXISTS.

Wrong as we think slavery is, we can yet afford to let it alone where it is, because that much is due to the necessity arising from its actual presence in the nation; but can we, while our votes will prevent it, allow it to spread into the national territories, and to overrun us here in these free States? ["No, never," and applause. A voice — "Guess not." Laughter.] If our sense of duty forbids this, then let us stand by our duty, fearlessly and effectively. Let us be diverted by none of those sophistical contrivances wherewith we are so industriously plied and belabored, — contrivances such as groping for some middle ground, between the right and the wrong, vain as the search for a man who should be neither a living man nor a dead man, — such as a policy of "don't care" on a question about which all men care,—such as Union appeals, beseeching true Union men to yield to disunionists, reversing the divine rule, and calling, not the sinners, but the righteous to repentance, — [prolonged cheers and laughter,] — such as invocations of Washington, imploring men to unsay what Washington said, and undo what Washington did. Neither let us be slandered from our duty by false accusations against us, nor frightened from it by menaces of destruction to the Government nor of dungeons to ourselves. [Applause.] Let us have faith that right makes might; and in that faith let us, to the end, dare to do our duty as we understand it.

THE ILLINOIS SENATORIAL CANVASS.

We extract from the various speeches of Mr. Lincoln, during the debates between himself and Judge Douglas, the following passages.

JEFFERSON, AND THE RIGHTS OF THE AFRICAN.

The Judge has alluded to the Declaration of Independence, and insisted that negroes are not included in that Declaration; and that it is a slander upon the framers of that instrument, to suppose that negroes were meant therein; and he asks you: Is it possible to believe that Mr. Jefferson, who penned the immortal paper, could have supposed himself applying the language of that instrument to the negro race, and yet held a portion of that race in slavery? Would he not at once have freed them? I only have to remark upon this part of the Judge's speech, (and that, too, very briefly, for I shall not detain myself, or you, upon that point for any great length of time,) that I believe the entire records of the world, from the date of the Declaration of Independence, up to within three years ago, may be searched in vain for one single affirmation, from one single man, that the negro was not included in the Declaration of Independence. I think I may defy Judge Douglas to show that he ever said so, that Washington ever said so, that any President ever said so, that any member of Congress ever said so, or that any living man upon the whole earth ever said so, until the necessities of the present policy of the Democratic party, in regard to slavery, had to invent that affirmation. And I will remind Judge Douglas and this audience, that while Mr. Jefferson was the owner of slaves, as undoubtedly he was, in speaking upon this very subject, he used the strong language that "he trembled for his country, when he remembered God was just;" and I will offer the highest premium in my power to Judge Douglas if he will show that he, in all his life, ever uttered a sentiment at all akin to that of Jefferson.

DOUGLAS'S NEGROPHOBIA.

Douglas accused his opponent of making speeches to suit the different opinions of the communities in which he spoke. Mr. Lincoln thus disposes of the statement.

Now a few words in regard to these extracts from speeches of mine which Judge Douglas has read to you, and which he supposes are in very great contrast to each other. Those speeches have been before the public for a considerable time, and if they have any inconsistency in them, if there is any conflict in them, the public have been able to detect it. When the Judge says, in speaking on this subject, that I make speeches of one sort for the people of the northern end of the State, and of a different sort for the Southern people, he assumes that I do not understand that my speeches will be put in print and read North and South. I knew all the while that the speech I made at Chicago, and the one I made at Jonesboro', and the one at Charleston, would all be put in print, and all the reading and intelligent men in the community would see them and know all about my opinions. And I have not supposed, and do not now suppose, that there is any conflict whatever between them. But the Judge will have it, that if we do not confess that there is a sort of inequality between the white and the black races, which justifies us in making them slaves, we must, then, insist that there is a degree of equality that requires us to make them our wives. Now, I have all the while taken a broad distinction in regard to that matter; and that is all there is in these different speeches which he arrays here, and the entire reading of either of the speeches will show that that distinction was made. Perhaps, by taking two parts of the same speech, he could have got up as much of a conflict as the one he has found. I have all the while maintained, that in so far as it should be insisted that there was an equality between the white and black races that should produce a perfect social and political equality, it was an impossibility. This you have seen in my printed speeches, and with it I have said, that in their right to "life, liberty, and the pursuit of happiness," as proclaimed in that old declaration, the inferior races are our equals. And these declarations I have constantly made in reference to the abstract moral question, to contemplate and consider when we are legislating about any new country which is not already cursed with the actual presence of the evil, slavery. I have never manifested any impatience with the necessities that spring from the actual presence of black people amongst us, and the actual existence of slavery amongst us where it does already exist; but I have insisted that, in legislating for new countries, where it does not exist, there is no just rule other than that of moral and abstract right! With reference to those new countries, those maxims as to the right of a people to "life, liberty, and the pursuit of happiness," were the just rules to be constantly referred to. There is no misunderstanding this, except by men interested to misunderstand it. I take it that I have to address an intelligent and reading community, who will peruse what I say, weigh it, and then judge whether I advance improper or unsound views, or whether I advance hypocritical, and deceptive, and contrary views in different portions of the country. I believed myself to be guilty of no such thing as the latter, though, of course, I cannot claim that I am entirely free from all error in the opinions I advance.

THE REPUBLICAN AND DOUGLAS SECTIONALISM.

The Judge has also detained us awhile in regard to the distinction between his party and our party. His he assumes to be a national party, — ours a sectional one. He does this in asking the question whether this country has any interest in the maintenance of the Republican party. He assumes that our party is altogether sectional, — that the party to which he adheres is national; and the argument is, that no party can be a rightful party,—can be based upon rightful principles,—unless it can announce its principles everywhere. I presume that Judge Douglas could not go into Russia and announce the doctrine of our national Democracy; he could not denounce the doctrine of kings and emperors and monarchies in Russia; and it may be true of this country, that in some places we may not be able to proclaim a doctrine as clearly true as the truth of Democracy, because there is a section so directly opposed to it that they will not tolerate us in doing so. Is it the true test of the soundness of a doctrine, that in some places people won't let you proclaim it? Is that the way to test the truth of any doctrine? Why, I understood that at one time the people of Chicago would not let Judge Douglas preach a certain favorite doctrine of his. I commend to his consideration the question, whether he takes that as a test of the unsoundness of what he wanted to preach..

There is another thing to which I wish to ask attention for a little while on this occasion. What has always been the evidence brought forward to prove that the Republican party is a sectional party? The main one was that, in the Southern portion of the Union, the people did not let the Republicans proclaim their doctrines amongst them. That has been the main evidence brought forward,—that they had no supporters, or substantially none, in the slave States. The South has not taken hold of our principles as we announce them; nor does Judge Douglas now grapple with those principles. We have a Republican State platform, laid down in Springfield in June last, stating our position all the way through the questions before the country. We are now far advanced in this canvass. Judge Douglas and I have made perhaps forty speeches apiece, and we have now for the fifth time met face to face in debate, and up to this day I have not found either Judge Douglas or any friend of his taking hold of the Republican platform, or laying his finger upon anything in it that is wrong. I ask you all to recollect that. Judge Douglas turns away from the platform of principles to the fact that he can find people somewhere who will not allow us to announce those principles. If he had great confidence that our principles were wrong, he would take hold of them and demonstrate them to be wrong. But he does not do so. The only evidence he has of their being wrong is in the fact that there are people who won't allow us to preach them. I ask again, is that the way to test the soundness of a doctrine?

I ask his attention also to the fact that by the rule of nationality he is himself fast becoming sectional. I ask his attention to the fact that his speeches would not go as current now south of the Ohio River as they have formerly gone there. I ask his attention to the fact that he felicitates himself to-day that all the Democrats of the free States are agreeing with him, while he omits to tell us that the Democrats of any slave State agree with him. If he has not thought of this, I commend to his consideration the evidence in his own declaration, on this day, of his becoming sectional too. I see it rapidly approaching. Whatever may be the result of this ephemeral contest between Judge Douglas and myself, I see the day rapidly approaching when his pill of sectionalism, which he has been thrusting down the throats of Republicans for years past, will be crowded down his own throat

THE VITAL DISTINCTION.

The Judge tells, in proceeding, that he is opposed to making any odious distinctions between free and slave States. I am altogether unaware that the Republicans are in favor of making any odious distinction between the free and slave States. But there still is a difference, I think, between Judge Douglas and the Republicans, in this. I suppose that the real difference between Judge Douglas and his friends, and the Republicans, on the contrary, is that the Judge is not in favor of making any difference between slavery and liberty, — that he is in favor of eradicating, of pressing out of view, the questions of preference in this country for free or slave institutions; and consequently every sentiment he utters discards the idea that there is any wrong in slavery. Everything that emanates from him or his coadjutors in their course of policy, carefully excludes the thought that there is anything wrong in slavery. All their arguments, if you will consider them, will be seen to exclude the thought that there is anything whatever wrong in slavery. If you will take the Judge's speeches, and select the short and pointed sentences expressed by him, — as his declaration that he "don't care whether slavery is voted up or down," — you will see at once that this is perfectly logical, if you do not admit that slavery is wrong. If you do admit that it is wrong, Judge Douglas cannot logically say he don't care whether a wrong is voted up or voted down. Judge Douglas declares that if any community want slavery, they have a right to have it. He can say that logically, if he says that there is no wrong in slavery; but if you admit that there is a wrong in it, he cannot logically say that anybody has a right to do wrong. He insists that, upon the score of equality, the owners of slaves and owners of property, — of horses and every other sort of property, — should be alike and hold them alike in a new territory. That is perfectly logical, if the two species of property are alike, and are equally founded in right. But if you admit that one of them is wrong, you cannot institute any equality between right and wrong. And from this difference of sentiment, — the belief on the part of one that the institution is wrong, and a policy springing from that belief which looks to the arrest of the enlargement of that wrong; and this other sentiment, that it is no wrong, and a policy sprung from that sentiment which will tolerate no idea of preventing that wrong from growing larger, and looks to there never being an end of it through all the existence of things, — arises the real difference between Judge Douglas and his friends on the one hand, and the Republicans on the other. Now, I confess myself as belonging to that class in the country who contemplate slavery as a moral, social, and political evil, having due regard for its actual existence amongst us, and the difficulties of getting rid of it in any satisfactory way, and to all the constitutional obligations which have been thrown about it; but, nevertheless, desire a policy that looks to the prevention of it as a wrong, and looks hopefully to the time when as a wrong it may come to an end.

THE SUPREME COURT AND DOUGLAS.

While we were at Freeport, in one of these joint discussions, I answered certain interrogatories which Judge Douglas had propounded to me, and there in turn propounded some to him, which he in a sort of way answered. The third one of these interrogatories I have with me, and wish now to make some comments upon it. It was in these words: "If the Supreme Court of the United States shall decide that the States cannot exclude slavery from their limits, are you in favor of acquiescing in, adhering to, and following such decision, as a rule of political action?"

To this interrogatory Judge Douglas made no answer in any just sense of the word. He contented himself with sneering at the thought that it was possible for the Supreme Court ever to make such a decision. He sneered at me for propounding the interrogatory. I had not propounded it without some reflection, and I wish now to address to this audience some remarks upon it.

In the second clause of the sixth article, I believe it is, of the Constitution of the United States, we find the following language: "This Constitution and the laws of the United States which shall be made in pursuance thereof, and all treaties made, or which shall be made, under the authority of the United States, shall be the supreme law of the land; and the judges in every State shall be bound thereby, anything in the Constitution or laws of any State to the contrary notwithstanding."

The essence of the Dred Scott case is compressed into the sentence which I will now read: "Now, as we have already said in an earlier part of this opinion, upon a different point, the right of property in a slave is distinctly and expressly affirmed in the Constitution." I repeat it: "*The right of property in a slave is distinctly and expressly affirmed in the Constitution!"* What is it to be "*affirmed*" in the Constitution? Made firm in the Constitution; so made that it cannot be separated from the Constitution without breaking the Constitution; durable as the Constitution, and part of the Constitution. Now, remembering the provision of the Constitution which I have read, affirming that that instrument is the supreme law of the land; that the judges of every State shall be bound by it, any law or constitution of any State to the contrary notwithstanding; that the right of property in a slave is affirmed in that Constitution, is made, formed into, and cannot be separated from it without breaking it; durable as the instrument; part of the instrument; — what follows as a short and even syllogistic argument from it? I think it follows, and I submit to the consideration of men capable of arguing, whether, as I state it, in syllogistic form, the argument has any fault in it?

Nothing in the constitution or laws of any State can destroy a right distinctly and expressly affirmed in the Constitution of the United States.

The right of property in a slave is distinctly and expressly affirmed in the Constitution of the United States.

Therefore, nothing in the constitution or laws of any State can destroy the right of property in a slave.

PROPERTY IN SLAVES NOT RECOGNIZED IN THE CONSTITUTION.

I believe that no fault can be pointed out in that argument; assuming the truth of the premises, the conclusion, so far as I have capacity at all to understand it, follows inevitably. There is a fault in it as I think, but the fault is not in the reasoning; but the falsehood in fact is a fault of the premises. I believe that the right of property in a slave *is not* distinctly and expressly affirmed in the Constitution, and Judge Douglas thinks it *is*. I believe that the Supreme Court and the advocates of that decision may search in vain for the place in the Constitution where the right of a slave is distinctly and expressly affirmed. I say, therefore, that I think one of the premises is not true in fact. But it is true with Judge Douglas. It is true with the Supreme Court who pronounced it. They are estopped from denying it, and, being estopped from denying it, the conclusion follows that the Constitution of the United States being the supreme law, no constitution or law can interfere with it. It being affirmed in the decision that the right of property in a slave is distinctly and expressly affirmed in the Constitution, the conclusion inevitably follows that no State law or constitution can destroy that right. I then say to Judge Douglas, and to all others, that I think it will take a better answer than a sneer to show that those who have said that the right of property in a slave is distinctly and expressly affirmed in the Constitution, are not prepared to show that no constitution or law can destroy that right. I say I believe it will take a far better argument than a mere sneer to show to the minds of intelligent men that whoever has so said is not prepared, whenever public sentiment is so far advanced as to justify it, to say the other. This is but an opinion, and the opinion of one very humble man; but it is my opinion that the Dred Scott decision, as it is, never would have been made in its present form if the party that made it had not been sustained previously by the elections. My own opinion is, that the new Dred Scott decision, deciding against the right of the people of the States to exclude slavery, will never be made if that party is not sustained by the elections. I believe, further, that it is just as sure to be made as to-morrow is to come, if that party shall be sustained. I have said, upon a former occasion, and I repeat it now, that the course of argument that Judge Douglas makes use of upon this subject (I charge not his motives in this), is preparing the public mind for that new Dred Scott decision. I have asked him again to point out to me the reasons for his first adherence to the Dred Scott decision as it is. I have turned his attention to the fact that General Jackson differed with him in regard to the political obligation of a Supreme Court decision. I have asked his attention to the fact that Jefferson differed with him in regard to the political obligation of a Supreme Court decision. Jefferson said, that "judges are as honest as other men, and not more so." And he said, substantially, that "whenever a free people should give up in absolute submission to any department of government, retaining for themselves no appeal from it, their liberties were gone." I have asked his attention to the fact that the Cincinnati platform, upon which he says he stands, disregards a time-honored decision of the Supreme Court, in denying the power of Congress to establish a National Bank. I have asked his attention to the fact that he himself was one of the most active instruments at one time in breaking down the Supreme Court of the State of Illinois, because it had made a decision distasteful to him, — a struggle ending in the remarkable circumstance of his sitting down as one of the new judges who were to overslaugh that decision; — getting his title ot Judge in that very way.

DOUGLAS'S ATHEISM TO LIBERTY.

So far in this controversy I can get no answer at all from Judge Douglas upon these subjects. Not one can I get from him, except that he swells himself up, and says, "All of us who stand by the decision of the Supreme Court are the friends of the Constitution; all you fellows that dare question it in any way are the enemies of the Constitution." Now, in this very devoted adherence to this decision, in opposition to all the great political leaders whom he has recognized as leaders, — in opposition to his former self and history, there is something very marked. And the manner in which he adheres to it, — not as being right upon the merits as he conceives, (because he did not discuss that at all,) but as being absolutely obligatory upon every one simply because of the source from whence it comes, — as that which no man can gainsay, whatever it may be, — this is another marked feature of his adherence to that decision. It marks it in this respect, that it commits him to the next decision, whenever it comes, as being as obligatory as this one, since he does not investigate it, and won't inquire whether this opinion is right or wrong. So he takes the next one without inquiring whether *it* is right or wrong. He teaches men this doctrine, and in so doing prepares the public mind to take the next decision when it comes, without any inquiry. In this I think I argue fairly (without questioning motives at all) that Judge Douglas is most ingeniously and powerfully preparing the public mind to take that decision when it comes; and not only so, but he is doing it in various other ways. In these general maxims about liberty, — in his assertions that he "don't care whether slavery is voted up or voted down;" that "whoever wants slavery has a right to have it;" that "upon principles of equality it should be allowed to go everywhere;" that "there is no inconsistency between free and slave institutions." In this he is also preparing (whether purposely or not) the way for making the institution of slavery national! I repeat again, for I wish no misunderstanding, that I do not charge that he means it so; but I call upon your minds to inquire, if you were going to get the best instrument you could, and then set it to work in the most ingenious way, to prepare the public mind for this movement, operating in the free States, where there is now an abhorrence of the institution of slavery, could you find an instrument so capable of doing it as Judge Douglas? or one employed in so apt a way to do it?

I have said once before, and I will repeat it now, that Mr. Clay, when he was once answering an objection to the Colonization Society, that it had a tendency to the ultimate emancipation of the slaves, said that "those who would repress all tendencies to liberty and ultimate emancipation, must do more than put down the benevolent efforts of the Colonization Society,—they must go back to the era of our liberty and independence, and muzzle the cannon that thunders its annual joyous return,—they must blot out the moral lights around us,—they must penetrate the human soul, and eradicate the light of reason and the love of liberty!" And I do think, — I repeat, though I said it on a former occasion, — that Judge Douglas, and whoever like him teaches that the negro has no share, humble though it may be, in the Declaration of Independence, is going back to the era of our liberty and independence, and, so far as in him lies, muzzling the cannon that thunders its annual joyous return; that he is blowing out the moral lights around us, when he contends that whoever wants slaves has a right to hold them; that he is penetrating, so far as lies in his power, the human soul, and eradicating the light of reason and the love of liberty, when he is in every possible way preparing the public mind, by his vast influence, for making the institution of slavery perpetual and national.

ON TERRITORIAL ACQUISITION.

There is, my friends, only one other point to which I will call your attention for the remaining time that I have left me, and perhaps I shall not occupy the entire time that I have, as that one point may not take me clear through it.

Among the interrogatories that Judge Douglas propounded to me at Freeport, there was one in about this language: "Are you opposed to the acquisition of any further territory to the United States, unless slavery shall first be prohibited therein?" I answered as I thought, in this way, that I am not generally opposed to the acquisition of additional territory. and that I would support a proposition for the acquisition of additional territory, according as my supporting it was or was not calculated to aggravate this slavery question amongst us. I then proposed to Judge Douglas another interrogatory, which was correlative to that: "Are you in favor of acquiring additional territory in disregard of how it may affect us upon the slavery question?" Judge Douglas answered, that is, in his own way he answered it. I believe that, although he took a good many words to answer it, it was a little more fully answered than any other. The substance of his answer was, that this country would continue to expand, — that it would need additional territory, — that it was as absurd to suppose that we could continue upon our present territory, enlarging in population as we are, as it would be to hoop a boy twelve years of age, and expect him to grow to man's size without bursting the hoops. I believe it was something like that. Consequently, he was in favor of the acquisition of further territory, as fast as we might need it, in disregard of how it might affect the slavery question. I do not say this as giving his exact language, but he said so substantially, and he would leave the question of slavery where the territory was acquired, to be settled by the people of the acquired territory. [" That's the doctrine."] May-be it is; let us consider that for a while. This will probably, in the run of things, become one of the concrete manifestations of this slavery question. If Judge Douglas's policy upon this question succeeds and gets fairly settled down, until all opposition is crushed out, the next thing will be a grab for the territory of poor Mexico, an invasion of the rich lands of South America, then the adjoining islands will follow, each one of which promises additional slave fields. And this question is to be left to the people of those countries for settlement. When we shall get Mexico, I don't know whether the Judge will be in favor of the Mexican people that we get with it settling that question for themselves and all others; because we know the Judge has a great horror for mongrels, and I understand that the people of Mexico are most decidedly a race of mongrels. I understand that there is not more than one person there out of eight who is pure white, and I suppose from the Judge's previous declaration, that when we get Mexico or any considerable portion of it, that he will be in favor of these mongrels settling the question, which would bring him somewhat into collision with his horror of an inferior race.

It is to be remembered, though, that this power of acquiring additional territory is a power confided to the President and Senate of the United States. It is a power not under the control of the representatives of the people any further than they, the President and the Senate, can be considered the representatives of the people. Let me illustrate that by a case we have in our history. When we acquired the territory from Mexico in the Mexican war, the House of Representatives, composed of the immediate representatives of the people, all the time insisted that the territory thus to be acquired should be brought in upon condition that slavery should be forever prohibited therein, upon the terms and in the language that slavery had been prohibited from coming into this country. That was insisted upon constantly, and never failed to call forth an assurance that any territory thus acquired should have that prohibition in it, so far as the House of Representatives was concerned. But at last the President and Senate acquired the territory without asking the House of Representatives anything about it, and took it without that prohibition. They have the power of acquiring territory without the immediate representatives of the people being called upon to say anything about it, and thus furnishing a very apt and powerful means of bringing new territory into the Union, and when it is once brought into the country, involving us anew in this slavery agitation. It is, therefore, as I think, a very important question for the consideration of the American people, whether the policy of bringing in additional territory, without considering at all how it will operate upon the safety of the Union in reference to this one great disturbing element in our national politics, shall be adopted as the policy of the country. You will bear in mind that it is to be acquired, according to the Judge's view, as fast as it is needed, and the indefinite part of this proposition is that we have only Judge Douglas and his class of men to decide how fast it is needed. We have no clear and certain way of determining or demonstrating how fast territory is needed by the necessities of the country. Whoever wants to go out fillibustering, then, thinks that more territory is needed. Whoever wants wider slave fields, feels sure that some additional territory is needed as slave territory. Then it is as easy to show the necessity of additional slave territory as it is to assert anything that is incapable of absolute demonstration. Whatever motive a man or a set of men may have for making annexation of property or territory, it is very easy to assert, but much less easy to disprove, that it is necessary for the wants of the country. — *From Mr. Lincoln's reply to Judge Douglas, at the Fifth Joint Debate, Galesburg, Oct.* 7, 1858.

A SELF-EVIDENT LIE.

At Galesburg, the other day, I said, in answer to Judge Douglas, that three years ago there never had been a man, so far as I knew or believed, in the whole world, who had said that the Declaration of Independence did not include negroes in the term "all men." I reassert it to-day. I assert that Judge Douglas and all his friends may search the whole records of the country, and it will be a matter of great astonishment to me if they shall be able to find that one human being three years ago had ever uttered the astounding sentiment that the term "all men" in the Declaration, did not include the negro. Do not let me be misunderstood. I know that more than three years ago there were men who, finding this assertion constantly in the way of their schemes to bring about the ascendency and perpetuation of slavery, *denied the truth of it.* I know that Mr. Calhoun, and all the politicians of his school, denied the truth of the Declaration. I know that it ran along in the mouth of some Southern men for a period of years, ending at last in that shameful though rather forcible declaration of Pettit, of Indiana, upon the floor of the United States Senate, that the Declaration of Independence was in that respect, "a self-evident lie," rather than a self-evident truth. But I say, with a perfect knowledge of all this hawking at the Declaration without directly attacking it, that three years ago there never had lived a man who had ventured to assail it in the sneaking way of pretending to believe it, and then asserting it did not include the negro. I believe the first man who ever said it was Chief Justice Taney, in the Dred Scott case, and the next to him was our friend, Stephen A. Douglas. And now it has become the catchword of the entire party. I would like to call upon his friends everywhere to consider how they have come, in so short a time, to view this matter in a way so entirely different from their former belief? to ask whether they are not being borne along by an irresistible current—whither, they know not?

. . . .

And when this new principle — this new proposition that no human being ever thought of three years ago — is brought forward, *I combat it* as having an evil tendency, if not an evil design. I combat it as having a tendency to dehumanize the negro, — to take away from him the right of ever striving to be a man. I combat it as being one of the thousand things constantly done in these days to prepare the public mind to make property, and nothing but property, of the *negro, in all the States of this Union.*

THE CONSTITUTION ON SLAVERY. — POSITIONS OF THE TWO PARTIES.

Again, the institution of slavery is only mentioned in the Constitution of the United States two or three times, and in neither of these cases does the word "slavery" or "negro race" occur; but covert language is used each time, and for a purpose full of significance. What is the language in regard to the prohibition of the African slave-trade? It runs in about this way: "The migration or importation of such persons as any of the States now existing shall think proper to admit, shall not be prohibited by the Congress prior to the year one thousand eight hundred and eight."

The next allusion in the Constitution to the question of slavery and the black race, is on the subject of the basis of representation, and there the language used is, "Representatives and direct taxes shall be apportioned among the several States which may be included within this Union, according to their respective numbers, which shall be determined by adding to the whole number of free persons, including those bound to serve for a term of years, and excluding Indians not taxed, — three fifths of all other persons."

It says "persons," not slaves, not negroes; but this "three fifths" can be applied to no other class among us than the negroes.

Lastly, in the provision for the reclamation of fugitive slaves, it is said: "No person held to service or labor in one State, under the laws thereof, escaping into another, shall in consequence of any law or regulation therein, be discharged from such service or labor, but shall be delivered up, on claim of the party to whom such service or labor may be due." There again there is no mention of the word "negro" or of slavery. In all three of these places, being the only allusions to slavery in the instrument, covert language is used; language is used not suggesting that slavery existed, or that the black race were among us; and I understand the contemporaneous history of those times to be that covert language was used with a purpose, and that purpose was that in our Constitution, which it was hoped and is still hoped will endure forever, — when it should be read by intelligent and patriotic men, after the institution of slavery had passed from among us, — there should be nothing on the face of the great charter of liberty suggesting that such a thing as negro slavery had ever existed among us. This is part of the evidence that the fathers of the Government expected and intended the institution of slavery to come to an end. They expected and intended that it should be in the course of ultimate extinction. And when I say that I desire to see the further spread of it arrested, I only say I desire to see that done which the fathers have first done. When I say I desire to see it placed where the public mind will rest in the belief that it is in the course of ultimate extinction, I only say I desire to see it placed where they placed it. It is not true that our fathers, as Judge Douglas assumes, made this Government part slave and part free. Understand the sense in which he puts it. He assumes that slavery is a rightful thing within itself, — was introduced by the framers of the Constitution. The exact truth is, that they found the institution existing among us, and they left it as they found it. But in making the Government, they left this institution with many clear marks of disapprobation upon it. They found slavery among them, and they left it among them because of the difficulty, — the absolute impossibility of its immediate removal. And when Judge Douglas asks me why we cannot let it remain part slave and part free, as the fathers of the Government made it, he asks a question based upon an assumption which is itself a falsehood; and I turn upon him and ask him the question, When the policy that the fathers of the Government had adopted in relation to this element among us was the best policy in the world, — the only wise policy, — the only policy that we can ever safely continue upon, that will ever give us peace, unless this dangerous element masters us all and becomes a national institution, — *I turn upon him and ask him why he could not leave it alone.* I turn and ask him why he was driven to the necessity of introducing a *new policy* in regard to it. He has himself said he introduced a new policy. He said so in his speech on the 22d of March of the present year, 1858. I ask him why he could not let it remain where our fathers placed it. I ask, too, of Judge Douglas and his friends why we shall not again place this institution upon the basis on which the fathers left it. I ask you, when he infers that I am in favor of setting the free and slave States at war, when the institution was placed in that attitude by those who made the Constitution, *did they make any war?* If we had no war out of it, when thus placed, wherein is the ground of belief that we shall have war out of it, if we return to that policy? Have we had any peace upon this matter springing from any other basis? I maintain that we have not. I have proposed nothing more than a return to the policy of the fathers.

WHAT IS RESPONSIBLE FOR THE AGITATION?

When have we had perfect peace in regard to this thing which I say is an element of discord in this Union? We have sometimes had peace, but when was it? It was when the institution of slavery remained quite where it was. We have had difficulty and turmoil whenever it has made a struggle to spread itself where it was not. I ask, then, if experience does not speak in thunder-tones, telling us that the policy which has given peace to the country heretofore, being returned to, gives the greatest promise of peace again. You may say, and Judge Douglas has intimated the same thing, that all this difficulty in regard to the institution of slavery is the mere agitation of office-seekers and ambitious northern politicians. He thinks we want to get "his place," I suppose. I agree that there are office-seekers amongst us. The Bible says somewhere that we are desperately selfish. I think we should have discovered that fact without the Bible. I do not claim that I am any less so than the average of men, but I do claim that I am not more selfish than Judge Douglas.

But is it true that all the difficulty and agitation we have in regard to this institution of slavery springs from office-seeking, — from the mere ambition of politicians? Is that the truth? How many times have we had danger from this question? Go back to the day of the Missouri Compromise. Go back to the Nullification question, at the bottom of which lay this same slavery question. Go back to the time of the Annexation of Texas. Go back to the troubles that led to the Compromise of 1850. You will find that every time, with the single exception of the Nullification question, they sprung from an endeavor to spread this institution. There never was a party in the history of this country, and there probably never will be, of sufficient strength to disturb the general peace of the country. Parties themselves may be divided and quarrel on minor questions, yet it extends not beyond the parties themselves. But does *not* this question make a disturbance outside of political circles? Does it not enter into the churches and rend them asunder? What divided the great Methodist Church into two parts, North and South? What has raised this constant disturbance in every Presbyterian General Assembly that meets? What disturbed the Unitarian Church in this very city two years ago? What has jarred and shaken the great American Tract Society recently, not yet splitting it, but sure to divide it in the end? Is it not this same mighty, deep-seated power that somehow operates on the minds of men, exciting and stirring them up in every avenue of society, — in politics, in religion, in literature, in morals, in all the manifold relations of life? Is this the work of politicians? Is that irresistible power, which for fifty years has shaken the Government and agitated the people, to be stilled and subdued by pretending that it is an exceedingly simple thing, and we ought not to talk about it? If you will get everybody else to stop talking about it, I assure you I will quit before they have half done so. But where is the philosophy or statesmanship which assumes that you can quiet that disturbing element in our society which has disturbed us for more than half a century, which has been the only serious danger that has threatened our institutions, — I say, where is the philosophy or the statesmanship based on the assumption that we are to quit talking about it, and that the public mind is all at once to cease being agitated by it? Yet this is the policy here in the north that Douglas is advocating, — that we are to care nothing about it! I ask you if it is not a false philosophy? Is it not a false statesmanship that undertakes to build up a system of policy upon the basis of caring nothing about *the very thing that every body does care the most about?* — a thing which all experience has shown we care a very great deal about?

FREEDOM OF THE TERRITORIES.

The Judge alludes very often, in the course of his remarks, to the exclusive right which the States have to decide the whole thing for themselves. I agree with him very readily, that the different States have that right. He is but fighting a man of straw when he assumes that I am contending against the right of the States to do as they please about it. Our controversy with him is in regard to the new territories. We agree that when the States come in as States, they have the right and the power to do as they please. We have no power as citizens of the free States, or in our federal capacity as members of the Federal Union through the General Government, to disturb slavery in the States where it exists. We profess constantly that we have no more inclination than belief in the power of the Government to disturb it; yet we are driven constantly to defend ourselves from the assumption that we are warring upon the rights of the *States*. What I insist upon is, that the new territories shall be kept free from it while in the territorial condition.

Judge Douglas assumes that we have no interest in them, — that we have no right whatever to interfere. I think we have some interest. I think that as white men we have. Do we not wish for an outlet for our surplus population, if I may so express myself? Do we not feel an interest in getting to that outlet with such institutions as we would like to have prevail there? If *you* go to the territory opposed to slavery, and another man comes upon the same ground with his slave, upon the assumption that the things are equal, it turns out that he has the equal right all his way, and you have no part of it your way. If he goes in and makes it a slave territory, and by consequence a slave State, is it not time that those who desire to have it a free State were on equal ground? Let me suggest it in a different way. How many Democrats are there about here [" A thousand "] who have left slave States and come into the free State of Illinois to get rid of the institution of slavery? [Another voice,—" A thousand and one."] I reckon there are a thousand and one. I will ask you, if the policy you are now advocating had prevailed when this country was in a territorial condition, where would you have gone to get rid of it? Where would you have found your free State or territory to go to? And when hereafter, for any cause, the people in this place shall desire to find new homes, if they wish to be rid of the institution, where will they find the place to go to?

Now, irrespective of the moral aspect of this question as to whether there is a right or wrong in enslaving a negro, I am still in favor of our new territories being in such a condition that white men may find a home, — may find some spot where they can better their condition, — where they can settle upon new soil, and better their condition in life. I am in favor of this not merely (I must say it here as I have elsewhere) for our own people who are born amongst us, but as an outlet for *free white people everywhere*, the world over, — in which Hans and Baptiste and Patrick, and all other men from all the world, may find new homes, and better their conditions in life.

THE REAL ISSUE—IS SLAVERY RIGHT OR WRONG?

I have stated upon former occasions, and I may as well state again, what I understand to be the real issue in this controversy between Judge Douglas and myself. On the point of my wanting to make war between the free and the slave States, there has been no issue between us. So, too, when he assumes that I am in favor of introducing a perfect social and political equality between the white and black races. These are false issues, upon which Judge Douglas has tried to force the controversy. There is no foundation, in truth, for the charge that I maintain either of these propositions. The real issue in this controversy—the one pressing upon every mind—is the sentiment on the part of one class that looks upon the institution of slavery *as a wrong*, and of another class that *does not* look upon it as a wrong. The sentiment that contemplates the institution of slavery in this country as a wrong is the sentiment of the Republican party. It is the sentiment around which all their actions, all their arguments circle, from which all their propositions radiate. They look upon it as being a moral, social, and political wrong; and while they contemplate it as such, they nevertheless have due regard for its actual existence among us, and the difficulties of getting rid of it in any satisfactory way and to all the constitutional obligations thrown about it. Yet having a due regard for these, they desire a policy in regard to it that looks to its not creating any more danger. They insist that it should, as far as may be, *be treated* as a wrong, and one of the methods of treating it as a wrong is to *make provision that it shall grow no larger*. They also desire a policy that looks to a peaceful end of slavery at some time, as being wrong. These are the views they entertain in regard to it, as I understand them; and all their sentiments, all their arguments and propositions, are brought within this range. I have said, and I repeat it here, that if there be a man amongst us who does not think that the institution of slavery is wrong in any one of the aspects of which I have spoken, he is misplaced and ought not to be with us. And if there be a man amongst us who is so impatient of it as a wrong as to disregard its actual presence among us, and the difficulty of getting rid of it suddenly in a satisfactory way, and to disregard the constitutional obligations thrown about it, that man is misplaced if he is on our platform. We disclaim sympathy with him in practical action. He is not placed properly with us.

THE TRUE MODE OF TREATMENT.

On this subject of treating it as a wrong, and limiting its spread, let me say a word. Has anything ever threatened the existence of this Union, save and except this very institution of slavery? What is it that we hold most dear amongst us? Our own liberty and prosperity. What has ever threatened our liberty and prosperity save and except this institution of slavery? If this is true, how do you propose to improve the condition of things by enlarging slavery,—by spreading it out and making it bigger? You may have a wen or cancer upon your person, and not be able to cut it out lest you bleed to death; but surely it is no way to cure it, to ingraft and spread it over your whole body. That is no proper way of treating what you regard a wrong. You see this peaceful way of dealing with it as a wrong,—restricting the spread of it, and not allowing it to go into new countries where it has not already existed. That is the peaceful way, the old-fashioned way, the way in which the fathers themselves set us the example.

THE DEMOCRATIC TREATMENT.

On the other hand, I have said there is a sentiment which treats it as *not* being wrong. That is the Democratic sentiment of this day. I do not mean to say that every one who stands within that range, positively asserts that it is right. That class will include all who positively assert that it is right, and all who like Judge Douglas treat it as indifferent, and do not say it is either right or wrong. These two classes of men fall within the general class of those who do not look upon it as a wrong.

And if there be among you anybody who supposes that he, as a Democrat, can consider himself "as much opposed to slavery as anybody," I would like to reason with him. You never treat it as a wrong. What other thing that you consider as a wrong, do you deal with as you deal with that? Perhaps you *say* it is wrong, *but your leader never does, and you quarrel with anybody who says it is wrong.* Although you pretend to say so yourself, you can find no fit place to deal with it as a wrong. You must not say anything about it in the free States, *because it is not here.* You must not say anything about it in the slave States, *because it is there.* You must not say anything about it in the pulpit, because that is religion, and has nothing to do with it. You must not say anything about it in politics, *because that will disturb the security of "my place."* There is no place to talk about it as being a wrong, although you say yourself it *is* a wrong. But finally, you will screw yourself up to the belief, that if the people of the slave States should adopt a system of gradual emancipation on the slavery question, you would be in favor of it. You would be in favor of it. You say that is getting it in the right place, and you would be glad to see it succeed. But you are deceiving yourself. You all know that Frank Blair and Gratz Brown, down there in St. Louis, undertook to introduce that system in Missouri. They fought as valiantly as they could for the system of gradual emancipation, which you pretend you would be glad to see succeed. Now I will bring you to the test. After a hard fight, they were beaten; and when the news came over here, you threw up your hats and *hurraed for Democracy!* More than that, take all the argument made in favor of the system you have proposed, and it carefully excludes the idea that there is anything wrong in the institution of slavery. The arguments to sustain that policy carefully excluded it. Even here to-day you heard Judge Douglas quarrel with me, because I uttered a wish that it might some time come to an end. Although Henry Clay could say he wished every slave in the United States was in the country of his ancestors, I am denounced by those pretending to respect Henry Clay for uttering a wish that it might some time, in some peaceful way, come to an end. The Democratic policy in regard to that institution will not tolerate the merest breath, the slightest hint, of the least degree of wrong about it. Try it by some of Judge Douglas's arguments. He says, he "don't care whether it is voted up or voted down" in the territories. I do not care myself, in dealing with that expression, whether it is intended to be expressive of his individual sentiments on the subject, or only of the national policy he desires to have established. It is alike valuable for my purpose. Any man can say that who does not see any wrong in slavery, but no man can logically say it who does see a wrong in it, — because no man can logically say he don't care whether a wrong is voted up or voted down. He may say he don't care whether an indifferent thing is voted up or down, but he must logically have a choice between a right thing and a wrong thing. He contends that whatever community wants slaves, has a right to have them. So they have, if it is not a wrong. But if it is a wrong, he cannot say people have a right to do wrong. He says that, upon the score of equality, slaves should be allowed to go in a new territory, like other property. This is strictly logical, if there is no difference between it and other property. If it and other property are equal, his argument is entirely logical. But if you insist that one is wrong, and the other right, there is no use to institute a comparison between right and wrong. You may turn over everything in the Democratic policy from beginning to end, whether in the shape it takes on the statute book, in the shape it takes in the Dred Scott decision, in the shape it takes in conversation, or the shape it takes in short maxim-like arguments,— it everywhere carefully excludes the idea that there is anything wrong in it.

THE COTTON-GIN BASIS.

That is the real issue. That is the issue that will continue in this country when these poor tongues of Judge Douglas and myself shall be silent. It is the eternal struggle between these two principles — right and wrong — throughout the world. They are the two principles that have stood face to face from the beginning of time; and will ever continue to struggle. The one is the common right of humanity, and the other the divine right of kings. It it the same principle in whatever shape it develops itself. It is the same spirit that says, "You work and toil and earn bread, and I'll eat it." No matter in what shape it comes, whether from the mouth of a king who seeks to bestride the people of his own nation, and live by the fruit of their labor, or from one race of men as an apology for enslaving another race, it is the same tyrannical principle. I was glad to express my gratitude at Quincy, and I re-express it here to Judge Douglas,—*that he looks to no end of the institution of slavery.* That will help the people to see where the struggle really is. It will hereafter place with us all men who really do wish the wrong may have an end. And whenever we can get rid of the fog which obscures the real question,— when we can get Judge Douglas and his friends to avow a policy looking to its perpetuation,— we can get out from among that class of men and bring them to the side of those who treat it as a wrong. Then there will soon be an end of it, and that end will be its "ultimate extinction." Whenever the issue can be distinctly made, and all extraneous matter thrown out, so that men can fairly see the real difference between the parties, this controversy will soon be settled; and it will be done peaceably too. There will be no war, no violence. It will be placed again where the wisest and best men of the world placed it. Brooks of South Carolina once declared that when this Constitution was framed, its framers did not look to the institution existing until this day. When he said this, I think he stated a fact that is fully borne out by the history of the times. But he also said they were better and wiser men than the men of these days; yet the men of these days had experience which they had not, and by the invention of the cotton-gin it became a necessity in this country that slavery should be perpetual. I now say that, willingly or unwillingly, purposely or without purpose, Judge Douglas has been the most prominent instrument in changing the position of the institution of slavery which the fathers of the Government expected to come to an end ere this,—*and putting it upon Brooks's cotton-gin basis,*—placing it where he openly confesses he has no desire there shall ever be an end of it.

A MONSTROUS DOCTRINE.

I understand I have ten minutes yet. I will employ it in saying something about this argument Judge Douglas uses, while he sustains the Dred Scott decision, that the people of the territories can still somehow exclude slavery. The first thing I ask attention to is the fact that Judge Douglas constantly said, before the decision, that whether they could or not, *was a question for the Supreme Court.* But after the court has made the decision, he virtually says it is *not* a question for the Supreme Court, but for the people. And how is it he tells us they can exclude it? He says it needs "police regulations," and that admits of "unfriendly legislation." Although it is a right established by the Constitution of the United States, to take a slave into a territory of the United States, and hold him as property, yet unless the territorial legislature will give friendly legislation, and, more especially, if they adopt unfriendly legislation, they can practically exclude him. Now, without meeting this proposition as a matter of fact, I pass to consider the real constitutional obligation. Let me take the gentleman who looks me in the face before me, and let us suppose that he is a member of the territorial legislature. The first thing he will do will be to swear that he will support the Constitution of the United States. His neighbor by his side in the territory has slaves, and needs territorial legislation to enable him to enjoy that constitutional right. Can he withhold the legislation which his neighbor needs for the enjoyment of a right which is fixed in his favor in the Constitution of the United States which he has sworn to support? Can he withhold it without violating his oath? And more especially, can he pass unfriendly legislation to violate his oath? Why, this is a *monstrous* sort of talk about the Constitution of the United States! *There has never been as outlandish or lawless a doctrine from the mouth of any respectable man on earth.* I do not believe it is a constitutional right to hold slaves in a territory of the United States. I believe the decision was improperly made, and I go for reversing it. Judge Douglas is furious against those who go for reversing a decision. But he is for legislating it out of all force while the law itself stands. I repeat, that there has never been so monstrous a doctrine uttered from the mouth of a respectable man.

DOUGLAS THE CHIEF OF ABOLITIONISTS.

I suppose most of us (I know it of myself) believe that the people of the Southern States are entitled to a congressional fugitive slave law, — that is a right fixed in the Constitution. But it cannot be made available to them without congressional legislation. In the Judge's language, it is a "barren right" which needs legislation before it can become efficient and valuable to the persons to whom it is guaranteed. And as the right is constitutional, I agree that the legislation shall be granted to it, — and that not that we like the institution of slavery. We profess to have no taste for running and catching niggers, — at least, I profess no taste for that job at all. Why then do I yield support to a fugitive slave law? Because I do not understand that the Constitution, which guarantees that right, can be supported without it. And if I believed that the right to hold a slave in a territory was equally fixed in the Constitution with the right to reclaim fugitives, I should be bound to give it the legislation necessary to support it. I say that no man can deny his obligation to give the necessary legislation to support slavery in a territory, who believes it is a constitutional right to have it there. No man can, who does not give the abolitionists an argument to deny the obligation enjoined by the Constitution to enact a fugitive slave law. Try it now. It is the strongest abolition argument ever made. I say if that Dred Scott decision is correct, then the right to hold slaves in a territory is equally a constitutional right with the right of a slaveholder to have his runaway returned. No one can show the distinction between them. The one is express, so that we cannot deny it. The other is construed to be in the Constitution, so that he who believes the decision to be correct, believes in the right. And the man who argues that by unfriendly legislation, in spite of that constitutional right, slavery may be driven from the territories, cannot avoid furnishing an argument by which abolitionists may deny the obligation to return fugitives, and claim the power to pass laws unfriendly to the right of the slaveholder to reclaim his fugitive. I do not know how such an argument may strike a popular assembly like this, but I defy anybody to go before a body of men whose minds are educated to estimating evidence and reasoning, and show that there is an iota of difference between the constitutional right to reclaim a fugitive, and the constitutional right to hold a slave, in a territory, provided this Dred Scott decision is correct. I defy any man to make an argument that will justify unfriendly legislation to deprive a slaveholder of his right to hold his slave in a territory, that will not equally, in all its length, breadth, and thickness, furnish an argument for nullifying the fugitive slave law. Why, there is not such an abolitionist in the nation as Douglas, after all.—*From the Seventh Joint Debate in Alton, Ill., Oct.* 15, 1858.

DOUGLAS'S DOCTRINE OF UNFRIENDLY LEGISLATION BY THE TERRITORIES ON SLAVERY.

At the end of what I have said here, I propose to give the Judge my fifth interrogatory, which he may take and answer at his leisure. My fifth interrogatory is this.

If the slaveholding citizens of a United States Territory should need and demand congressional legislation for the protection of their slave property in such territory, would you, as a member of Congress, vote for or against such legislation?

Judge Douglas — "Will you repeat that? I want to answer that question."

Mr. Lincoln — If the slaveholding citizens of a United States Territory should need and demand congressional legislation for the protection of their slave property in such territory, would you, as a member of Congress, vote for or against such legislation ?

I am aware that, in some of the speeches Judge Douglas has made, he has spoken as if he did not know or think that the Supreme Court had decided that a territorial legislature cannot exclude slavery. Precisely what the Judge would say upon the subject, — whether he would say definitely that he does not understand they have so decided, or whether he would say he does understand that the court have so decided, I do not know; but I know that in his speech at Springfield he spoke of it as a thing they had not decided yet; and in his answer to me at Freeport, he spoke of it so far again, as I can comprehend it, as a thing that had not yet been decided. Now I hold that if the Judge does entertain that view, I think that he is not mistaken in so far as it can be said that the Court has not decided anything save the mere question of jurisdiction. I know the legal arguments that can be made, — that after a court has decided that it cannot take jurisdiction in a case, it then has decided all that is before it, and that is the end of it. A plausible argument can be made in favor of that proposition, but I know that Judge Douglas has said in one of his speeches that the court went forward, *like honest men as they were*, and decided all the points in the case. If any points are really extra-judicially decided because not necessarily before them, then this one as to the power of the territorial legislature to exclude slavery is one of them, as also the one that the Missouri Compromise was null and void. They are both extra-judicial, or neither is, according as the court held that they had no jurisdiction in the case between the parties, because of want of capacity of one party to maintain a suit in that court. I want, if I have sufficient time, to show that the court did *pass its opinion*, but that is the only thing actually done in the case. If they did not decide, they showed what they were ready to decide whenever the matter was before them. What is that opinion? After having argued that Congress had no power to pass a law excluding slavery from a United States territory, they then used language to this effect: That inasmuch as Congress itself could not exercise such a power, it followed as a matter of course that it could not authorize a territorial government to exercise it, for the territorial legislature can do no more than Congress could do. Thus it expressed its opinion emphatically against the power of a territorial legislature to exclude slavery, leaving us in just as little doubt on that point as upon any other point they really decided. — *From the Third Joint Debate at Jonesboro', September* 15, 1858.

THE REPUBLICAN METHOD.

We have in this nation this element of domestic slavery. It is a matter of absolute certainty that it is a disturbing element. It is the opinion of all the great men who have expressed an opinion upon it, that it is a dangerous element. We keep up a controversy in regard to it. That controversy necessarily springs from difference of opinion, and if we can learn exactly, can reduce to the lowest elements, what that difference of opinion is, we perhaps shall be better prepared for discussing the different systems of policy that we would propose in regard to that disturbing element. I suggest that the difference of opinion, reduced to its lowest terms, is no other than the difference between the men who think slavery a wrong, and those who do not think it wrong. The Republican party think it wrong, — we think it is a moral, a social, and a political wrong. We think it is a wrong not confining itself merely to the persons or the States where it exists, but that it is a wrong in its tendency, to say the least, that extends itself to the existence of the whole nation. Because we think it wrong, we propose a course of policy that shall deal with it as a wrong. We deal with it as with any other wrong, in so far as we can prevent its growing any larger, and so deal with it that in the run of time there may be some promise of an end to it. We have a due regard to the actual presence of it amongst us, and the difficulties of getting rid of it in any satisfactory way, and all the constitutional obligations thrown about it. I suppose that in reference both to its actual existence in the nation, and to our constitutional obligations, we have no right at all to disturb it in the States where it exists, and we profess that we have no more inclination to disturb it than we have the right to do it. We go further than that; we don't propose to disturb it where, in one instance, we think the Constitution would permit us. We think the Constitution would permit us to disturb it in the District of Columbia. Still, we do not propose to do that, unless it should be in terms which I don't suppose the nation is very likely soon to agree to, — the terms of making the emancipation gradual, and compensating the unwilling owners. Where we suppose we have the constitutional right, we restrain ourselves in reference to the actual existence of the institution, and the difficulties thrown about it. We also oppose it as an evil so far as it seeks to spread itself. We insist on the policy that shall restrict it to its present limits. We don't suppose that in doing this we violate anything due to the actual presence of the institution, or anything due to the constitutional guaranties thrown around it.

THE DECLARATION OF INDEPENDENCE.

The Declaration of Independence was formed by the representatives of American liberty from thirteen States of the Confederacy,— twelve of which were slaveholding communities. We need not discuss the way or the reason of their becoming slaveholding communities. It is sufficient for our purpose that *all of them* greatly deplored the evil, and that they placed a provision in the Constitution which they supposed would gradually remove the disease by cutting off its source. This was the abolition of the slave-trade. So general was the conviction, — the public determination, — to abolish the African slave-trade, that the provision which I have referred to as being placed in the Constitution, declared that it should *not* be abolished prior to the year 1808. A constitutional provision was necessary to prevent the people, through Congress, from putting a stop to the traffic immediately at the close of the war. Now, if slavery had been a good thing, would the fathers of the Republic have taken a step calculated to diminish its beneficent influences among themselves, and snatch the boon wholly from their posterity? These communities, by their representatives in old Independence Hall, said to the whole world of men :—

We hold these truths to be self-evident; that all men are created equal; that they are endowed by their Creator with certain inalienable rights; that among these are life, liberty, and the pursuit of happiness." This was their majestic interpretation of the economy of the universe. This was their lofty, and wise, and noble understanding of the justice of the Creator to his creatures. [Applause.] Yes, gentlemen, to *all* his creatures, to the whole great family of man. In their enlightened belief, nothing stamped with the divine image and likeness was sent into the world to be trodden on, and degraded, and imbruted by its fellows. They grasped not only the whole race of man then living, but they reached forward and seized upon the farthest posterity. They erected a beacon to guide their children and their children's children, and the countless myriads who should inhabit the earth in other ages. Wise statesmen as they were, they knew the tendency of prosperity to breed tyrants, and so they established these great self-evident truths, that when in the distant future some man, some faction, some interest, should set up the doctrine that none but rich men, or none but white men, or none but Anglo-Saxons, were entitled to life, liberty, and the pursuit of happiness, their posterity might look up again to the Declaration of Independence, and take courage to renew the battle which their fathers began,— so that truth, and justice, and mercy, and all the humane and Christian virtues might not be extinguished from the land; so that no man hereafter would dare to limit and circumscribe the great principles on which the temple of liberty was being built. [Loud cheers.]

Now, my countrymen, if you have been taught doctrines conflicting with the great landmarks of the Declaration of Independence; if you have listened to suggestions which would take away from its grandeur, and mutilate the symmetry of its proportions; if you have been inclined to believe that all men are *not* created equal in those inalienable rights enumerated by our chart of liberty, let me entreat you to come back. Return to the fountain whose waters spring close by the blood of the Revolution. Think nothing of me, — take no thought for the political fate of any man whomsoever, — but come back to the truths that are in the Declaration of Independence. You may do anything with me you choose, if you will but heed these sacred principles. You may not only defeat me for the Senate, but you may take me and put me to death. While pretending no indifference to earthly honors, I *do claim* to be actuated in this contest by something higher than any anxiety for office. I charge you to drop every paltry and insignificant thought for any man's success. It is nothing; I am nothing; Judge Douglas is nothing. *But do not destroy that immortal emblem of humanity, — the Declaration of American Independence.*

MR. LINCOLN IN CONGRESS. .

In illustration of Mr. Lincoln's position on the Mexican war, Bounty Lands, Disposal of the Public Domain, etc., we annex some extracts from congressional speeches. Most of the issues are dead which then excited the nation. The extracts will serve to show Mr. Lincoln's position, and be the best answer to any statements by his opponents, based thereon.

MEXICAN WAR — RESOLUTIONS OF INQUIRY.

On the 22d of December, Mr. Lincoln moved the following preambles and resolutions, which were read and laid over under the rule :—

"Whereas, the President of the United States, in his message of May 11, 1846, has declared that 'the Mexican Government not only refused to receive him, (the envoy of the United States,) or listen to his propositions, but after a long-continued series of menaces, have at last invaded our territory and shed the blood of our fellow-citizens on our own soil.'"

And again in his message of December 8, 1846, that "we had ample cause of war against Mexico long before the breaking out of hostilities, but even then we forebore to take redress into our own hands until Mexico herself became the aggressor, by invading our soil in hostile array, and shedding the blood of our citizens."

And yet again in the message of December 7, 1847, that "the Mexican Government refused even to hear the terms of adjustment which he (our minister of peace) was authorized to propose, and finally, under wholly unjustifiable pretexts, involved the two countries in war, by invading the territory of the State of Texas, striking the first blow, and shedding the blood of our citizens on our own soil."

And whereas this House is desirous to obtain a full knowledge of all the facts which go to establish whether the particular spot on which the blood of our citizens was so shed, was or was not at that time our own soil. Therefore,

Resolved, by the House of Representatives, That the President of the United States be respectfully requested to inform this House.

1. Whether the spot on which the blood of our citizens was shed, as in his messages declared, was or was not within the Territory of Spain, at least after the treaty of 1819, until the Mexican revolution.

2. Whether that spot is or is not within the territory which was wrested from Spain by the revolutionary Government of Mexico.

3. Whether that spot is or is not within a settlement of people, which settlement has existed ever since long before the Texas revolution, and until its inhabitants fled before the approach of the United States army.

4. Whether that settlement is or is not isolated from any and all other settlements by the Gulf and the Rio Grande, on the south and west, and by wide, uninhabited regions, on the north and east.

5. Whether the people of that settlement, or a majority of them, or any of them, have ever submitted themselves to the government or laws of Texas or of the United States, by consent or by compulsion, either by accepting office, or voting at elections, or paying tax, or serving on juries, or having process served upon them, or in any other way.

6. Whether the people of that settlement did or did not flee from the approach of the United States army, leaving unprotected their homes and their growing crops, before the blood was shed, as in the message stated; and whether the first blood, so

shed, was or was not shed within the enclosure of one of the people who had thus fled from it.

7. Whether our citizens, whose blood was shed, as in his messages declared, were or were not, at that time, armed officers and soldiers sent into that settlement by the military order of the President, through the Secretary of War.

8. Whether the military force of the United States was or was not so sent into that settlement after General Taylor had more than once intimated to the War Department that, in his opinion, no such movement was necessary to the defence or protection of Texas.

SOLDIERS' BOUNTY.

Mr. Lincoln spoke against the bill granting land to the soldiers of the Mexican war. We extract as follows: —

If there was a general desire on the part of the House to pass the bill now, he should be glad to have it done, concurring, as he did generally, with the gentleman from Arkansas, (Mr. Johnson,) that the postponement might jeopard the safety of the proposition. If, however, a reference was to be made, he wished to make a very few remarks in relation to the several subjects desired by gentlemen to be embraced in amendments to the ninth section of the act of the last session of Congress. The first amendment declared by members of this House, had for its only object to give bounty lands to such persons as had served for a time as privates, but had never been discharged as such, because promoted to office. That subject, and no other, was embraced in this bill. There were some others who desired, while they were legislating on this subject, that they should also give bounty lands to the volunteers of the war of 1812. His friend from Maryland said there were no such men. He (Mr. L.) did not say there were many, but he was very confident there were some. His friend from Kentucky, near him, (Mr. Gaines) told him he himself was one.

There was still another proposition touching this matter, — that was, that persons entitled to bounty land should, by law, be entitled to locate those lands in parcels, and not be required to locate them in one body, as was provided by the existing law.

Now, he had carefully drawn up a bill embracing these three separate propositions, which he intended to propose as a substitute for all these bills in the House, or in Committee of the Whole on the State of the Union, at some suitable time. If there was a disposition on the part of the House to act at once on this separate proposition, he repeated that, with the gentleman from Arkansas, he should prefer it, lest they should lose all. But, if there was to be a reference, he desired to introduce his bill embracing the three propositions, thus enabling the Committee and the House to act at the same time, whether favorably or unfavorably, upon all.

THE PUBLIC LANDS.

Mr. Lincoln moved to reconsider the vote by which the bill was passed. He stated to the House that he had made this motion for the purpose of obtaining an opportunity to say a few words in relation to a point raised in the course of the debate on this bill, which he would now proceed to make, if in order. The point in the case to which he referred, arose on the amendment that was submitted by the gentleman from Vermont, (Mr. Collamer,) in Committee of the Whole on the State of the Union, and which was afterwards renewed in the House, in relation to the question whether the reserved sections, which, by some bills heretofore passed, by which an appropriation of land had been made to Wisconsin, had been enhanced in value, should be reduced to the minimum price of the public lands. The question of the reduction in value of those sections was, to him, at this time, a matter very nearly of indifference. He was inclined to desire that Wisconsin should be obliged by having it reduced. But the gentleman from Indiana, (Mr. C. B. Smith,) the Chairman of the Committee on the Territories, yesterday associated that question with the general question, which is now, to some extent, agitated in Congress, of making appropriations of alternate sections of land to aid the States in making internal improvements, and enhancing the prices of the section reserved, and the gentleman from Indiana took ground against that policy. He did not make any special argument in favor of Wisconsin; but he took ground generally against the policy of giving alternate sections of land, and enhancing the price of the reserved sections. Now he (Mr. L.) did not, at this time, take the floor for the purpose of attempting to make an argument on the general subject. He rose simply to protest against the doctrine which the gentleman from Indiana had avowed in the course of what he (Mr. L.) could not but consider an unsound argument.

It might however be true, for anything he knew, that the gentleman from Indiana might convince him that his argument was sound; but he (Mr. L.) feared that gentleman would not be able to convince a majority in Congress that it was sound. It was true, the question appeared in a different aspect to persons in consequence of a difference in the point from which they looked at it. It did not look to persons residing east of the mountains as it did to those who lived among the public lands. But, for his part, he would state that if Congress would make a donation of alternate sections of public lands for the purpose of internal improvement in his State, and forbid the reserved sections being sold at $1.25, he should be glad to see the appropriation made, though he should prefer it if the reserved sections were not enhanced in price. He repeated, he should be glad to have such appropriations made, even though the reserved sections should be enhanced in price. He did not wish to be understood as concurring in any intimation that they would refuse to receive such an appropriation of alternate sections of land because a condition enhancing the price of the reserved sections should be attached thereto. He believed his position would now be understood, if not, he feared he should not be able to make himself understood.

But before he took his seat he would remark that the Senate, during the present session, had passed a bill making appropriations of land on that principle for the benefit of the State in which he resided, — the State of Illinois. The alternate sections were to be given for the purpose of constructing roads, and the reserved sections were to be enhanced in value in consequence. When the bill came here for the action of this House, it had been received, and was now before the Committee on Public Lands, — he desired much to see it passed as it was, if it could be put in a more favorable form for the State of Illinois. When it should be before this House, if any member from a section of the Union in which these lands did not lie, whose interest might be less than that which he felt, should propose a reduction of the price of the reserved sections to $1.25, he should be much obliged; but he did not think it would be well for those who came from the section of the Union in which the lands lay, to do so. He wished it, then, to be understood, that he did not join in the warfare against the principle which had engaged the minds of some members of Congress who were favorable to improvements in the western country.

There was a good deal of force, he admitted, in what fell from the Chairman of the Committee on Territories. It might be that there was no precise justice in raising the price of the reserved sections to $2.50 per acre. It might be proper that the price should be enhanced to some extent, though not to double the usual price; but he should be glad to have such an appropriation with the reserved sections at $2.50; he should be better pleased to have the price of those sections at something less; and he should be still better pleased to have them without any enhancement at all.

There was one portion of the argument of the gentleman from Indiana, the Chairman of the Committee on Territories, (Mr. Smith,) which he wished to take occasion to say that he did not view as unsound. He alluded to the statement that the General Government was interested in these internal improvements being made, inasmuch as they increased the value of the lands that were unsold, and they enabled the Government to sell lands which could not be sold without them. Thus, then, the Government gained by internal improvements, as well as by the general good which the people derived from them, and it might be, therefore, that the lands should not be sold for more than $1.50, instead of the price being doubled. He, however, merely mentioned this in passing, for he only rose to state, as the principle of giving these lands for the purposes which he had mentioned had been laid hold of and considered favorably, and as there were some gentlemen who had constitutional scruples about giving money for these purposes, who would not hesitate to give land, that he was not willing to have it understood that he was one of those who made war against that principle. This was all he desired to say, and having accomplished the object with which he rose, he withdrew his motion to reconsider.

May 11, 1848.

SLAVERY IN THE DISTRICT OF COLUMBIA.

In the debate on the slave-trade in the District of Columbia, Mr Lincoln introduced an amendment to a bill before the House.

Mr. L. read as follows: —

Strike out all after the word "resolved," and insert the following :—

That the Committee on the District of Columbia be instructed to report a bill in substance as follows:

Section 1. Be it enacted by the Senate and House of Representatives of the United States in Congress assembled, That no person not now within the District of Columbia, nor now owned by any person or persons now resident within it, nor hereafter born within it, shall ever be held in slavery within said District.

Sect. 2. That no person now within said District, or now owned by any person or persons now resident within the same, or hereafter born within it, shall ever be held in slavery without the limits of said District: Provided, That officers of the Government of the United States, being citizens of the slaveholding States, coming into said District on public business, and remaining only so long as may be reasonably necessary for that object, may be attended into and out of said District, and while there, by the necessary servants of themselves and their families, without their right to hold such servants in service being impaired.

Sect. 3. That all children born of slave mothers within said District, on or after the 1st day of January, in the year of our Lord, 1850, shall be free; but shall be reasonably supported and educated by the respective owners of their mothers, or by their heirs or representatives, and shall serve reasonable service as apprentices to such owners, heirs, or representatives, until they respectively arrive at the age of —— years, when they shall be entirely free: And the municipal authorities of Washington and Georgetown, within their respective jurisdictional limits, are hereby empowered and required to make all suitable and necessary provision for enforcing obedience to this section, on the part of both masters and apprentices.

Sect. 4. That all persons now within this District, lawfully held as slaves, or now owned by any person or persons now resident within said District, shall remain such at the will of their respective owners, their heirs, or legal representatives: Provided, that such owner, or his legal representatives, may, at any time, receive from the Treasury of the United States the full value of his or her slave, of the class in this section mentioned, upon which such slave shall be forthwith and forever free: And provided further, That the President of the United States, the Secretary of State, and the Secretary of the Treasury, shall be a board for determining the value of such slaves as their owners desire to emancipate under this section, and whose duty it shall be to hold a session for the purpose on the first Monday of each calendar month, to receive all applications, and, on satisfactory evidence in each case, that the person presented for valuation is a slave, and of the class in the section mentioned, and is owned by the applicant, shall value such slave at his or her full cash value, and give to the applicant an order on the treasury for the amount, and also to such slave a certificate of freedom.

Sect. 5. That the municipal authorities of Washington and Georgetown, within their respective jurisdictional limits, are hereby empowered and required to provide active and efficient means to arrest and deliver up to their owners all fugitive slaves escaping into said District.

Sect. 6. That the elective officers within said District of Columbia are hereby empowered and required to open polls at all the usual places of holding elections, on the first Monday of April next, and receive the vote of every free male white citizen above the age of twenty-one years, having resided within said District for the period of one year or more next preceding the time of such voting for or against this act, to proceed in taking said votes in all respects not herein specified, as at elections under the municipal laws, and with as little delay as possible to transmit correct statements of the votes so cast to the President of the United States; and it shall be the duty of the President to count such votes immediately, and if a majority of them be found to be for this act, to forthwith issue his proclamation giving notice of the fact; and this act shall only be in full force and effect on and after the day of such proclamation.

Sect. 7. That involuntary servitude for the punishment of crime, whereof the party shall have been duly convicted, shall in no wise be prohibited by this act.

Sect. 8. That for all purposes of this act, the jurisdictional limits of Washington are extended to all parts of the District of Columbia not included within the present limits of Georgetown.

Mr. Lincoln then said, "that he was authorized to say that of about fifteen of the leading citizens of the District of Columbia to whom this proposition had been submitted, there was not one but approved of such a proposition. He did not wish to be misunderstood. He did not know whether or not they would vote for his bill on the first Monday of April; but he repeated that out of fifteen persons to whom it had been submitted, he had authority to say that every one of them desired that some such proposition as this should pass."

RIGHTS OF NATURALIZED CITIZENS.

The Illinois *Staats-Anzeiger* publishes a letter of Abraham Lincoln, written just a year since, on the Naturalization question and the Massachusetts amendment, as well as on the propriety of a fusion of the Republican with other parties. The following is the letter.

SPRINGFIELD, MAY 17, 1859.

DR. THEODORE CANISIUS: —

DEAR SIR: I have received your letter, in which you ask, for yourself and other German citizens, whether I am for or against the constitutional provision, in relation to naturalized citizens, which has lately been adopted by Massachusetts; and whether I am for or against a fusion of the Republican and other opposition elements for the election campaign of 1860.

Massachusetts is a sovereign and independent State, and I have no title to advise or admonish her as to her course, what she shall do. But when any one, from that which she has done, seeks to draw a conclusion as to what I shall do, I may, without being charged with presumption, speak my mind. I say, then,, that, so far as I understand the Massachusetts amendment, I am against the adoption of the same, as well in Illinois as in all other places where I have the right to oppose it. Since I interpret the spirit of our institutions as tending to the elevation of man, I am opposed to everything which leads to his degradation. Since, as is pretty well known, I commiserate the oppressed condition of the negroes, I should be guilty of a remarkable inconsistency, were I to favor any measure, whose tendency is to abridge the existing rights of *white men*, whether born in another country, or speaking another language than my own.

As regards the question of a fusion of parties, I am for it, if it can be effected upon a Republican basis; upon no other terms am I in favor of it. A fusion upon any other terms would be as unwise as it would be unprincipled. Its effect would be to lose thereby the whole North, while the common enemy would certainly carry the entire South. The question in relation to men is a different one. There are good and patriotic men, and able statesmen in the South, whom I would cheerfully support, if they stood upon Republican ground; but I am opposed to lowering the Republican standard by so much as a hair's-breadth.

I have written this in haste, but I believe that it substantially answers your questions.

Respectfully yours,
ABRAHAM LINCOLN.

LINCOLN'S VOTE IN THE ILLINOIS SENATORIAL CANVASS OF 1858.

The following table shows the popular vote of Mr. Lincoln's supporters in the Legislature elected at the termination of the memorable struggle between Mr. Lincoln and Judge Douglas. The figures show how rascally must have been the apportionment by which Mr. Lincoln was defeated:—

For Members of the Legislature.

Lincoln, 125,275; Lecompton, 5,071; Douglas, 121,090.

For Treasurer.

Miller, 125,430; Dougherty, 5,071; Fondey, 121,609.

For Superintendent of Public Instruction.

Bateman, 124,556; Reynolds, 5,173; French, 122,413.

SPEECH

OF

HON. HANNIBAL HAMLIN

OF MAINE.

SPEECH.

DEMOCRACY.

The following manly speech was delivered in the U. S. Senate Chamber, June 12, 1856, when Senator Hamlin formally abandoned party affiliation with his old associates. His democracy was of the rugged Silas Wright school, and for several years had the Maine Senator felt himself becoming isolated in the ranks of his old friends. It was a bold and manly speech. The occasion which called it forth was the platform adopted at Cincinnati by the National Democratic Convention, and the outrages perpetrated in Kansas, by the connivance and under the protection of, the administration of Mr. Pierce. All who read the following speech will agree that Senator Hamlin did a manly act in a manly way.

A PERSONAL MATTER.

Mr. President, I arise for a purpose purely personal, such as I have never before risen for in the Senate. I desire to explain some matters personal to myself and to my own future course in public life. I ask the Senate to excuse me from further service as Chairman on Commerce. I do so because I feel that my relations hereafter will be of such a character as to render it proper that I should no longer hold that position. I owe this act to the dominant majority in the Senate. When I cease to harmonize with the majority, or tests are applied by that party with which

I have acted to which I cannot submit, I feel, certainly, that I ought no longer to hold that respectable position. I propose to state briefly the reasons that have brought me to that conclusion.

"SPEECH IS SILVERN, BUT SILENCE IS GOLDEN."

During nine years of service in the Senate I have preferred rather to be a working than a talking member, and so I have been almost a silent one. On the subjects which have so much agitated the country, Senators know that I have rarely uttered a word. I love my country more than I love my party. I love my country above my love for any interest that can too deeply agitate or disturb its harmony. I saw, in all the exciting debates through which we have passed, no particular good that would result from my active intermingling in them. My heart has often been full, and the impulses of that heart have often been felt upon my lips, but I have repressed them there.

WRONG OF THE NEBRASKA ACT.

Sir, I hold that the repeal of the Missouri Compromise was a gross moral and political wrong, unequalled in the annals of the legislation of this country, and hardly equalled in the annals of any other free country. Still, sir, with a desire to promote harmony and concord and brotherly feeling, I was a quiet man under all the exciting debates which led to that fatal result. I believed it wrong then; I can see that wrong lying broadcast all around us now. As a wrong I opposed that measure, — not indeed by my voice, but with consistent and steady and uniform votes. I so resisted it in obedience to the dictates of my own judgment. I did it also cheerfully, in compliance with the instructions of the legislature of Maine, which were passed by a vote almost unanimous. In the House of Representatives of Maine, consisting of 151 members, only six, I think, dissented; and in the Senate, consisting of 31 members, only one member non-concurred.

A WISE FORBEARANCE.

But the Missouri restriction was abrogated. The portentous evils that were predicted have followed, and are yet following, along in its train. It was done, sir, in violation of the pledges of that party with which I have always acted, and with which I have always voted. It was done in violation of solemn pledges of the President of the United States, made in his inaugural address. Still, sir, I was disposed to suffer the wrong, until I should see that no evil results were flowing from it. We were told by almost every Senator who addressed us upon that occasion, that no evil results would follow; that no practical difference in the settlement of the country, and the character of the future State would take place, whether the act was done or not. I have waited calmly and patiently to see the fulfilment of that prediction; and I am grieved, sir, to say now, that they have at least been mistaken in their predictions and promises. They all have signally failed.

THE CAUSE OF DISTURBANCE.

That Senators might have voted for that measure under the belief then expressed, and the predictions to which I have alluded, I can well understand. But how Senators can now defend that measure, amid all its evils, which are overwhelming the land, if not threatening it with a conflagration, is what I do not comprehend. The whole of the disturbed state of the country has its rise in, and is attributable to, that act alone,— nothing else. It lies at the foundation of all our misfortunes and commotions. There would have been no incursions by Missouri borderers into Kansas, either to establish slavery or control elections. There would have been no necessity either for others to have gone there partially to aid in preserving the country in its then condition. All would have been peace there. Had it not been done, that repose and quiet which pervaded the public mind then, would hold it in tranquillity to-day. Instead of startling events, we would have quiet and peace within our borders, and that fraternal feeling which ought to animate the citizens of every part of the Union toward those of all other sections.

WHERE DUTY LIES.

Sir, the events that are taking place are indeed startling. They challenge the public mind, and appeal to the public judgment; they thrill the public nerve as electricity imparts a tremulous motion to the telegraphic wire. It is a period when all good men should unite in applying the proper remedy to secure peace and harmony to the whole country. Is this to be done by any of us by remaining associated with those who have been instrumental in producing these results, and who now justify them? I do not see my duty lying in that direction.

I have, while temporarily acquiescing, stated here and at home, everywhere uniformly, that when the tests of those measures were applied to me as one of party fidelity, I would sunder them as flax is sundered by the touch of fire. I do it now.

A MORAL QUESTION.

The occasion involves a question of moral duty; and self-respect allows me no other line of duty but to follow the dictates of my own judgment and the impulses of my own heart. A just man may cheerfully submit to many enforced humiliations; but a self-degraded man has ceased to be worthy to be deemed a man at all.

THE ACTION AT CINCINNATI.

Sir, what has the recent Democratic Convention at Cincinnati done? It has indorsed the measure I have condemned, and has sanctioned its destructive and ruinous effects. It has done more, — vastly more. That principle of policy of territorial sovereignty which once had, and I suppose now has, its advocates within these walls, is stricken down, and there is an absolute denial of it in the resolutions of the Convention, if I draw right conclusions,—a denial equally to Congress, and even to the people of the territories, of the right to settle the question of slavery therein. On the contrary, the Convention has actually incorporated into the platform of the Democratic party that doctrine which, only a few years ago, met nothing but ridicule and contempt, here and elsewhere, namely, that the flag of the Federal Union, under the Constitution of the United States, carries slavery wherever it floats. If this baneful principle be true, then that national ode which inspires us always as on a battlefield, should be rewritten by Drake, and should read thus:—

"Forever float that standard sheet,
Where breathes the foe that falls before us,
With SLAVERY'S soil beneath our feet,
And SLAVERY'S banner streaming o'er us."

WHERE IS TERRITORIAL SOVEREIGNTY?

Now, sir, what is the precise condition in which this matter is left by the Cincinnati Convention? I do not design to trespass many moments on the Senate; but allow me to read and offer a very few comments upon some portions of the Democratic platform. The first resolution that treats upon the subject is in these words. I read just so much of it as is applicable to my present remarks.

"That Congress has no power, under the Constitution, to interfere with or control the domestic institutions of the several States, and that such States are the sole and proper judges of everything appertaining to their own affairs, not prohibited by the Constitution."

I take it that this language, thus far, is language which meets a willing and ready response from every Senator here; certainly it does from me. But, in the following resolution, I find these words:—

"That the foregoing propositions cover, and were intended to embrace, the whole subject of slavery agitation in Congress."

The first resolution which I read was adopted years ago in

Democratic conventions. The second resolution which I read was adopted in subsequent years, when a different state of things had arisen, and it became necessary to apply an abstract proposition, relating to the States, to the territories. Hence the adoption of the language contained in the second resolution which I have read.

THE POWER OF CONGRESS.

Now, sir, I deny the position thus assumed by the Cincinnati Convention. In the language of the Senator from Kentucky, (Mr. Crittenden,) so ably and appropriately used on Tuesday last, I hold that the entire and unqualified sovereignty of the territories is in Congress. That is my judgment; but this resolution brings the territories precisely within the same limitations which are applied to the States in the resolution which I first read. The two taken together, deny to Congress the power of legislation in the territories.

DENIAL OF POWER.

Follow on, and let us see what remains. Adopted as a part of the present platform, and as necessary to a new state of things, and to meet an emergency now existing, the Convention says: —

"*Resolved*, That the American Democracy recognize and adopt the principles contained in the organic laws establishing the territories of Kansas and Nebraska, as embodying the only sound and safe solution of the slavery question, upon which the great national idea of the people of this whole country can repose in its determined conservatism of the Union, — NON-INTERFERENCE BY CONGRESS WITH SLAVERY IN STATES AND TERRITORIES."

Then follows the last resolution: —

"*Resolved*, That we recognize the right of the people of all the territories, including Kansas and Nebraska, acting through the legally and fairly expressed will of a majority of actual residents, and whenever the number of inhabitants justifies it, to form a constitution, with or without domestic slavery, and be admitted into the Union upon terms of perfect equality with the other States."

"ET TU BRUTE."

Take all these resolutions together, and the deduction which we must necessarily draw from them is a denial to Congress of any power whatever to legislate upon the subject of slavery. The last resolution denies to the people of the territory any power over the subject, save when they shall have a sufficient number to form a constitution, and become a State, and also denies that Congress has any power over the subject; and so the resolutions hold that power is at least in advance while the territory is in a territorial condition. This is the only conclusion which you can draw from these resolutions. Alas for short-lived territorial sovereignty! It came to its death in the house of its friends; it was buried by the same hands that gave it baptism!

THE PLATFORM — THE NOMINEE.

But, sir, I did not rise for the purpose of discussing these resolutions, but only to read them. I may, I probably shall, take some subsequent occasion when I shall endeavor to present to the Senate and the country a fair account of what is the true issue presented to the people for their consideration and decision.

My object now is to show only that the Cincinnati Convention has indorsed and approved the repeal of the Missouri Compromise, from which many evils have already flowed; from which, I fear, more and worse evils must yet be anticipated. It would, of course, be expected that the presidental nominee of that convention would accept, cordially and cheerfully, the platform prepared for him by his party friends. No person can object to that. There is no equivocation on his part about the matter. I beg leave to read a short extract from a speech of that gentleman, made at his own home, within the last few days. In reply to the Keystone Club, which paid him a visit there, Mr. Buchanan said: —

"Gentlemen, two weeks since I should have made you a longer speech, but now I have been placed upon a platform of which I most heartily approve, and that can speak for me. Being the representative of the great Democratic party, and not simply James Buchanan, I must square my conduct according to the platform of the party, and insert no new plank, nor take one from it."

THE RIGHT STEP.

These events leave me but one unpleasant duty, which is to declare here that I can maintain political association with no party that insists upon such doctrines; that I can support no man for President who avows and recognizes them, and that the little of that power with which God has endowed me shall be employed to battle manfully, firmly, and consistently for his defeat, demanded as it is by the highest interest of the country which owns all my allegiance.

LETTERS OF ACCEPTANCE OF MESSRS. LINCOLN AND HAMLIN.

The following is the correspondence between the officers of the Republican National Convention and the candidates thereof for President and Vice-President.

CHICAGO, MAY 18, 1860.

To the Honorable ABRAHAM LINCOLN, of Illinois.

SIR: The representatives of the Republican party of the United States, assembled in convention in Chicago, have, this day, by an unanimous vote, selected you as the Republican candidate for the office of President of the United States to be supported at the next election; and the undersigned were appointed a committee of the Convention to apprise you of this nomination, and respectfully to request that you will accept it. A declaration of the principles and sentiments adopted by the Convention accompanies this communication.

In the performance of this agreeable duty we take leave to add our confident assurances that the nomination of the Chicago Convention will be ratified by the suffrages of the people.

We have the honor to be, with great respect and regard, your friends and fellow citizens.

Signed by, GEO. ASHMUN, of Massachusetts,
President of the Convention,
And the Chairmen of the various State delegations.

SPRINGFIELD, ILL., MAY 23, 1860.

Hon. GEORGE ASHMUN, President of the Republican National Convention.

SIR: I accept the nomination tendered me by the Convention, over which you presided, and of which I am formally apprised in the letter of yourself and others, acting as a committee of that Convention, for that purpose.

The declaration of principles and sentiments, which accompanies your letter, meets my approval; and it shall be my care not to violate, or disregard it, in any part.

Imploring the assistance of Divine Providence; and with due regard to the views and feelings of all who were represented in the Convention; to the rights of all the States and territories, and people of the nation; to the inviolability of the Constitution, and the perpetual union, harmony, and prosperity of all, I am most happy to co-operate for the practical success of the principles declared by the Convention.

Your obliged friend and fellow-citizen,

ABRAHAM LINCOLN

A similar letter was sent to the nominee for the Vice-Presidency, to which the following is the reply.

WASHINGTON, MAY 30, 1860.

Gentlemen: Your official communication of the 18th instant, informing me that the representatives of the Republican party of the United States, assembled at Chicago, on that day, had, by a unanimous vote, selected me as their candidate for the office of Vice-President of the United States, has been received, together with the resolutions adopted by the Convention as its declaration of principles.

Those resolutions enunciate clearly and forcibly the principles which unite us, and the objects proposed to be accomplished. They address themselves to all, and there is neither necessity nor propriety in my entering upon a discussion of any of them. They have the approval of my judgment, and in any action of mine will be faithfully and cordially sustained.

I am profoundly grateful to those with whom it is my pride and pleasure politically to co-operate, for the nomination so unexpectedly conferred; and I desire to tender through you, to the members of the Convention, my sincere thanks for the confidence thus reposed in me. Should the nomination, which I now accept, be ratified by the people, and the duties devolve upon me of presiding over the Senate of the United States, it will be my earnest endeavor faithfully to discharge them with a just regard to the rights of all.

It is to be observed, in connection with the doings of the Republican Convention, that a paramonnt object with us, is, to preserve the normal condition of our territorial domain as homes for free men. The able advocate and defender of Republican principles, whom you have nominated for the highest place that can gratify the ambition of man, comes from a State which has been made what it is, by special action in that respect, of the wise and good men who founded our institutions. The rights of free labor have there been vindicated and maintained. The thrift and enterprise which so distinguished Illinois, one of the most flourishing States of the glorious West, we would see secured to all the territories of the Union; and restore peace and harmony to the whole country, by bringing back the government to what it was under the wise and patriotic men who created it. If the republicans shall succeed in that object, as they hope to, they will be held in grateful remembrance by the busy and teeming millions of future ages.

I am, very truly, yours, H. HAMLIN.

Hon. GEORGE ASHMUN, President of the Convention, and others of the Committee.

www.ingramcontent.com/pod-product-compliance
Lightning Source LLC
LaVergne TN
LVHW020226110826
845151LV00003B/837
* 9 7 8 1 4 2 5 5 3 2 3 3 8 *